GLOBALIZATION & TECHNOLOGY

Best wishes,

Rajneesh

hope you will find
some of it entertaining,
perhaps even useful!

24.4.04

GLOBALIZATION & TECHNOLOGY

Interdependence, Innovation Systems and Industrial Policy

RAJNEESH NARULA

polity

First published in 2003 by Polity Press in association with Blackwell Publishing Ltd

Editorial office:
Polity Press
65 Bridge Street
Cambridge CB2 1UR, UK

Marketing and production:
Blackwell Publishing Ltd
108 Cowley Road
Oxford OX4 1JF, UK

Distributed in the USA by
Blackwell Publishing Inc.
350 Main Street
Malden, MA 02148, USA

A catalogue record for this book is available from the British Library.

Library of Congress Cataloging-in-Publication Data
Narula, Rajneesh, 1963–
Globalization and technology: interdependence, innovation systems and industrial policy/Rajneesh Narula.
      p. cm.
Includes bibliographical references and index.
ISBN 0-7456-2456-1—ISBN 0-7456 2457-X (pbk.)
1. Technological innovations. 2. Industrial policy.
3. Globalization. I. Title.
HC79.T4N37 2003
338'.064—dc21
                                                          2002155021
Typeset in 10.5pt on 12pt Palatino
by Kolam Information Services Pvt. Ltd., Pondicherry, India
Printed and bound in Great Britain by MPG Books Ltd, Bodmin, Cornwall
For further information on Polity, visit our website: www.polity.co.uk

Contents

Figures

Tables

Boxes

Abbreviations

BERD	business expenditures on R&D
CAD	computer-aided design
CIS	Community Innovation Survey
EETs	Eastern European Economies in Transition
FDI	foreign direct investment
GATT	General Agreement on Tariffs and Trade
GPN	Global Production Network
ICTs	information and communications technologies
IMF	International Monetary Fund
IS	import-substitution
LDCs	least developed countries
M&A	mergers and acquisitions
MNE	multinational enterprise
NAFTA	North American Free Trade Agreement
NFR	Norwegian Research Council
NICs	newly industrializing countries
OECD	Organization for Economic Cooperation and Development
OS	operating system
PCB	printed circuit board
PDA	personal digital assistant
R&D	research and development
SAP	Structural Adjustment Programme
SDI	strategic defence initiative
SEM	Single European Market
SI	systems of innovation
SINTEF	Stiftelser for Industriell og Teknisk Forskning ved NTH

SME   small- and medium-sized enterprise
STP   strategic technology partnering
WIPO   World Intellectual Property Organization
WTO   World Trade Organization

Acknowledgements

Books, most unfortunately, do not write themselves. But this is a matter of time: I am an unbridled optimist in all matters technological, and I feel certain that Nokia's next line of mobile phones will have just such a feature. Failing Nokia, I have my hopes pinned on the Swiss Army Knife folks.

This particular exercise in masochism has been two years in the making, most of which were spent vegetating in front of the TV (thank you, Seven of Nine, MTV and Buffy). Before inflicting the actual contents of this volume on your unsuspecting mental faculties, it is tradition to share the blame for its contents with the people behind the person behind the book.

First, I would like to thank the four people without whose direct intervention I would probably be drifting around the Amazon as an unemployed tour guide wearing a very smelly shirt and nursing a perpetual hangover (although some may consider that being a professional academic is no real improvement over being a professional barfly). These are John Dunning, John Hagedoorn, Jan Fagerberg and Keith Smith, all of whom have taken my ramblings seriously and have provided me with opportunities for which I am sure I was largely unqualified. I have made some of their intellectual biases my own, as the reader of this book will discover.

The second group consists of people who have added texture to my thought. Tine Bruland and Olav Wicken for introducing me to economic history; Robin Cowan for a crash course on technological lock-in and tacit knowledge; Gabriel Benito for reading every word I have ever written and commenting on *everything*. Special thanks must go to Chris Freeman, Daniele Archibugi, David Held and Nikos Kastrinos for comments on the first version of the manuscript. Nikos's comments on the first paragraph of the first page were particularly earth-shattering. It is a small detail that this was in fact as far as he got.

There is a third group: those who have contributed immeasurably in keeping me sane and holding my intellectual and social proclivities in check. This group is large, so I shall single out just a few (in the interests of brevity): Paola Criscuolo, John Cantwell, Lou Anne Barclay, Annelies Hogenbirk, Anthony Arundel, Michael Meissner, Elena Baldini, Akin Okelana, Bart Verspagen, Peter Gray, Pat Rotonda, Amir Moghaddam, Charmaine Liew, Monica Narula and Virginia Acha.

Fourth, I would like to thank Bert Sadowski for permission to use some of our jointly authored material in chapter 6, John Dunning for parts of chapter 7, and Mona Wibe for parts of chapter 2.

I must also thank the various institutions that have provided me with the perfect environment to study. The Centre for Technology Innovation and Culture (TIK) at the University of Oslo; the Department of International Economics and Management at the Copenhagen Business School; MERIT and its entire staff (past and present) for being my refuge for so many years. Last but not least, I would like to acknowledge the staff of the Department of Electrical Engineering, Ahmadu Bello University, Zaria, Nigeria, 1979–1983. Although I may not have been the most diligent of undergraduates, some of that engineering stuff did stick, as the contents of this book would suggest. No condition is permanent, it seems, even ignorance.

Special thanks go to Paola Criscuolo for her research assistance and Sudha Menon for her assistance in indexing.

Partial research funding by the Norwegian Research Council is gratefully acknowledged.

Acknowledgement is also due to the copyright holders for permission to reprint the following: chapter 3 was originally published as 'Innovation Systems and "Inertia" in R&D Location: Norwegian Firms and the Role of Systemic Lock-in', *Research Policy*, 31/5 (2002), 795–816; chapter 5 is a revised version of 'Choosing between Internal and Non-internal R&D Activities: Some Technological and Economic Factors', *Technology Analysis & Strategic Management*, 13 (2001), 365–87; chapter 6 is adapted from 'Technological Catch-up and Strategic Technology Partnering in Developing Countries' (with B. Sadowski), *International Journal of Technology Management*, 23 (2002), 599–617.

Finally, thank you, dear reader: I await my obscenely large royalty cheques so I can buy that phone.

RN
Copenhagen,
November 2002

Introduction

Globalization is a controversial subject where possibly the only feature that everyone seems to agree on is that it is an ongoing *process*, rather than an *event*. Economic globalization as used here implies the growing interdependence of locations and economic units across countries and regions. I use the word 'interdependence' very deliberately. Cross-border linkages between economic entities do not imply globalization, merely internationalization. Trading activities do not necessarily result in interdependence. If we concentrate on measures of international trade, levels of global activity are roughly at the same level as they were 100 years ago (Bairoch and Kozul-Wright 1998). The new element of international business is the growth of FDI (foreign direct investment) and the multinational corporation. When we discriminate between trade, long-term capital flows, portfolio investment and FDI, we come to an important differentiation. For while international business activity was broad-based in the past, it was dominated by the development of vertical linkages, with a flow of goods between locations, in response to varying elasticities of supply and demand. Raw materials were transported from one location to another, manufactured, and transported to a third location for sale. Factors of production were immobile, and although capital did in fact get relocated, these were capital flows rather than capital embodied in physical assets or personnel, and there was no significant integration of operations in disparate locations within the control and management of the same individuals. Firms were *international*, but not *multinational*. International business and economic activity was *extensive* in the sense that the value of goods and capital exchanged were considerable, and involved numerous countries and actors, who were all dependent upon each other's patronage. But it was not *intensive*, in that activities were largely not integrated across borders, with the possible exception of the large trading companies and other state-sanctioned *de facto* monopolies (Held et al. 1999).

Technological change and innovation are acknowledged almost universally as determinants of globalization. However, technology is another highly imprecise word, and if I am to proceed further without doing violence to any of these concepts, it is essential that the reader understand what I mean. Technology implies the application of scientific knowledge for practical aims. Technology is the application of scientific concepts that help us understand our environment, and allow us to convert this knowledge to develop and fabricate artefacts. Technology and science are *cumulative*, and build upon previous science and technology. The *practical* dividing line between science and technology is not always clear. Science and technology advance through *innovation*, which represents change in the stock of knowledge. Technology and science are subsets of knowledge. The difference is sometimes considered to be in the intent of the work, in that science is conducted in the altruistic thirst for information, while increases in the knowledge base of firms is with a specific intent in order to create a product or a service. But this difference has also blurred.

In a very general sense, 'innovation' may mean the introduction of *any* novelty, but in the economics and technology literature it has come to have a more precise meaning or meanings since Schumpeter made his distinction between 'invention' and 'innovation'. An invention is an idea, sketch or model of any new or improved device, product, process or system. Innovations occur only when the new product, device or process is involved in a commercial transaction. Multiple inventions may be involved in achieving an innovation. In the Schumpeterian sense, scientific discoveries as well as inventions would not come within the compass of 'innovation' although they might fall within a second, broader, type of definition, which is concerned with the entire *process* of an innovation, including antecedent work not necessarily undertaken by the entrepreneur who attempts the first type.[1] The broad definition of innovation as used here implies *changes in the knowledge, ability and techniques required to produce goods and services of higher or better quality per unit price*, while technology represents the cumulative stock of these innovations. Technology therefore – for the purposes of this volume – includes all activities that provide assets with which an economic unit can generate products or services. Science provides us with more generic knowledge, which may or may not generate products and services.[2] Although it is not strictly accurate, I will use knowledge creation and innovation as synonyms here, since my interest here is with the process through which economic units evolve their knowledge bases.

Knowledge creation is often associated with formal activities within research and development (R&D) that is undertaken in a systematic manner within universities, specialized public and private R&D facilities. However, these formal means represent only a small proportion of knowledge creation. Knowledge creation is a much larger and more systemic phenomenon, although formal facilities account for a large percentage of output. One can do no better than to quote Freeman and Soete (1997: 45) on this point:

> But this [formal] Research and Development system is at the heart of the whole complex, for in contemporary society it originates a large proportion of the new and improved materials, products, processes and systems, which are the ultimate source of economic advance. This is not to underestimate the importance of dissemination of knowledge through the education system, industrial training, the mass media, information services and other means. Nor is it to deny the obvious fact that in the short run rapid progress may be

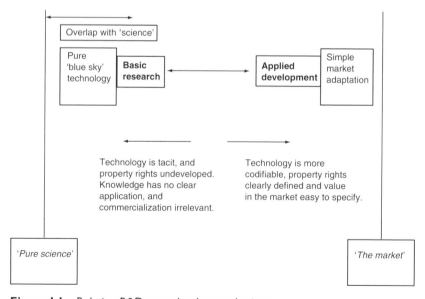

Figure I.1 Relating R&D to technology and science

made simply by the application of the existing stock of knowledge. Nor yet is it to deny the importance of feedback from production and from markets to R&D and scientific activities. It is only to assert that the fundamental point that for any given technique of production, transport or distribution, there are long-run limitations on the growth of productivity, which are technologically determined. In the most fundamental sense the winning of new knowledge is the basis for human civilization.

Knowledge development is incremental and radical. This is a function of the way all learning takes place. Economic units – be they firms or individuals – acquire knowledge by exploring in the vicinity of their existing knowledge assets, by undertaking routines, which leads to incremental innovations (*learning-by-doing*). Knowledge is acquired by interaction with the external environment. In the case of firms it may be through interaction (*inter alia*) with customers, suppliers, competitors, government agencies. This is referred to as *learning-by-interacting*. Firms (like individuals, who make up firms) are generally averse to radical change, in that they are likely to repeat successful patterns of behaviour, learning and interaction that have been successful in the past. This is referred to as *routinized learning*.

Routinized learning can be further characterized as 'exploitative learning' which adds to the existing knowledge and competences of a firm without fundamentally changing the nature of its activities. Non-routinized learning or 'exploratory learning' involves changes in company routines and experimentation with new alternatives (see e.g. Dodgson 1993; March 1991).

Much of the innovative activities of firms comes under the rubric of non-formal R&D. Indeed, as Smith (2000) points out, innovation rests not on discovery but on learning, and evidence from the EU-sponsored Community Innovation Survey (CIS) confirms this view. Generally speaking, industries that are regarded as having a low R&D intensity (which tends to be based on measures of formal R&D) tend to undertake a greater amount of informal innovation. Indeed, innovation undertaken through the acquisition of new plant and equipment tends to be the largest contributor to total innovation expenditures. That is, firms acquire new equipment that is then modified or adapted, and new and improved routines to use these technologies are gradually developed (see e.g. Laestadius 2000).

'The globalization of technology' vs. 'Globalization and Technology'

The work of Archibugi and associates (e.g., Archibugi and Michie 1994, 1995, Archibugi and Iammarino 2000, Archibugi and Pietrobelli 2002) is worth mentioning in the context of this volume. The focus of Archibugi and associates is on the globalization *of* technology, and seeks to classify the different modalities through which technology and innovation have a growing cross-border nature. They build around a taxonomy that classifies individual innovations according to the way these are produced, exploited and diffused internationally. This taxonomy is presented in Table I.1, and identifies three main categories of technology generation:

1 The international *exploitation* of nationally produced technology. This concerns the use by innovators to exploit their technological competences in markets other than the domestic one. This category can be labelled 'international' as opposed to 'global' since the innovation preserves its own national identity, even when it is diffused and marketed in more than one country.
2 The global *generation* of innovation. This category focuses on innovations generated by single proprietors on a global scale, usually multinational enterprises (MNEs). The innovations in this category are generated based on inputs from multiple research and technical centres, which may be located in different countries.
3 Global technological *collaborations*.

Archibugi's three modes of globalization of technology are clearly very different, although it is somewhat difficult to disentangle them empirically. The starting points (and assumptions) of this volume and their work are the same. First, we both acknowledge that there is a convergence between countries in the kinds of knowledge being used. Second, there is consensus that there is a rapid convergence in the way in which knowledge is created and disseminated.

My interest in this book is to focus on understanding the *why* of this taxonomy. I accept that the globalization of technology can be seen in terms of these three categories, but I seek to enquire as to the reasons for this. Why are some MNEs more likely than others to generate innovations globally? Why do a majority of innovatory activities – even by MNEs – continue to be nationally generated, even though large shares of their sales and production are undertaken abroad?

Table 1.1   A taxonomy of the globalization of technology

Categories	Actors	Forms
International *exploitation* of nationally produced innovations	Profit-seeking firms and individuals	• Exports of innovative goods • Sale of licences and patents • Foreign production of innovative goods internally generated
Global *generation* of innovations	Multinational enterprises	• R&D and innovative activities both in the home and in the host countries • Acquisitions of existing R&D laboratories or greenfield R&D investment in host countries
Global techno-scientific *collaborations*	• Universities and public research centres	• Joint scientific projects and R&D networks • Scientific exchanges, sabbatical years • International flows of students
	• National and multinational firms	• Joint ventures for specific innovative projects • Productive agreements with exchange of technical information and/or equipment

Source: adapted from Archibugi and Michie (1995).

Why do firms increasingly undertake global techno-scientific collaborations, and are these a substitute for the other two categories, or complementary to them? In asking *why*, I intend to explain that these three categories are not independent of each other, but overlap in their nature and extent. There is – yet again – considerable interdependence between these categories.

There is a small – but important – semantic point that should be noted. This volume is not about the globalization *of* technology, but about globalization *and* technology. Furthermore, it is not my intention to examine all the issues associated with technology and globalization, despite the title of the book. Within this wide field, *I will be focusing my attention on the growing nature of cross-border interdependence in the creation and diffusion of technology.* I take it as a given that economic growth occurs because of the ability of a nation's industries to develop and sustain their competitive position, and that this requires growth of productivity of its capital and labour (see Fagerberg 1994 for a review). Further, I will assume that economic growth concerns not just the acquisition and development of knowledge through innovation and learning, but also the diffusion and efficient utilization of this knowledge. My own humble contribution here is to shed on the international aspect of this interdependence or cooperation by examining the growing nature of cross-border interdependence at two levels. *First, between locations, by examining the role of cross-border interdependence in the innovation process. Second, between firms, by studying the dynamics of inter-firm R&D collaboration.*

Interdependence between economic units as per the definition of globalization used here implies cross-border cooperation, whether by design or otherwise, and this is what has led to the 'fuzziness' aspect associated with globalization. There are specific outcomes that have become blurred through the changes wrought by globalization and technological change, and have led to what seem like paradoxical outcomes. Concepts that have traditionally been clear and precise are now less clear and imprecise. Specifically, the nature and boundaries of several hitherto clearly defined economic entities are no longer as easy to define. I use the term 'economic entity' deliberately, because I wish to include firms and countries (and the in-between entities) within the same frame of reference. This is not a matter of convenience: the fuzzy issue rears its (indeterminate) head because it is no longer clear what is the appropriate unit. Academics and policy makers bemoan the loss of sovereignty that globalization has wrought, and it has become increasingly obvious that countries are unable to make and implement economic decisions unilaterally, because porous borders, MNEs and international markets determine prices, exchange rates, the use of resources and technological trajectories (see e.g., Boyer and Drache 1996). That is, countries are obliged to consider external conditions in maintaining the welfare of their citizens, and are thus more or less obliged to consider external (non-domestic) dimensions. They are obliged to move towards *cooperation* or *an interdependence* with other nation-states, supra-national institutions and even firms in an attempt to seek Pareto-optimal outcomes. The MNE figures large in such matters: FDI-based industrial development policies are now commonplace in most countries. Although there has been a growth in the global FDI flows, there is also increased competition for certain kinds of foreign capital, particularly those that provide opportunities for indigenous spillovers of technology and organizational capability. Firms too (whether uninational or multinational) are increasingly integrated with firms, customers, suppliers, governments and organizations in other locations creating a multi-level and multi-dimensional arena of cooperation and interdependence.

It is obvious that these issues go well beyond those of economics and business; and must necessarily include socio-political considerations as well. This is particularly the case with globalization, which has increased the vulnerability of hitherto relatively closed economies to the external shocks and influences from the world economy at large. As Stopford and Strange (1991) well illustrate, firm–government interaction is also influenced by the dynamics of government–government and firm–firm relationships. These are the issues that raise the spectre of fuzzy borders.

Despite the growing role of cross-border interdependence, however, societies and systems change only very slowly: there remains a fundamental distinctness of national identities and cultures, nations and firms. There is little evidence that economic units are becoming generic and identical any more than during the heyday of the Roman, Persian or British empires. In other words, the environment within which economic activity is undertaken still remains largely the same and changes only very slowly. Unilever may supply similar products to almost every household under the sun, it may have alliances with a variety of firms, depend on a large number of partners for inputs, but its control structure and its 'core' activities remain largely embedded in its home countries. The very fact that debates lamenting the loss of national sovereignty exist is because people and the ecology within which economic activity is undertaken are integrated within systems that are bound together by routines, procedures and traditions ('institutions'), which cause embeddedness. Institutions complement economic actors: institutions cannot be changed without radically affecting the whole system. New concepts, technologies and practices are more easily introduced across borders in an interdependent world, but their introduction is not costless: they tend to disequilibrate systems (Kogut 2000).

While a large literature has mushroomed describing the increasingly interwoven nature and cross-border dependence of locations and firms, there is considerable variation by location, firm, and industrial sector. Indeed, it has resulted in a widening in the created assets[3] and income gap between the industrialized countries and a handful of wealthier developing countries on the one hand, and the poorer developing countries at the other. The literature on economic catch-up and convergence,[4] for instance, tends to categorize countries into three broad groups. The first consists of the wealthy industrialized countries which, over the last two decades, have experienced a convergence in income levels, consumption patterns and technological capabilities. The second comprises the more advanced developing countries (primarily the Asian newly industrializing countries – NICs), which are catching up and converging with the first group. The third category is made up of a large number of poorer developing countries, which far from converging with the first and second group are diverging from them, either because they have 'fallen behind' relative to the first group, or because they have 'stumbled back' in both a relative and absolute sense (Hikino and Amsden 1994). Put another way, the homogeneity among markets that is usually associated with globalization has occurred only partially, and in a very selective way. Similar behaviour has been noted for FDI (see e.g. Narula 1996a). Indeed, as argued by Gray (1996), globalization, while benefiting the middle income developing countries, has so far brought relatively few economic gains to the least developed countries, for example, most of sub-Saharan Africa. The simultaneous divergence of the growth and income levels between richer and poorer economies, and the convergence amongst industrial (and rich) economies, harks back to the vicious cycle of poverty. The inability of the least developed countries to escape from the vicious cycle, and therefore to converge, can be explained by the absence of the same conditions that underlie convergence within the developed countries, namely, that while technological spillovers assist productivity growth in industrialized economies, non-industrialized, poorer economies are unable to utilize such spillovers either because they are not available to them or because the countries do not have the appropriate social-institutional systems and the necessary technological and organizational capability.[5] Thus, when one speaks of globalization, one speaks of the globalization of selected groups of countries or industrial sectors. Naturally, any discussion invoking globalization therefore has significant policy implications for both developing and developed countries. However, in this book I do not intend to dwell on the dichotomy *per se*.

Globalization is also by no means an irreversible or a linear process. Globalization can be said to be largely an evolutionary process, and an incredibly complex one at that. Increasing interdependence is co-determined by so many processes that are themselves evolutionary in nature. Primary (but not solely) amongst these co-evolutionary processes is that of technological change. The outcome of evolutionary processes is generally always non-obvious except with hindsight. Evolutionary processes have two fundamental features. First, they occur in historical time and are non-reversible. Second, they are about the creation of novelty, and this creative process involves selection mechanisms in which the environment determines which novelties survive. Thus, by extension, it is about both creation and destruction of novelties, and the cumulative processes that these entail.

How this book is organized

The rest of this book will proceed as follows. **Chapter 1** expands on this introduction, delving somewhat deeper into some of the nature and causes of cross-border interdependence. It introduces the reader to the main forces underlying globalization of technology, highlighting the complex and intertwining nature of some of these forces that simultaneously underlie fuzzy borders and precise boundaries. These are not – as should be obvious by now – limited solely to economic issues, or to the forces of technological change, or the spread of the MNE. Each contributes – by its very nature – to the fundamental inequities, paradoxes, concentrations and imbalances that mark any evolutionary phenomenon.

The **first main theme** of this book is the tendency for locations to be interdependent in the creation of knowledge. **Chapters 2 and 3** focus on discussing the questions related to the location and dynamics of innovation and its relationship to globalization. I discuss the process of knowledge creation within economies, and the important role of international actors in an innovation system, and why firms and countries are largely reluctant globalizers, at least as far as R&D is concerned. This is an area of some paradox. On the one hand, locations are increasingly interdependent. On the other, locations remain distinct and idiosyncratic. At the same time, the line of reasoning I develop here suggests that – over the long term – it is reasonable to expect that boundaries will become increasingly fuzzy and indistinct as globalization progresses. My central argument builds around the concept of 'inertia', the process of evolutionary change, and a 'systems of innovation' understanding of learning.

Chapter 3 seeks to enquire why firms – *ceteris paribus* – tend to concentrate their R&D activities at home, using a systems of innovation approach. I argue that R&D inertia is associated with structural inertia and resultant systemic lock-in. Interaction within an innovation system is a self-reinforcing mechanism that may or may not lead to *ex post* efficiency. Lock-in can be efficient when technologies and institutions maintain the competitiveness of firms. On the other hand, radical innovations or technological discontinuities may require new institutions and resources, but systemic lock-in may prevent rapid reaction. Firms can use a 'voice' strategy by intervening to modify the appropriate institutions in the existing innovation system, or an 'exit' strategy by seeking alternative innovation system which more closely fit their needs.

The **second theme** of the book is the growing interdependence of firms in the innovation process. **Chapter 4** starts the ball rolling by examining the reasons for the growth in R&D collaboration by firms. I develop a framework to understand the welfare and social rationale for government involvement in promoting and partaking in R&D activities in general and alliances in particular, paying special attention to the evolution of *international* strategic technology partnering.

Chapter 5 expands further on the growth of alliances, making a clearer distinction between various types of R&D collaboration, and evaluating how firms make the choice between in-house R&D and non-internal R&D. I recount the reasons for the growth in non-internal activities, and explain why these are not as prevalent for R&D as other value-adding activities, and highlight that outsourcing is most often undertaken where multiple, substitutable sources are available. I then develop two frameworks. First, a static framework is developed, which evaluates the choice of mode based on a firm's distribution of competences, and their strategic importance. Second, a dynamic framework is developed that demonstrates how the static framework differs depending on whether the firm is engaged in pre-paradigmatic, paradigmatic or post-paradigmatic sectors.

Chapter 6 tries to connect the issue of R&D collaboration with the question of national capabilities and innovation systems. I examine the kinds and types of organizational modes of strategic technology alliances utilized by developing country firms. I examine the reasons for the growth of strategic alliance activity by developing country firms, and, in particular, propose explanations for the considerable variation between countries and regions, both in terms of propensity and organizational modes. I propose that while the issue of economic divergence and 'falling behind' remains valid, there are convincing arguments that the failure of developing countries to participate is also a result of fundamental structural differences in the economies of these countries.

I present some conclusions and observations in **Chapter 7**. I demonstrate the possible sub-optimal outcome of nation-states attempting to 'target' innovatory activity by particular companies. I discuss the role of governments in promoting and engaging in the generation and diffusion of intellectual capital in general, and in facilitating inter-firm technological alliances and in being able to implement effective industrial policy. I also evaluate the efficacy of techno-nationalism, in light of the welfare and social responsibilities of governments, particularly in an age of globalization.

1

Technology and Globalization as Concatenated Processes: A Brief Commentary on the Causes of Globalization

1.1 Introduction

To reiterate what has been stated in the introduction, evolutionary processes have two fundamental features. First, they occur in historical time and are non-reversible. Second, they are about the creation of novelty, and this creative process involves selection mechanisms in which the environment determines which novelties survive. Thus, by extension, it is about both creation and destruction of novelties, and the cumulative processes that these entail. Technology and globalization are both evolutionary, but it is essential to emphasize that they are by no means synchronized. They are instead *co-evolutionary*. That is, they represent different systems that are evolutionary, but are to some extent independent. By extension, this implies that they are also to some extent interdependent. The word 'concatenation' describes this well. It implies that technology and globalization are inextricably linked together, yet are not the same object. There are other co-determinants of globalization, some of which are also linked to technological change, and also bound to evolutionary principles. It is essential that we understand their principal components before we get to the heart of the matter, which is to understand the changing interdependence of firms and countries on a cross-border basis. To this end we also need to have an understanding of globalization's tangible properties and causes; it is a sum of its parts, no more and no less.

There are two secondary issues that I want to illustrate by example in this chapter, but not seek to prove in any rigorous fashion. First, that globalization is a summation and accumulation of various other evolutionary processes. There are myriad other processes and events which through an unlikely and complex intertwining define the *essence* of globalization. It is a slippery beast, precisely because it does not really exist. But as with all myths it has real foundations, and this is what much of this chapter will attempt to do. Second, that globalization is not new (Drucker 1997). Its equivalent Latin word was probably in daily use during the heyday of the Roman Empire. It is simply fashionable once again. Yet it grips our imagination, fascinating and horrifying us simultaneously. Globalization – and its constituent processes – has occurred largely incrementally, punctuated by numerous discontinuities. Various aspects of globalization are more intense than they were in the past, but globalization in the sense of interdependence has historical, *past dependence*.

This chapter seeks to put the rest of this volume in context: although much of the rest of this book purports to focus explicitly on technology and globalization, globalization is a much larger and more involved phenomenon. Chapter 1 sets the stage by going through some of various elements that intermediate between globalization and technology.

1.2 Mapping globalization

It is no simple task to map out the causes of globalization: a whole literature has evolved in pursuit of this elusive goal, most recently reviewed by Ietto-Gillies (2002), and probably most thoroughly by Dicken (1998) and Held et al. (1999). The problem, as I see it, is that any analysis of the causes of globalization requires an *anti-monde* test. That is, what might be the case 'in another world'? This is different from simply comparing an *ex ante* situation with the *ex post* environment, which is the most prevalent means of economic analysis. This is not simply because economists are lacking in imagination, but that economics (despite the best efforts of some) is not a science but a *social science*. The beauty of science is in its clear-cut boundaries. An experiment in physics or engineering is regarded as successful only if it can be repeated *ad infinitum* with exactly the same results, regardless by whom or where or when. Furthermore, it is possible to exclude certain processes in the repetition, to create a 'control'. In the social sciences, we are obliged to throw in a '*ceteris paribus*' clause even into our theorizing. In order to test these arguments we sometimes introduce numerous restrictive and often implausible assumptions. Unfortunately all else rarely is equal. Time moves on, and with it there are numerous other factors that have changed. We cannot, for instance, study how Bismarck might have helped create a coherent nation-state in the Balkans. Even when our analysis is drawn to rather simple questions, there remains a non-replicable element, because there are a hundred other factors, which cannot be precisely identified, much less controlled. The various social science disciplines are largely inseparable when dealing with questions of even reasonable magnitude.

In addition to the non-replicability bottleneck, we are faced with the chicken and egg dilemma. Are economic units more interdependent because of improved transportation opportunities? There is no denying that there is a relationship between the two, but might it not also be the case that the need of economic units to transport goods more efficiently leads to improved transportation? Similar arguments can be made about information and communications technologies (ICTs), other new technologies, international institutions, and the like.

I believe the best we can reasonably expect to say is that there are numerous factors that are interrelated, and should not worry too much about the direction of the causality or the relative importance of each. Academics (myself included) sometimes get mired in technicalities and miss the big picture.

After such an opening, it seems rather bold to attempt to map out the primary forces underlying globalization, but this is exactly what I have attempted to do in figure 1.1. This is not a complete taxonomy, and the layout, order and arrows are for illustrative purposes only, since cause and effect are hard to determine. I have tried to classify the *causes* of globalization into three distinct categories, as distinct from *outcomes* of globalization. However, there is a decided fuzziness between the two categories, and in this chapter I discuss some (but not all) elements from each of the categories:

1 Those associated with *political economy* and the environment (figure 1.1). Sections 1.3, 1.5, 1.6, 1.7, and 1.10 briefly discuss some of these forces. Note that there is considerable overlap between these variables, and with FDI and trade.
2 Those associated with *technology* are on the right-hand side of figure 1.1. In this chapter, I shall only discuss *new technologies* (section 1.8) and the multi-technology firm (section 1.9). This oversight is intentional, since technology is one of the main themes of the subsequent chapters.
3 Variables associated with the *growth, spread and the intensity of MNE activity* (figure 1.1), and are analysed in section 1.4. Note

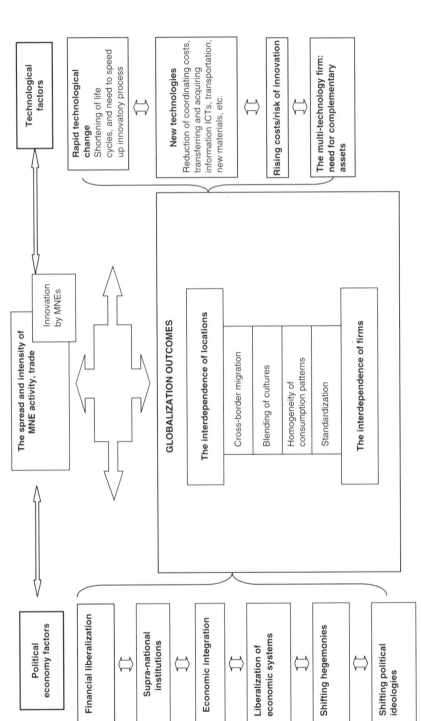

Figure 1.1 Mapping globalization

that, strictly speaking, the growth of MNE activity is a subset of *financial liberalization*, which itself is a function of numerous other political economy variables.

4 Variables that are most commonly identified as *outcomes* of globalization (figure 1.1). In this chapter I provide some brief comments on *the homogeneity of consumption patterns and standardization* (section 1.11).

Note that the MNE category is purposely not sub-categorized, with the exception of *globalization of innovation by MNEs* (section 1.5). This is because MNE activity is itself a function of the various other primary forces. For instance, one can say that increased MNE activity is a result of increased cross-border competition. However, cross-border competition is a function of economic and regional integration. It is also a result of financial liberalization, the shift towards market economies and neo-liberal economic policies. These in turn are partly caused by the ascendancy of the US as a singular hegemonic power. There is also a process of positive feedback: the greater the spread of any given MNE, the greater the pressure on its competitors to spread likewise.

It should be patently obvious that the creation of four clear and distinct categories is fraught with difficulty. To give another example, new information and communication technologies may have reduced transaction costs, and made economic integration (both *de facto* and *de jure*) possible. But economic integration itself would not have been possible without the reduction of trade and investment barriers. Such reductions would not have occurred had not economic actors (such as MNEs) engaged in trade and investment demonstrated the positive social returns of increased cross-border activity. The increases in trade and investments have driven the need to improve appropriability of MNEs' intellectual property rights, and the ability to enforce contracts across borders, prompting the development of supra-national institutions and international agreements. Such agreements are essential for economic integration, but creating such agreements depends on participants having sufficiently compatible legal frameworks. It should be obvious from these two examples that trying to map all inter-linkages is futile, because the links between all these factors are self-reinforcing and rampant.

It is important to re-emphasize that while most change occurs incrementally, discontinuities play a significant and unpredictable role, although hindsight has the advantage of always being perfect. Such discontinuities can be political (e.g., the collapse of the USSR), technological (e.g., the invention of the transistor), or even natural (e.g., El Niño, the AIDS epidemic). It is tempting to include 'chance' as an important variable, but this would be universal platitude and thereby a tautology.

The next few sections deal with some of these main forces underlying globalization, all described with the caveat that each is a function of the others, but keeping the focus on technology and globalization. The categorization is simply a device to aid the reader by providing simplicity of presentation, without, it is hoped, oversimplification. In each section I will highlight three points: I provide a brief historical context and its development to the current state of affairs; I provide some brief discussion on how the factor in question relates to the other factors; and where relevant, I hope to highlight that interdependence is at an early – and not necessarily stable – stage of evolution.

1.3 Financial liberalization

Liberalization has come to have many meanings, and these vary to include the liberalization of capital flows, the liberalization of trade regimes, and the liberalization of markets and economic systems. In this section my interest is on financial liberalization, and in particular on international capital flows, although the liberalization of economic systems is an associated process, which is discussed in section 1.6. It is no exaggeration to claim that the liberalization of capital flows has been a decisive feature of the post-1945 'liberalization'.

International capital flows can be differentiated into several types (Held et al. 1999):

- foreign direct investment;
- international bank lending;
- international bonds and other credit instruments;
- portfolio investment, which implies ownership of shares or bonds of firms located overseas without the control associated with direct investment;
- international equities and other financial instruments (such as options and derivatives);
- development assistance and aid (both government to government aid, and NGO-controlled flows);
- monetary flows (through the sales and purchase of foreign currencies).

As admirably narrated by Held et al. (1999: ch. 4), there has been a gradual globalization of such activities over the last 150 years or so. In other words, liberalization too has occurred largely incrementally over the long term, dating back to the establishment of the formal gold standard in 1878. The gold standard as a concept – that currencies were backed by reserves of gold – survived until the end of the twentieth century, although the institutions associated with the gold standard were superseded by new regulations (and organizations to monitor and enforce these regulations) established under the terms of the Bretton Woods agreement in 1944.

The liberalization of capital flows in the Bretton Woods scenario was not all-inclusive. It led to the growth of multinational banking, international money markets, derivatives trading, debt trading and the cross-border listing and multiple listing of firms in several stock markets, to mention but a few developments. However, capital control, monetary and fiscal policies remain under national control. National central banks therefore have considerable sway in determining the extent and nature of capital flows activities. Although most Organization for Economic Cooperation and Development (OECD) countries have eliminated national controls, eliminating the formal barriers between international and domestic financial markets, monetary and fiscal policies remain the realm of central banks. Furthermore, the agreement is applicable only upon member countries of the International Monetary Fund (IMF), thereby limiting its geographical scope, since membership originally excluded the centrally planned economies of Central and Eastern Europe and Asia.

The liberalization of capital flows within the Bretton Woods agreement thus demonstrates its ideological origins, and reflects certain market capitalism-based value systems and institutions. A large number of countries have liberalized only reluctantly, as part of Structural Adjustment Programmes (SAP) that are often preconditions for World Bank loans. Others have voluntarily (but still somewhat reluctantly) accepted liberalization as a means to attract international investment.

The increasing globalization of capital markets has led to considerable loss in economic autonomy of individual governments. Short-term interest rates, for instance, may still be nationally controlled, but long-term rates tend to be determined by international markets. Determining exchange rates, too, is largely in the hands of international markets, and it requires deep pockets to intervene to stabilize them. The internationalization of credit and the variety of sources and types of assets make it difficult for countries to control money supply. The ensuing lack of control over domestic economic development has seen the need for governments to pursue largely convergent macroeconomic policies designed to minimize disruptive financial flows. However, the current international economic system à la Bretton Woods is less able to handle the relatively chaotic financial consequences of global financial markets (see Stiglitz 2002).

The next section discusses what is arguably the most controversial aspect of financial liberalization – that of foreign direct investment – and its much maligned conduit, the multinational enterprise.

1.4 Multinational enterprises

Despite the hyperbole produced by the anti-globalization movement, globalization cannot be credited as a primarily MNE-driven process. Nonetheless, the *importance* of the MNE to globalization is possibly the only point anti-globalization and pro-globalization factions agree on. MNEs are simply the most visible of these processes, and while their role in promoting globalization is undeniable, they are a function of numerous other factors, as much of this volume will illustrate.

Their attractiveness as a scapegoat is partly associated with what looks a meteoric appearance from the ashes of World War II. Also, MNEs have managed to pick up for themselves an unsavoury image as exploitative emblems of unfettered and shameless capitalism, greed and power – the large faceless mega-corporation conglomerate that is answerable to no government, ethos or value. This is not the place to debunk or confirm either of these myths authoritatively. But it is worth noting that the first MNEs – in the sense that operations were integrated across borders and there existed some level of overall strategic control and coordination between affiliates in different locations – came to being towards the end of the nineteenth century.[1] During the eighteenth century the large trading houses (state-owned or state-sanctioned) engaged primarily as traders, moving natural resources from the developing world to Europe, and manufactures in the other direction. Although there were considerable foreign investments abroad, these were mainly associated with long-term capital flows, with the financing of debts, bonds and other financial instruments, required to support large-scale private and public projects in the colonies. In addition, where private investments by individuals occurred, these were what Wilkins (1986, 1988) calls 'free-standing companies' in that they were companies established by investors of a home country nationality who were located in a host country, but did not form part of any firm located in the nominal home country. They were not strictly domestic firms, since their capital (and entrepreneurial basis) came from abroad, but they did not represent a direct investment since *the foreign-located firm was not a subsidiary of another firm in another country*. Jones (1996) reviews this issue in some detail and notes that such investments were often associated with colonial interests. That is, Dutch entrepreneurs established free-standing companies in the Dutch East Indies, just as the French and British did in their colonies. Indeed, even by 1914, the number of free-standing companies far outnumbered 'true' MNE subsidiaries by a large order of magnitude. Both types of MNE were predominantly in services and natural resource extraction. Most activities were *trade-supportive* in nature, and largely did not support much transfer of technology.

Large firms were the exception rather than the rule at this time, both in Europe and in the colonies. Even as late as 1789, the biggest bank in Paris had fewer than thirty employees (Braudel 1992: 443). Braudel goes on to state, 'Numerous small firms remained the rule. Size of firm only increased significantly when the state was concerned: the most colossal of modern companies, the state, helped others to grow as it increased in stature itself.'

The first MNEs as we know them today did not blossom till well into the twentieth century, because the concept of large firms did not make its debut until late in the nineteenth century. The importance of size arose for a number of reasons, some of them technological. First, this was about the time of the 'second' industrial revolution, with innovations associated with mass production techniques. These innovations particularly benefited more capital-intensive industries that were characterized by economies of scale and scope, such as refineries (for both sugar and petroleum), animal and vegetable oils, chemicals, iron, copper and aluminium (both primary processing and products), packaging and processing of food products, standardized machinery and the development of large-scale enterprises (Chandler 1990). Second, developments in transportation and communication made it much more feasible to coordinate far-flung activities efficiently. Third, the brief period of free trade that had flourished in the nineteenth century was replaced after about 1880 by high trade barriers. FDI continued to be dominated by MNEs from the major European colonial powers – the Netherlands, UK and France – and the US, which was by this time firmly established as the technological and economic hegemon. These four countries accounted for about 87 per cent of FDI stock in 1938 (Jones 1996).

MNEs were not highly integrated across borders until well into the latter half of the twentieth century, partly owing to global restrictions on cross-border capital flows and limited liquidity during the inter-war years. Trade played a much larger role than FDI. Activities of MNEs were organized in a multi-domestic fashion, in the sense that a French MNE's US operations duplicated activities of its (say) UK affiliate, and so on. Indeed, the Bretton Woods conference of 1944, which established rules and organizations (such as the International Monetary Fund, the World Bank and the International Bank for Reconstruction and Development) in the post-war financial era, did not consider FDI as a major concern (Ito and Krueger 2000). Indeed, to this day, few countries collect comprehensive national statistics on FDI, and when they do so, they are often hard to compare since they use different methodologies. (Most other important financial and economic measures are collected and published in a standardized way based on recommendations deriving from the Bretton Woods institutions.) The tendency to ignore FDI and MNEs, except with regard to their effect on trade, is still largely the case within much of mainstream economic theory.

There are a number of excellent studies that have examined the changing structure of international production, and I do not intend to duplicate these here[2]. Suffice to say that there has been a meteoric growth in FDI activities since the end of World War II. FDI stocks as a percentage of GDP[3] stood at 21.46 per cent in 2001, up from just 6.79 per cent as recently as 1982 (table 1.1). Furthermore, MNEs engage in considerable intra- and inter-firm trade, and (as table 1.1 indicates) about a third of world trade is undertaken by MNEs.

The primary source of outbound FDI continues to be the industrialized countries. Of outward FDI stocks 88.1 per cent emanated from the developed countries in 2001, as illustrated by figure 1.2a; the EU as a bloc accounted for the largest share of outward FDI, with the Netherlands, UK, France and Germany accounting for fully 41.3 per cent of all outward FDI stock from the developed world. Around 68 per cent of inward FDI is directed towards Triad countries – North America, Europe and Japan (figure 1.2b). Although there has been an increase in the share of inward FDI to developing countries, this increase almost entirely represents an increase to a small group of developing countries which primarily includes the Asian NICs and China. Indeed, as table 1.2 shows, in most geographical regions in the developing world, just five countries account for at least 70 per cent of all inward FDI.

The point here is that although the activities of MNEs has increased, this has remained concentrated within a small group of firms – the 100 largest MNEs account for 18 per cent of all employment by MNEs worldwide – and between and from a few countries.

Table 1.1   Selected indicators of FDI and international production, 1982 and 2001 (US$ billions, unless otherwise indicated)

	1982	2001
FDI inflows	59	735
FDI outflows	28	621
FDI inward stock	734	6,846
FDI outward stock	552	6,582
Sales of foreign affiliates	2,541	18,517
Employment of foreign affiliates ('000)	17,987	53,581
Total assets of foreign affiliates	1,959	24,592
Exports of foreign affiliates	670	2,600
Inward FDI stock to GDP ratio (%)	6.79	21.46
Foreign affiliates' exports to total exports (%)	32.20	34.99

Source: UNCTAD (2002) table 1.1; for explanatory footnotes see UNCTAD (2002).

Table 1.2   FDI to developing regions, two periods, as % to all developing countries

	1980	2000
Africa	6.7	4.8
Nigeria	1.0	1.0
North Africa	2.3	1.7
Rest of Africa	2.1	1.4
concentration ratio in 2000 (5 largest recipients):		
Algeria, Nigeria, Tunisia, Angola, Morocco		68.8
Asia	72.5	63.9
Asian NICs	61.7	31.8
China	2.6	17.5
Rest of Asia	8.2	14.6
concentration ratio in 2000 (5 largest recipients):		
China, Hong Kong, Malaysia, Singapore, Indonesia		80.9
Latin America	20.7	30.7
Brazil	7.3	10.0
Mexico	3.4	4.6
Rest of Latin America	10.1	16.1
concentration ratio in 2000 (5 largest recipients):		
Brazil, Argentina, Chile, Mexico, Bermuda		74.9

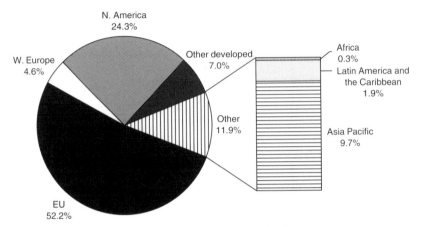

Figure 1.2a   Distribution of outward FDI stock, 2000

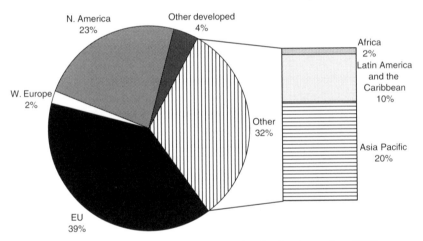

Figure 1.2b   Inward FDI stock: percentage distribution by region, 2000

Of the world's 100 largest MNEs in 1999, just three hailed from developing countries (the EU accounted for forty-six, North America for twenty-eight and Japan for eighteen). Just twenty developing countries continue to account for roughly 80 per cent of total FDI flows to all developing countries.

MNEs tend to be large, and they tend to be in a position to utilize the advantages of size. These advantages are most visible in the area of innovation. Furthermore, they have superior access to capital markets. These advantages allow MNEs to legitimately (and sometimes illegitimately) undermine smaller players to achieve a monopoly position. This is especially so in countries where regulatory authorities do not have the power to challenge MNEs. Monopolists are not loved, especially where they are large and foreign, and the underdog is small and domestic. Many sectors of industry in the least developed countries are entirely foreign-owned, and in some instances dominated by a single large MNE.

MNEs have also demonstrated no aversion in trying to influence the political economy of their host countries, and although this is quite normal for any commercial establishment, in a few – but well publicized – instances, in an attempt to pursue their own interests they have destabilized host governments. Given that a majority of MNEs are associated with former colonial powers and major economic and political hegemons, it is no wonder that MNEs are sometimes seen to represent neo-colonialism, and suspicion of their intentions is still rife[4].

The anti-MNE movement reached its peak during the 1960s when these attitudes became enshrined within the concept of import-substitution and national self-sufficiency (not just in the developing world), and policies to promote this view were adopted through much of the developing world. Inward FDI was largely controlled and limited in its scope, unless it met stringent conditions that promoted the self-sufficiency view by enhancing the host country's domestic sector. This entailed building and supporting 'national champions'. I should emphasize that although this is nowadays often associated with the import-substituting era in the developing countries, the concept of national champions was prevalent worldwide albeit much earlier in Europe and America (towards the latter half of the nineteenth century), and was a cornerstone of Japanese industrial development for much of the twentieth century. Indeed, techno-nationalism remains an important force in certain countries and in certain sectors (see e.g., Ostry and Nelson 1995 and chapter 3).

Nonetheless, international agreements including the various General Agreement on Tariffs and Trade (GATT) rounds, regional integration agreements, bilateral treaties and changing political and economic dogma have largely rehabilitated the market as the most efficient basis for allocation of resources. This has happened much more gradually in the developed world. Partly because foreign MNEs have been present in these markets for much longer, they have gradually come to be regarded on an equal basis with national firms. In addition, these countries are also home to significant numbers of MNEs and realize that the *quid pro quo* nature of international agreements would mean that restrictions on inward FDI in their domestic market will probably exclude the outward FDI of their own MNEs. The rehabilitation of the MNE has happened much more recently in the developing countries, but to a lesser extent. This is in part because this is a relatively recent event, having occurred somewhat involuntarily as part of economic liberalization and structural adjustment programmes (see discussion in next section).

Thus, by and large, over the last twenty years, MNEs have been rehabilitated, in the sense that they are not viewed with as much suspicion. This has happened from all ends, with the attitudes of MNEs, host and home countries changing. MNEs have become – if not good corporate citizens – less explicitly political, and the relationship with governments has experienced a *volte face*. Most countries are now trying to promote economic growth through FDI and international trade – what has been referred to as the 'New Economic Model' (Reinhardt and Peres 2000). This 'new view' is a pragmatic one, given the limited success of other non-hierarchical means to redistribute capital and technology, and recognizes the potential of the MNE as a means to promote economic development. This is discussed at length in section 1.6.

1.5 The globalization of innovation by MNEs

In general, despite the large amounts of investment in terms of capital values, MNEs still tend largely to concentrate their more strategic and core activities 'close to home'. In other words, they remain more deeply embedded in their home country than elsewhere. A large proportion of even the most internationalized MNEs tend to exhibit significant inertia with regard to their more 'strategic' activities, such as R&D and headquarters functions that tend to stay at home (Benito et al. forthcoming). General Electric, for instance, has approximately 1,600 researchers in its US facility, and about 400 in its two international corporate research labs. One point that derives indirectly from these data is that if FDI by developed country firms in other developed countries tends to have such low levels of embeddedness in locations where they have been present for many years, it is not surprising that MNEs in developing countries have an even lower level of embeddedness. It is a moot point that perhaps they are regarded as outsiders *because* they have not embedded themselves.

Nonetheless, as table 1.3 shows, the share of foreign firms' R&D in domestic R&D varies quite considerably, even within the Triad countries. In general, foreign-owned R&D activities in Europe represent higher percentages of national expenditure than in the US.

Figures on patenting (which is a measure of innovatory output, as opposed to expenditures, which indicate inputs) suggest that MNEs account for a much larger share in smaller countries, but by and large, innovatory activities of MNEs seem to remain at home. In general, firms from EU countries show a higher tendency to adopt international research strategies relative to US and Japanese MNEs. As table 1.4 shows, during the period 1987–95, 32.5 per cent of patents from EU-owned affiliates was produced outside the continent, while less than 9 per cent of the innovation activities of US-owned subsidiaries was undertaken outside the US, and for Japan this figure is around 1 per cent.

A considerable amount of the foreign-located R&D activities done by MNEs is located in the US, and in terms of patents this figure is close to 50 per cent. This reflects two things. First, it is indicative of the high levels of FDI that the US attracts by virtue of being the single most important market for MNEs in technology-intensive sectors. Foreign-owned MNEs in the US explicitly seek to augment their asset base by seeking technological spillovers from their US competitors, customers and suppliers. Second, it reflects the technological advantages of the US relative to European and Japanese counterparts in certain industries. Table 1.5 shows that, on average, the number of patents granted to European affiliates in the

Table 1.3 R&D expenditure of foreign affiliates as a percentage of total R&D expenditures in selected host economies, 1998 or latest year

Canada	34.2
Finland (1999)	14.9
France	16.4
Japan	1.7
Netherlands	21.8
Spain (1999)	32.8
UK (1999)	31.2
US	14.9
Czech Republic (1999)	6.4
Hungary	78.5
India (1994)	1.6

Source: UNCTAD (2002), table I.10.

US corresponds to more than half of all patents from R&D activity performed abroad. In particular for firms operating in the chemicals and pharmaceutical sector and the aircraft and aerospace industry, the data show a high and increasing concentration of research activity in the US. Growing trends are noticeable also in the electrical equipment and computing industries.

The growth of MNE R&D and its spread is one of the themes of this book, because it directly influences the interdependence of locations, and is further discussed in chapters 2 and 3.

Table 1.4 Share of US patents of the world's largest firms attributable to research in foreign locations, 1987–1995

Nationality of parent firm	%
US	8.3
Japan	1.0
European countries (total)	32.5
Germany	19.0
UK	53.0
Italy	13.5
France	26.9
Netherlands	54.8
Belgium–Lux	47.7
Switzerland	47.7
Sweden	36.5

Source: adapted from Cantwell and Janne (2000): elaboration from US patent database developed by John Cantwell at the University of Reading.

Table 1.5 Patenting activity attributable to European-owned research outside the home country in the US, 1978–1995

Industrial group of the European-owned parent firm	1978–1986 (%)	1987–1995 (%)
Chemicals and pharmaceuticals	57.4	61.6
Electrical equipment and computing	38.6	40.8
Motor vehicles	26.9	18.2
Aircraft and aerospace	44.0	69.8
Other transportation equipment	11.8	14.3
Professional and scientific instruments	45.1	32.2

Source: adapted from Cantwell and Janne (2000): elaboration from US patent database developed by John Cantwell at the University of Reading.

Box 1.1   Globalization of R&D: not as new a phenomenon?

John Cantwell and his associates at the University of Reading have worked intensively with US patent data. Their research seems to indicate that when examined on a historical basis, countries such as Switzerland, UK and the Netherlands which have historically been home to large MNEs (and thus have always had a high level of international technological activity) have seen large increases in international R&D since the 1950s. Another group of countries (such as France and Germany) which have few large MNEs have seen a gradual increase in their international R&D over the last eighty years. The third group are countries such as the US and Sweden, whose MNEs have historically tended to seek technology internationally, and were in fact as highly internationalized before the Second World War as they are today (having actually experienced a dip, only returning to their pre-war levels relatively recently).

Shares of US patenting of largest nationally owned industrial firms due to research located abroad

	1920–39 (%)	1940–68 (%)	1969–90 (%)
US	6.81	3.57	6.82
UK	27.71	41.95	43.17
Germany	4.03	8.68	13.72
Italy	29.03	24.76	14.24
Sweden	31.04	13.18	25.51
Netherlands	15.57	29.51	52.97

Source: Adapted from Cantwell (1995).

1.6 Liberalization of economic systems

Economic liberalization – in the sense of moving towards political and economic ideologies that emphasize markets – has much to do with the process of globalization, as most countries have embraced more market-friendly systems that promote and nurture (relatively) free trade and investment regimes. However, while this has happened gradually through the Triad countries over the post-World War II era, it has happened much more suddenly within the developing countries. The point I want to illustrate in this section is that economic policies have gradually evolved over fifty years, while almost all of the developing countries have attempted to restructure since the late 1980s, and along with the formerly centrally planned economies, only seriously during the 1990s. Thus this aspect of globalization is much more recent, and is still at an early and nascent stage in the developing world. The liberalization of economic systems towards a more laissez-faire approach that eschews central planning and state-interventionism is a consequence of a variety of developments, but is possibly the aspect of globalization that has caused the most umbrage.

The developing economies are individually very different, with different languages, geographies, histories and resource endowments. Nonetheless, they share a few common features. First, a majority of the developing countries (with the exception of a handful of Asian economies – mainly the NICs) pursued an import-substituting, inward-looking policy orientation for the several decades prior to the current trend towards liberalization, roughly until the early 1990s. Second – but not entirely unrelated to the first point – there has been a long love–hate relationship between the former colonies and the colonial powers stretching back for centuries. Third, they have had a historical dependence on natural resource and extractive industries, a trend which the import-substitution (IS) policies implemented in the 1950s and 1960s were to have helped reduce. These issues have – intentionally or not – coloured the attitudes of government policies towards industrial development, as well as their involvement in trade and investment within the current wave of economic liberalization.

At the risk of oversimplifying a complex set of developments,[5] the doctrine of import-substitution took hold in the post-World War II era, whereby leading economists of the day rejected the market solution as a means for the underdeveloped south to catch up with the developed north, by moving away from exporting primary commodities and importing manufactures, towards developing a domestic industrial base. This, it was argued, would capture the rents that derived to the developed economies from value adding to the primary commodities imported from the south, and the resulting structural change would spur economic development, as well as promoting economic independence. The implementation of import-substitution generally involved a high degree of central planning, combined with protection. Protection was undertaken through tariffs, exchange rate manipulation, quotas and exchange controls.

Domestic industry was to be developed by seeking capital and technology from abroad, since it was largely accepted at the time that physical capital and know-how could be transferred relatively easily through the flow of aid, turn-key projects and the provision of technical experts from the north to the south. Indeed, this view was widely held, with agencies such as the World Bank promoting these technology transfer programmes (Bruton 1998).

The role of MNEs was seen as a means to actualize the process of technology transfer. Investments in most countries were permitted in targeted sectors with the explicit understanding that control, ownership and technology would gradually transfer to the domestic sector. In addition, intermediate inputs were to be phased out as domestic suppliers acquired the competence to meet the (graduated and increasing) local content stipulations that were generally included in the investment agreements. FDI was largely undertaken with the intention of supplying the local market, since neighbouring countries had implemented their own import-substitution programmes. Captive markets meant that MNEs were able to pass on the costs of producing at an inefficient scale. A considerable share of productive assets was, furthermore, in state ownership, as a part of the belief in central planning, and the need to support large capital-intensive and scale-intensive projects which the private sector could not afford to maintain.

Import-substitution policies did lead to economic growth in most developing countries during the 1950s and 1960s, and even in the 1970s, although the anticipated growth of the domestic manufacturing sector did not go quite as planned. Despite increasing awareness of the problems of import-substitution and its effective implementation, however, many countries continued to pursue these policies, in many instances increasing the role of state ownership as a means to increase efficiency and to promote social welfare.

Unlike the East Asian NICs, the rest of the developing world did not voluntarily seek to move towards promoting an outward orientation in tandem with its import-substituting regime, but was pressured into structural adjustment programmes due to problems with macroeconomic stability and the ensuing economic crises that engulfed them in the 1980s.

The point of this quick romp through the political economy of development is that developing countries have reluctantly switched from an inward-looking, interventionist ideological basis to a market-friendly, market-driven regime that requires them to exist – suddenly – in a new multilateral milieu, but one in which they have little experience. They have hitherto operated their economies on a national basis, and by looking inward they have been able to minimize exposure to external shocks. Institutions continue to remain largely independent and national. By institutions we mean the 'sets of common habits, routines, established practices, rules, or laws that regulate the interaction between individuals and groups' (Edquist and Johnson 1997). Institutions create the milieu within which economic activity is undertaken and establishes the ground rules for interaction between the various economic actors, and represents a sort of a 'culture'. Institutions are both formal and informal, and will probably have taken years – if not decades – to create and sustain. To modify and develop institutions is a complex and slow process, particularly since they cannot be created simply by government fiat. Such change is even more complex where the new institutions require synchronization between countries. The Triad countries have taken fifty years to adjust and reform institutions, but even here there is inertia. The EU, for instance has failed to reform its agricultural sector. Norway remains largely mired in an import-substituting world, with a strong tendency towards central planning and state-owned economic actors.

Liberalization is an important force in economic globalization since it requires a multilateral view on hitherto domestic issues, and promotes interdependence of economies. It is implicit within this view that FDI and MNE activity can be undertaken with much greater ease than previously. This view is enforced because countries have explicitly sought to encourage MNE activity as a source of much-needed capital and technology. In addition to financial crises, the general warming of the attitudes towards FDI emanate from an accelerating pace of technical change and the emergence of integrated production networks of MNEs (Lall 2000).

Although systems may not yet be *de facto* liberalized, there is reason to believe that there is a tendency towards a broad global liberalization. This is partly enhanced by the establishment of the World Trade Organization (WTO), and the preceding GATT rounds, which encouraged liberalization, have in fact acted as an important force in establishing common rules and frameworks. Certainly, the various agreements within WTO have serious ramifications for member countries. In principle WTO agreements encourage an easier flow of technology and knowledge, and more alternative sources. Also, firms situated in least developed countries (LDCs) potentially have greater (and less impeded) access to important markets such as those of the OECD countries (Lall 1997). There is also the opportunity for binding arbitration and redress through the WTO. Brewer and Young (1998) point out that dispute settlement through the WTO is a preferable alternative to 'the uncertainties of unilateralism', particularly for developing countries.

Nonetheless, liberalization (among other forces related to the Washington Consensus) has acted as a major 'shock' to the institutions within most countries, since it has introduced not just new economic actors (MNEs), but it has also required major restructuring of existing institutions (legal codes, political structures, policy orientation). Despite the view of the Washington Consensus, the sudden exposure of these economies to the vagaries of international competition will not necessarily facilitate their institutional setting (as best illustrated by the chaotic state of the ex-Soviet economies). As Kogut (2000: 34) notes:

> Institutions, however, do not travel by the arteries of multinational corporations. They reflect patterns of behaviour that are inscribed in legal codes and political and economic relationships. Outside the power of any one actor to change, institutions are social agreements that guide and coordinate the interdependent acts of economic actors in a country.

1.7 Regional and economic integration

Is regional economic integration simply a *fait accompli*, a result of naturally declining economic distances between economic units and the needs of firms to reduce transaction costs? In other words, do nation-states simply 'evolve' towards *de facto* regional integration because of globalization? Certainly, *de facto* integration was enhanced by *de jure* integration in the case of the North American Free Trade Agreement Countries (NAFTA). However, one might readily say the opposite for the EU, where *de jure* integration occurred first as a political imperative, which was followed by structural programmes designed to create *de facto* integration.

There is no question that globalization (with all its caveats) has resulted in *de facto* economic integration. This has led to a revival of previously unsuccessful or dormant schemes and the establishment of a clutch of new agreements. Although estimates vary, there are close to 100 regional integration schemes in existence. Part of this renewed enthusiasm has to do with the benefits that have accrued to members associated with various European regional integration schemes and NAFTA, and in particular, the experience of Mexico in NAFTA.

It is not a coincidence that this renewed interest in regional integration has occurred while the concept of globalization pervades our understanding of the world economy. The two are not unrelated, and some have argued that regional integration projects appear to represent an opportunity to redress the inequities of multilateral agreements (Baldwin 1997), and to increase their autonomy from outside forces (Vernon 1996). Globalization has been uneven, in the sense that the primary beneficiaries have been the countries of the Triad and a handful of developing countries.

There are several similarities between globalization and regional integration. Both are processes and closely associated with cross-border economic activity, although globalization is more a consequence of increased cross-border activity, while regional integration is intended to *cause* it. The proliferation of cross-border activity is regarded as a primary symptom of globalization. Both globalization and regional integration are believed to provide opportunities for more rapid economic growth, associated in large part with increased FDI and trade that are consequent from increased opportunities to exploit economies of scale.

One of the primary conditions for integration is that countries have complementarities. However, they must also share similar institutions, and – especially for deep integration – have similar levels of social and economic development. Indeed, Friederich List pointed this out in his classic *National System of Political Economy*:

> A simpleton only could maintain that a union for free commercial intercourse between themselves is not as advantageous to the different states included in the United States of North America, to the various departments of France, and to the various German allied states, as would be their separation by internal provincial customs tariffs.... Let us only suppose all other nations of the earth to be united in a similar manner, and the most vivid imagination will not be able to picture to itself the sum of prosperity and good fortune which the whole human race would thereby acquire. Unquestionably the idea of a universal confederation and a perpetual peace is commended both by common sense and religion... A union of the nations of the earth whereby they recognize the same conditions of right among themselves and renounce self-redress, can only be realized if a large number of nationalities attain to as nearly the same degree as possible of industry and civilization, political cultivation, and power.

However, there is often a lack of common institutions, and the lack of political consensus in creating these. Take for instance the various and overlapping Latin American regional integration schemes, some of whose members have been in the throes of regional integration on a sporadic basis for over two decades. A recent study by the Inter-American Development Bank (IDB 2000) highlights the various problems in regulatory and institutional frameworks between Latin American countries. For instance, a truck carrying goods from Brazil to Chile requires 200 hours for a 3,500 km journey, of which 50 per cent is spent at the two border crossings. As I have highlighted before, the development of common institutions is a slow and gradual process. It is here that the benefit of a history of regional integration attempts and a similarity of cultures helps the most. Previous cooperative institution building allows countries to continue in that vein, but political differences and a lack of congruity in goals means that regional integration schemes remained largely incomplete.

1.8 The role of new technologies in globalization

New technologies are only new until an even newer technology comes along. This may sound facetious, but history teaches us to be humble, and this lesson is often lost as each generation and civilization gets wrapped up in hubris. But despite the earlier assertion that globalization is not new, it bears repeating that there have been numerous waves of new technologies, each of which has contributed to an industrial revolution, or, at the very least, to industrial *evolution*. Schumpeter (1939) first highlighted the role of technological paradigms in determining the long-term cyclical trends in economic development originally suggested by Kondratieff (1925). This line of reasoning has been further fleshed out and developed by Chris Freeman (for a review, see Freeman and Soete 1997). I am suspicious of the regularity of Kondratieff waves because of the perfect nature of hindsight, and thus any such classification is deterministic. That notwithstanding, it is undeniable that there has been a series of new technologies that have each resulted in a discontinuity, and have had a pervasive influence on a wide variety of industries, and sectors of the economy. The first industrial revolution was instigated in part by the development of centralized production units (the factory), the mass production of textiles, the use of water power and access to cheap cotton (from the colonies). A century or so later, the harnessing of steam power resulted in a second industrial revolution. Electricity underlay another revolution during the beginning of the twentieth century. Mass production technologies ('Fordism') drove yet another.

It is true that each of the technologies credited has fundamentally affected the organization of economic activity, and has had knock-on effects on a wide variety of sectors. But as David (1991) illustrates, it takes considerable time to adopt, internalize and appreciate the benefits of new technologies. It is also not always clear why certain technologies are regarded as more important than others. By way of an example, not enough credit is given to the discovery of petroleum derivatives such as plastics and petrol, and the process technologies that are needed to extract these derivatives efficiently. To my reading, these technologies constituted a new paradigm that shares the distinctive features of creating a technological *discontinuity*, and having significant cross-industry influences – at least as much as electricity. But this is a small quibble.

Each of these new technologies has, in its turn, promoted the increasing interdependence of economic units. Steam power made transportation much more reliable and rapid. Electricity and radio technologies improved communications. That the British managed to maintain an empire as far-flung and disparate as it did owes much to these technological changes: goods transported to and from colonies efficiently and cheaply; colonial administrators able to keep in touch with London; civil unrest curtailed by the use of machine guns. At the same time, these new technologies have allowed firms to coordinate and control (much more efficiently and reliably) their activities in different countries, and utilize differences in factor costs and inputs to better exploit comparative advantages and scale economies. Thus, as discussed in a previous section, the boundary-spanning MNE might never have come to exist in the absence of each of these 'new' technologies.

1.8.1 Information and communications technologies: a new revolution?

Technological revolutions and 'new' technologies come and go. The smart money is on information and communications technologies (ICTs) both as a 'new' technology and as a revolutionary technology. Their influence is pervasive in the sense that ICTs have affected numerous other industries. Biotechnology – another 'new' technology – is highly dependent on advances in automation and data processing. In the absence of ICTs, mapping and cloning genes would be a tedious and slow process. Without these technologies, the human genome project might have taken several times as long. But the role of ICTs is multiple (Santangelo 2002). First, it has affected other products where the importance of data processing and communications was hitherto marginal or negligible. Take the humble automobile, which was hitherto primarily a mechanical product. The average new automobile boasts several microprocessors controlling everything from the positioning of the seats, the anti-lock braking system, electronic fuel injection and ignition system. As the BMW advertisements proclaimed in the 1990s, cars now have more computing power than the Apollo spacecraft had. These developments in turn have forced technological change on yet other technologies. In the case of automobiles, the growing use of ICTs has increased power consumption, such that the existing 12 volt-based electrical system is increasingly insufficient, forcing car companies to develop and design a 45 volt Bus system. Other new applications are less significant. For instance, lawnmowers remain largely unchanged by the ICT revolution, as does (largely) agricultural activity. In these industries, ICTs may have become more important, but they remain a marginal or peripheral technology. On the other hand, a whole gamut of new industries has evolved where ICTs are a core and central technology: internet service providers, e-bookshops, mobile telephony, Personal Digital Assistants (PDAs), pagers, global positioning systems, to mention but a few.

What I am trying to highlight here is that there are products and processes where innovations in 'new' technologies have only an *autonomous* role, while there are yet others where these developments have a *systemic* influence.

The second role of ICTs is as a facilitating technology. Along with improvements in transport systems, it is a space-shrinking technology (Dicken 1998). The various aspects of ICTs – satellites, fixed line networks, mobile networks, the internet, networked computers – have acted to reduce costs of communications while improving reliability, efficiency and coverage. Distances have 'shrunk', and this has happened not just among the OECD countries, but in the developing countries as well. It is no longer necessary to wait several years to get a fixed line phone connection in many countries, and then to wait an unreasonable number of hours trying to get an audible connection in many developing countries.

Space-shrinking technologies do indeed make it easier for cross-border exchanges of information to occur: one can have one's MTV wherever one desires (if one can afford it). The latest escapade of the Bob the Builder or Commissar Rex can be viewed at will, BBC and CNN will give you the latest stock market action, and the low-down on holiday destinations. But, as I will discuss later, the effect on the convergence of consumption patterns is far from clear. However, ICTs as a *facilitator* of economic activity is important whether used by firms, individuals, or governments, whether by disseminating information, collecting information or reducing transaction, information and communication costs. These developments have had a significant effect on the ability of even small- and medium-sized enterprises (SMEs) to coordinate overseas activities (be they sales or manufacturing subsidiaries), as well as better undertake outsourcing and alliances (Narula 2002a).

1.9 The knowledge-intensive, multi-technology firm

It has long been the case that undertaking any form of economic activity requires access to a variety of skills and knowledge. Thus I find it rather facile to refer to the knowledge-intensive nature of most forms of value-adding activity as a feature of globalization. The only difference from yesteryear is that there is an increasing need for non-traditional and non-intuitive skills. By traditional, intuitive skills I mean those that an able-bodied person might reasonably acquire by instinct, by observing, by imitating and being good with one's hands. Many of the skills and knowledge that are required in the workplace today require a certain level of education in areas that are non-obvious. In other words, 'basic skills' that one acquired through basic education are less relevant in today's workplace. While it may still be possible to be a master carpenter and make chairs, if the carpenter wishes to go beyond a one-man operation she must know about accounting, marketing, law and even webpage design. Although many technologies have an intuitive aspect to them, these are often traditional sectors. Newer technologies have a greater non-intuitive aspect. Understanding how to repair or design a Volkswagen Beetle, a bicycle, a cassette deck or a water heater requires simply to spend a certain amount of time unscrewing and unbolting parts to observe the mechanisms, and perhaps a basic knowledge of physics. Understanding how to fix or make a CD player, a 2001 model Mercedes Benz or a digital mobile phone requires specialized knowledge and skills such as digital circuit design, control engineering, laser technology.

Of course, what is new today will be old tomorrow; becoming diffused, it will be regarded as basic knowledge. Two decades ago, subjects such as 'principles of microprocessor design', 'integrated circuit fabrication' or even 'printed circuit board (PCB) design' were specialist topics in engineering departments, the subject of masters-level and doctoral theses. Today the first of these two are taught in advanced bachelor-level courses, and the last is such a general topic that amateur books teach one pretty much all there is to know. The point I am trying to make is that technology matures over time: there is a proportional (but non-linear) decline in its uncertainty and a corresponding increase in its appropriability.

Box 1.2   The power of change: the end of a paradigm and the start of a new one?

One of the most standardized and diffused product technologies is the light bulb, largely unchanged (in principle and in appearance) since Thomas Edison. This, if anything, can be regarded as a relatively low technology-intensive, mature product, which is very much intuitive in that secondary school students anywhere can put one together. But this may be about to change. Many of the larger firms such as GE and Philips are experimenting with a successor based on light emitting diodes (LEDs) which currently are used for electronic displays. LEDs are more reliable, last longer, are more rugged, consume less electricity and are more efficient, because they convert more energy to light and give off less heat.

Early versions of LED-based light sources are beginning to find their way into industrial applications, and within a decade or so, another old technology will be replaced by a new, and more sophisticated one. What does this mean for old technology bulb manufacturers who do not have the resources to invest in upgrading?

Knowledge has always been a prerequisite of any sort of efficient economic activity. But it is true to say that economic activity has become *increasingly* knowledge-intensive. Furthermore, technology is now less intuitive (we will delve more deeply into learning as a systemic process in the next chapter), because it goes further than requiring intuitive skills.

It is another matter when one observes that products and production are increasingly multi-technology in nature. Seemingly independent technologies are required for products and processes, which have hitherto been seen as mono-technology products. Again, this is not an entirely new phenomenon, but its intensity has increased. A car is no longer simply a mechanical engineering product, but requires technological competence in areas as diverse as ceramics, computing, communications and plastics, among others. It is true that there are products and processes which remain largely mono-technology in nature, such as fish-hooks, and will probably remain so. Most multi-technology firms maintain multiple or 'distributed' competences, by maintaining a minimum level of in-house expertise in several fields in order to monitor externally developed knowledge and integrate it with its other production inputs.

Even where products are mono-technology-based, the processes used to manufacture them often utilize several technologies. Furthermore, within a given technology there are several technological paradigms at play, as firms base products on the current dominant design, yet develop nascent technologies with the long-term intention of replacing the current technology with a new dominant design. This is discussed at length in chapters 4 and 5.

The increasing cross-fertilization of technologies across disciplines and resultant broader portfolio of competences has become fundamental to the competitiveness of technology-based firms. There has also, however, been a concurrent increase in competition, due, *inter alia*, to the liberalization of markets, and the reduction of transaction and transportation costs. This has led to a decline in the profit margins due to increased cross-border competition (Buckley and Casson 1998). Consequently the increased costs of requiring more technological competences is not offset by greater profits, but quite the opposite. In addition, R&D in new technologies has been seen to be increasingly capital-intensive. So, the need to reduce costs (and maintain profits), while maintaining the firm's technological assets has become an important managerial balancing act.

1.10 Political economy: shifting hegemonies and discontinuities

Discontinuities are not always technological. Events do not always proceed in a linear way, and – to use a thoroughly unscientific word – there are surprises and coincidences, some of which are historically dependent (such that, with hindsight, these events might have been predicted). Wars, for instance, have sometimes played a fundamental role in fostering interdependence between economic units. European regional integration came largely out of the desire to avoid further European conflict – the desire to Europeanize Germany, before Germany Germanized Europe. It was encouraged at various stages by the US, in the hope of creating a united Western Europe that might act to prevent Soviet expansionism. On a smaller scale, the Norwegian economy benefited financially from World War I, by providing its considerable shipping tonnage to all sides during the war, and by supplementing Western Europe's depleted shipping capacity after the war (Stonehill 1965). This helped support the large-scale nationalization of foreign firms' assets and its being much more closed than any other Western European country (Kvinge and Narula 2001). Norwegian barriers to trade and investment are still on average at least double of those in most EU countries, and compared to countries such as Germany, the UK and Italy more than three times as high (OECD 2000). Likewise, wartime profits allowed Sweden's SKF to become the world's largest manufacturer of ball bearings, by buying the entire German ball bearing industry in the 1920s (Jones 1996). The OPEC oil crisis in the 1970s instigated technological change in offshore oil exploration and extraction (as increased prices made this more viable), and the North Sea as a major source of petroleum. It has also led to increased R&D into alternative technologies and energy sources. The great depression in the 1920s contributed to the reform of the global financial system and the rise of fascism, the New Deal, and Keynesian economics.

The Cold War answers for much. Competition policies implemented during the US occupation of Japan designed to prevent the pre-war domination of the *Zaibatsu* in the post-war economy were relaxed in order to promote production to support the Korean War. Thailand and Korea likewise benefited from the Vietnam War. Indeed, all the Asian NICs (and Japan as well as the 'new' NICs) share several features in common. They were prominent US allies, the US turned a blind eye to uncompetitive and undemocratic policies in these countries, and they were given access to US technology and capital with few strings attached. I am oversimplifying greatly, and not giving enough credit to domestic reasons such as the entrepreneurial spirit of the population, well-designed economic policies and long-term investment in education and infrastructure, to name a few.

The end of the Cold War and the subsequent US political and economic hegemony has also played a prominent role in globalization (Gray 1998). The US has begun to promote US-style capitalism quite explicitly to the rest of the world in several ways. First, it has used its economic clout to demand concessions for American corporations in the form of privileged market access. The most prominent recent example has been its holding up China's entry to the WTO in exchange for numerous concessions, such as majority ownership in the finance sector, the purchase of US capital goods and technology over European alternatives, etc. Second, in its capacity as host and principal sponsor of the IMF and the World Bank, it has been the intellectual light behind the 'Washington Consensus'. Negotiations between client countries and the World Bank are undertaken with active US Treasury Department participation, and US-style policy prescriptions are part of the structural adjustment programmes prescribed (Wade 2002).

Other exogenous events may have lesser influence, and some of them may speed up technological change, affect the relative bargaining power of individual countries or MNEs, or alter the outcome of supra-national, bi-national or multilateral treaties. These events are 'shocks' or discontinuities in that they affect the otherwise gradual and evolutionary process of change, are difficult to predict, and have unknown outcomes, just as technological discontinuities do.

1.11 Standardization and homogeneity across borders

Strictly speaking, standardization and the homogeneity of consumption patterns cannot be said to be a cause of globalization, but an outcome. A number of populist writers have postulated that globalization implies that we shall all be turning into Americans in rather short order. Other more cautious souls suggest that we are losing our own cultures and national identities. Indeed, this trend is itself taken to be the primary content of globalization. Both ideas are largely unfounded. The idea is largely social legend. One only need travel a small distance away from a major city to note a complete lack of cosmopolitan lifestyle in most countries. In Europe one need not leave the city to discover the absence of a global world: except for the capitals of some former superpowers with large ex-colonies such as France, the UK and the Netherlands, much of Europe remains mono-cultural. Less than 10 per cent of R&D scientists (people whose qualifications make it relatively easy to relocate) live more than 100 km from where they were born. Academics may be forgiven for their belief in the global village: they are one among a few – rather privileged – *global tribes*.

Nonetheless, homogeneity across borders has occurred and there has been a growing interdependence because of this. I have earlier raised the spectre of empires, hegemons and Rome on purpose, because standardization as a trend predates *Pax Americana*. Conquests and empires have always played their role in standardizing tastes – where might we be today, had not five cultures asserted themselves – the Spaniards, the French, the British, the Arabs and the Han Chinese, and created a world dominated by just a few languages, rather than several thousands?

There is something to be said about the role of the British Empire, for example, in creating legal, political and social institutions and infrastructure in a similar manner across all its former dominions that persist to this day. Lundan and Jones (2001) refer to this as a 'commonwealth effect'. However, some of these 'British' institutions date back even further to the Romans, such as common law, civil law and international law. Roman law has affected the development of law in most of Western civilization as well as in parts of the East (e.g., the Byzantine Empire until 1453). It forms the basis for the law codes of most countries of continental Europe. Each European country has of course modified Roman law owing to local influences and subsequent changes in political control, as have their former dominions. For example, South African law is a hybrid of Roman-Dutch law (itself superseded in the Netherlands since 1809 several times) and English law.

Indeed, the basis for globalization derives from colonialism and empire building. The Spanish, British, French, Americans, Russians and Chinese, not to mention other empire-builders such as the Arabs, Ottomans, Romans, Mughals, and Fulanis, defined most of the boundaries of the political and social units as we know them today. They also bequeathed common languages, legal systems, and the infrastructure and institutions upon which the modern states have been further built. There are two dominant bases for legal systems worldwide – the Roman code and the Islamic code.

Homogenization forces are not necessarily one-way. The entire world is beholden to the mighty tomato, the humble potato, the wispy maize cob, all originally from Latin America. The Chinese have contributed numerous technological breakthroughs to the road towards globalization, among which number paper, gunpowder and block printing. The Arabs provided the astrolabe and the basis of much of Western knowledge on mathematics, astronomy and medicine.

All these elements – technology, laws, political systems – are part of the intricacies that make up institutions in the sense of routines make up the 'glue' between economic actors. These evolve over time and are largely complementary to one another. Changes in any one element within a system may adversely affect other elements, and for this reason new institutional change is slow, or when rapid (through discontinuities in technology or exogenous shocks), causes considerable ripple effects on other elements in a national system. Increased interdependence between locations or countries (à la globalization) force change, and when these changes have happened suddenly (such as through Napoleon's conquest of much of mainland Europe and the introduction of the Napoleonic code) they have often been rejected where the exogenous shock has not lasted long enough for societies to respond with revising all complementary elements.

Increasing homogeneity across economic units is a continuous process of learning, forgetting and adapting that has been going on since the beginning of time, and circumstantial evidence suggests that this is happening more extensively. That is, the effect of homogenization is occurring more rapidly, and is inclusive of many more cultures and countries than in the past. There is very little variation in the brand names on offer on most main streets.

That said, this stereotype is valid only superficially. There are people in Uganda or Bolivia or Laos buying and wearing the same Polo shirts, Hugo Boss suits, drinking their frothy cappuccinos as they discuss their latest stock purchase with their business associates in New York or Tokyo. Such well-heeled types exist in every developing country, and do so very obviously. They speak English fluently, typically attend universities abroad, and have never flown economy class. A street or a block away, almost cheek-by-jowl, there are several times as many people – in every developing country – who have never been to the airport, think cappuccino is some sort of Mexican dog, do not own a tie, and are often functionally illiterate.

In other words, there is a very great unevenness in the distribution of wealth, and consequently a correspondingly great variation in the extent to which consumption patterns are standardized, both between countries and within countries. It is a big leap of faith to assume that if all else were equal, consumption patterns and tastes would be identical. Even in the entertainment sector, that most global of sectors, there is no clear homogeneity, and no sign that there is a convergence towards homogeneity. True, MTV is available on every TV from Vientiane to Santiago, but each is different. Indian MTV largely features Bollywood songs; MTV Germany has a different line-up from MTV Italy. In other words, there is no evidence to suggest that we live in a global village. While it is true that tastes may have shown some level of similarity amongst the richer OECD countries, and that this similarity may well have increased over the last fifty years since *Pax Americana*, there is no sign of convergence. The most we can say is that there are *global tribes and that there are global brands*. The bourgeoisie in every country exhibits similar spending habits, and as the middle classes become more affluent in each country this number may well be on the increase. But only relative to themselves, since the poorer sections of society still dominate both relatively and absolutely, especially in the developing world.

1.12 The dynamics of international interdependence: countries and firms

The discussion in this chapter raises two related issues: the import-ance of cooperative agreements, and the international search for assets.

1.12.1 Growing inter-locational interdependence: the international search for technological assets

The evidence regarding R&D internationalization by MNEs is varied, heterogeneous and ambiguous. It is true that large MNEs play a dominant role in the innovative activities of their home countries and control or own a large part of the world's stock of advanced technologies. These same MNEs undertake a growing share of their total production activities in host locations. A major-ity of overseas R&D activities of MNEs are associated with adapting and modifying their existing technological assets in response to demand conditions ('asset-exploiting R&D'). On the other hand, evidence clearly suggests that this is intermediated by industry-level effects (see e.g., Lall 1979, Patel 1996), and there is considerable inertia in the internationalization of R&D. That is, firms have not internationalized their innovative activity propor-tionally to the growth in their overall production activities (Zanfei 2000, Patel and Pavitt 2000). This non-internationalization is associated – *inter alia* – with the complex nature of systems of innovation, the embeddedness of the MNEs' activities in the home environment (see chapter 3), and the need for internal cohesion within the MNEs (Blanc and Sierra 1999, Zanfei 2000). Thus, the R&D intensity of MNEs' overseas activities tends to be quite low.

However, over the last decade there is evidence of a growing significance of overseas R&D activities by MNEs in order to aug-ment their existing assets by specifically establishing R&D facilities ('asset-augmenting' R&D) to absorb and acquire technological spillovers, either from the local knowledge base (public infrastruc-ture or to benefit from agglomerative effects in a specific sector), or from specific firms (see e.g., Dunning and Narula 1995, Cantwell and Janne, 1999, Patel and Vega 1999, Kuemmerle 1996, Le Bas and Sierra 2002, Criscuolo et al. 2002).

Although internalizing local technological spillovers also occurs when MNEs engage in asset-exploiting R&D, it is not the primary intent, as is the case with asset-augmenting R&D. Although there are other means by which technological spillovers can be acquired, such as through technological collaboration and licensing, these options are not always available to the firm, particularly where the technology sought is proprietary to another firm which does not wish to sell it. Even where a market for the knowledge in question exists, the tacit and firm-specific nature of technology means that they are more efficiently internalized when in close physical proximity to the transferring firm. In other words, there is often an important local component, that is, spillovers are stronger within a small geographical unit (see e.g. Jaffe et al. 1993, Jaffe and Trajtenberg 1996, Sjöholm 1996, Maurseth and Verspagen 2001). The empirical results in this literature seem to confirm that geographical distance negatively affects the scope for spillovers. This suggests that technological spillovers generated by the R&D activities of MNEs are geographically concentrated, and hence we should observe a greater knowledge flow between (for instance) European foreign affiliates operating in the US and headquarters and subsidiaries of US MNEs than between European and US MNEs' headquarters. Indeed, recent research suggests that asset-augmenting activities are on the rise, as figure 1.3 suggests.

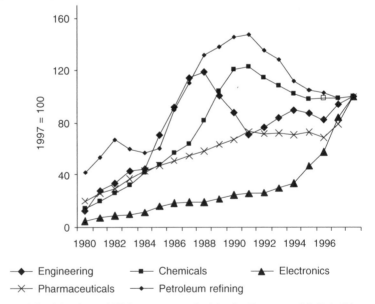

Figure 1.3 Number of EPO patents applied for by European MNEs' affiliates in the US (3-year moving average, 1997 = 100)
Source: Criscuolo et al. (2002).

Foreign sources of knowledge are thus increasingly important to firms and to countries. There is no question that globalization exerts itself by the way firms have to seek complementary assets – whether by FDI, alliances, outsourcing or licensing – in other locations. This trend has to do with the distinct nature of technological specializations of each country. Technological accumulation is incremental, and highly path-dependent, whether one views it from a firm, industry or national perspective. Thus, technological specialization patterns are distinct across countries, despite the economic and technological convergence associated with economic globalization (Archibugi and Pianta 1992, Narula 1996a). Other studies have shown that these patterns of technological specialization are fairly stable over long periods (see Cantwell 1989, Zander 1995) and change only very gradually. The kinds of technology across countries have been shown to have converged because of, *inter alia*, increasing cross-border competition and the increasing interdependence of economic actors in different locations. Cantwell and Sanna-Randaccio (1990) have shown, for instance, that firms seek to emulate the technological advantages of leading competitors in the same industry, regardless of their national location. Similarly, Narula and Hagedoorn (1999) have shown that firms seek to engage in R&D alliances with technological leaders in the same industry, irrespective of their national origins. Thus there is a growing mismatch between what home locations can provide and what firms require. In general, *national innovation systems and industrial and technological specialization of countries change only very gradually, and – where there is institutional inertia – much more slowly than the technological needs of firms*. Firms must seek either to import and acquire the technology they need from abroad, or venture abroad and seek to internalize aspects of other countries' innovation systems.

It is important to realize two points. First, that few systems are purely based around national sources. The presence of inward FDI (*ceteris paribus*) provides domestic firms with linkages to economic actors outside their national boundaries. The same is true through international collaborative activities by non-firm actors. Few systems are purely national, because knowledge flows occur through the collaboration between universities, government organizations and the like. Second, systems do not always suffer from inertia. Non-firm organizations (and particularly government institutions) play a fundamental role in overcoming such system failure (Freeman 1992) and can seek to remedy weaknesses and suboptimality in an innovation system. Systems can also survive discontinuities without major modifications. Harding (2001) illustrates – based on a study of the German innovation system – that systems can respond to new challenges and methods of organizing innovative activity without requiring a major restructuring. These issues are dealt with in greater detail in chapters 2, 3 and 7.

1.12.2 Growing inter-firm interdependence: the growth of cooperative agreements

From the perspective of the firm, the preceding discussion leads us quite naturally to the growth of alliances and outsourcing activities as a distinctive feature of globalization. Dunning (1995, 1997) goes further to propose that we are moving to a new age where flexible economic arrangements find increasing favour, in what he describes as one of *alliance capitalism*, shifting from the older paradigm of *hierarchical capitalism* where economic activity was conducted through hierarchies. The exact means and nature of this shift, as well as the implications of alliance capitalism and globalization are a matter of some debate.

Alliance activity has increased across the board, in all sectors of the economy, and in all kinds of activity. As a general phenomenon, it is associated with reductions in transaction costs. These have occurred due to, *inter alia*, (1) the introduction of new space-shrinking technologies (particularly information and computer technologies, which have reduced cross-border communication costs and organizational costs; (2) the harmonization of regulations and barriers as a result of growing economic liberalization. These have been further enhanced by the establishment of supra-national regional and inter-regional agreements such as NAFTA, and the EU, as well as multilateral protocols and agreements under the auspices of the World Trade Organization (WTO), World Intellectual Property Organization (WIPO), etc. These agreements have, *ceteris paribus*, reduced the risks of shirking contractual obligations as the costs of monitoring and enforcing cross-border alliances have fallen. The harmonization of regulations within the Single European Market (SEM) initiative, in such a view, represents a more advanced version of this activity, and further lowers transaction costs for firms within the European Union.

In addition, alliances have grown because of the increased competition due to liberalization of markets and the globalized nature of the operations of MNEs. Such increased competition has led to a low-growth scenario over the past two decades or so, and firms need to seek cheaper sources of inputs or divert sales from slow or negative growth markets (Buckley and Casson 1998). Such changes often need to be undertaken with rapidity. Declining transaction costs associated with contractual or quasi-internalized relationships in addition to falling profits margins has led to a *dis-integration* of certain firms in particular industries, as they seek flexibility and lower risk, which have hitherto preferred vertical integration. Indeed, some notice has been made of the process of dis-investment that, coincidentally or not, appears to have become quite common-place during the last decade (Benito 1997).

But the point that is most relevant for our discussion here is the technology-specific aspect. It is simply no longer possible for firms to meet all their technological needs *at the level of competence* that is needed, except for the largest of firms with unlimited resources.

The cross-fertilization of technological areas has meant that firms need to have an increasing range of competences (Granstrand et al. 1997). This encourages the use of alliances to seek complementary assets. As has been emphasized by others (e.g., Kogut 1988), the use of mergers and acquisitions (M&A) is not a viable option where the technology being sought is a small part of the total value of the firm. Greenfield investment does not represent a viable option either, in most instances, as the time and costs of building new competences from scratch may be prohibitive. It should be noted that in some instances alliances are used as a precursor to M&A (Hagedoorn and Sadowski 1999). In connection with this, there has also been a growing cost of development, and of acquiring the resources and skills necessary to bring new products and services to market. Increasing the market size, and the sharing of costs and risks associated with staying on the cutting edge of technology, creates strong motivation to undertake alliances, no matter how much firms may prefer to go it alone (Narula 1999, Narula 2001b. See also ch. 4).

Firms interested in acquiring knowledge in other aspects of value-adding such as production or sales have a broader choice of options that include wholly owned subsidiaries and arm's-length technology acquisition. However, some of these options are simply not available to firms that are seeking to undertake R&D. First, because knowledge has an uncodified, user-specific element which makes it hard to transfer efficiently. A greater extent of uncodified knowledge requires closer, face-to-face interaction if it is to be successfully transferred (Cantwell and Santangelo 1999). Arms-length transactions are simply not as effective, particularly in technology-intensive sectors or new, 'emerging' sectors, even if markets for these technologies were to exist. The further away these technologies are from the market (that is, more research-oriented than development-oriented) the less likely that technology can be obtained through market mechanisms (Narula 1999). Besides, its partly public good nature prevents prospective selling firms from making technologies available for evaluation, and without their doing so, the prospective buyer is unable to determine its worth. Markets, therefore, are liable to fail or will function inefficiently. This is the subject of chapters 4, 5 and 6.

2

Cross-border Interdependence between Locations: Learning, Growth and Systems of Innovation

2.1 Introduction

As chapter 1 has asserted, globalization as a process owes much to both the evolution of the MNE and the process of innovation and technological change, and that these two processes are themselves co-dependent and co-evolutionary. Furthermore, globalization – in the sense of a deepening of inter-linkages between and amongst economic units, and an increasing interdependence between them – is highly uneven, and at a rather early stage. Chapters 2 and 3 will focus on discussing the questions related to the location and dynamics of innovation and its relationship to globalization. I will discuss the process of knowledge creation within economies, and the important role of international actors in an innovation system, and why firms and countries are largely reluctant globalizers, at least as far as R&D is concerned. This is an area of some paradox: there is evidence to highlight two apparently contradictory situations. One the one hand, locations are apparently increasingly interdependent, and borders fuzzy. On the other, there is compelling evidence that locations remain distinct and idiosyncratic. I will seek to explain why these two states of nature can exist simultaneously. At the same time, the line of reasoning I develop here suggests that – over the long term – it is reasonable to expect that boundaries will become even more fuzzy and indistinct as globalization progresses. My central argument will build around the concept of 'inertia', the process of evolutionary change, and a 'systems of innovation' understanding of learning.

There is a clear link between geographical spread of the MNE and the process of technological change. Firms (of which MNEs are a subset) expand their (international) activities depending upon the strength (or weakness) of their competitive assets. These are not only confined to technological assets in the sense of ownership of plant, equipment and technical knowledge embodied in their engineers and scientists. Firms of all sizes also possess competitive advantages that derive from (1) the ability (that is, knowledge) to create efficient internal hierarchies (or internal markets)) within the boundaries of the firm and (2) from being able to utilize external markets efficiently. These ownership-specific assets are unique to each individual firm, because firms themselves consist of uniquely individual human beings. Even where two firms have the same product, one may be more profitable than the other because its managers are more efficient in utilizing its resources. Some of these are associated with the efficiency with which hierarchies are organized, and are referred to as organizational innovations[1]. Improvements in the quality of these assets lead to a greater quality per unit price; thus they can be regarded as innovations and as part of the firm's core assets. Such assets form a necessary (and sometimes sufficient) basis for a firm to remain competitive. Such assets include *inter alia* knowledge of overseas locations, capabilities associated with organizing multi-location operations, marketing and logistics, transfer pricing, etc. (for a discussion, see e.g., Dunning 1993, Madhok and Phene 2001). If we accept that economic growth depends on the ability of a nation's industries to develop and sustain their competitive position, and that this requires growth of productivity of its capital and labour, then we may postulate that economic growth concerns not just the development of knowledge through innovation, but also the diffusion of knowledge such that it may be utilized and exploited in an efficient manner. In other words, accumulated technology is an engine of growth *only* if it can be harnessed to make the best use of the available resources, and therefore must also consist of the knowledge to organize transactions efficiently, whether intra-firm, intra-industry or intra-market. The point here is that ownership-specific assets – be they technological in the narrow sense, or organizational – all share the common characteristics that they are cumulative, and evolve over time. That is, firms seek to maintain a stock of these assets, and *learn*.

Knowledge development is incremental and radical. This is a function of the way all learning takes place. Economic units – be they firms or individuals – acquire knowledge by exploring in the vicinity of their existing knowledge assets, by undertaking routines, which leads to incremental innovations (*learning-by-doing*).

Knowledge is acquired by interaction with its external environment. In the case of firms it may be through interaction (*inter alia*) with customers, suppliers, competitors, government agencies. This is referred to as *learning-by-interacting*. Firms (like individuals, who make up firms) are generally averse to radical change, in that they are likely to 'stay close' to successful patterns of behaviour, learning and interaction that have been successful in the past. This is referred to as *routinized learning*.

Routinized learning can be further characterized as 'exploitative learning' which adds to the existing knowledge and competences of a firm without fundamentally changing the nature of its activities. Non-routinized learning or 'exploratory learning' involves changes in company routines and experimentation with new alternatives (see e.g. Dodgson 1993; March 1991).

Another important factor in understanding the dynamics of technology and globalization is that these evolutionary processes do not occur in a vacuum. That is, firms do not make decisions about the kinds of product they will seek to develop, nor where they intend to develop and produce these goods and services, based simply on firm-specific issues and profit-maximizing motives (see Hagedoorn and Narula 2001). This may seem obvious to the lay reader, but to the economics profession this borders on the heretical, or something that – like a sibling or child born on the wrong side of the marital blanket – is discussed only *sotto voce* in polite company. Firms exist as part of 'systems', much as individuals exist as part of society. They are embedded through historical, social and economic ties to other economic units, just as individuals are linked to a particular location through social, historical and cultural links to other individuals (friends, family, job, etc.).

Finally, economic units of whatever size have finite resources. There are cognitive limits to what a firm can and cannot do, because it is constrained by its asset base or its potential to acquire these. Small- and medium-sized enterprises (SMEs) for instance, are limited by their size. A Danish IT firm with 100 employees may wish to establish R&D facilities in Silicon Valley, but there are limits to the size of any such affiliate. It might – with considerable additional capital – set up an R&D facility of twenty, perhaps even thirty employees, but it is unlikely to be able to muster the resources to establish a facility with 500 employees. Resources also include managerial assets, and other ownership advantages, and these are also finite. Although the resources available to mega-firms such as IBM, General Electric or Sony are much larger, they too have their limits in terms of the breadth and depth of their ownership-specific assets.

Firms are also constrained in the kinds of knowledge competences they can acquire and internalize by the extent of their absorptive capabilities (Cohen and Levinthal 1990). It takes years to develop new competences, and decades to achieve a level of expertise that will provide them with a technological advantage to be a technological front-runner. The skills to acquire and successfully internalize these external assets are non-trivial. In other words, *firms are constrained in what they can learn by what they know.*

The problem of finite resources also applies to systems and countries. Some of the characteristics of small economies are a function of size *per se.* The demand conditions restrain the sectors and kind of ownership advantages that firms of a particular nationality develop. Small market size constitutes a disadvantage in the development of process technology as the economies of scale are not present, but may provide a competitive advantage in product innovation (Walsh 1988). This applies to the kind of created asset location advantages small countries can provide.[2] They have fewer resources, and must either spread resources more thinly over the various disciplines, or must select areas as priorities, and these often (but not always) are those in which they have a natural-asset advantage and lead to a specialization of domestic firms in particular niche sectors (Soete 1987, Archibugi and Pianta 1992, Narula 1996a). The industrial structure of small open economies tends to demonstrate a 'niche' character, with a high level of specialization in few areas, where firms act as specialist suppliers, and thereby show a low level of product diversification. Bellak and Cantwell (1997) posit that these sectors will tend to be those in which they can achieve price-setter positions.

Understanding the systems view of technology accumulation, and the underlying dynamics of learning, also helps us to understand the creation of competitive advantage on an industry or a national level. It also – if one takes a linear and developmental view of technological accumulation and innovation systems – helps us to understand how industrial development occurs. What I intend to illustrate by this line of thought is that systems always exist, but they do not always result in an efficient outcome in the sense that firms in that location are able to sustain a comparative advantage. Furthermore, systems may be 'incomplete' or 'unbalanced' because some aspects of the systems are inefficient, or simply non-existent. Nor, even where an efficient, complete and balanced system exists, does this imply that this happy state of affairs will continue *ad infinitum.*

The causes of inefficiency are many, and it is not my intention to go through all of these mechanisms here in any great detail. One issue that I will raise continuously over the course of these two chapters – mainly because it has not received much attention in the economics of innovation literature (but much studied within the international business literature) – is the role of the MNE. Of the importance of cross-border flows of knowledge and capital there can be no doubt, and this is causally related to the spread of the MNE.

It is important to realize that few countries have truly 'national' systems. Of course, some innovation systems are more 'national' than others, and the term is indicative rather than definitive. For instance, smaller countries' innovation systems may have a larger dependence on non-national actors. Others have argued that innovation systems need to be viewed from an industry level (Nelson and Rosenberg 1993). It is certainly true that certain sectors (such as biotechnology) are less national and more global, while others are regional. However, by and large, most economic actors within an innovation system have a growing interdependence on economic actors outside their national boundaries.

Inter alia, this is as a result of the increasing internationalization of production, through FDI and strategic alliances, as well as the growing need for complementary technological competences. However, despite the growth of international production and sales networks, empirical work on R&D internationalization (e.g., Granstrand et al. 1992, Pearce and Singh 1992, Patel and Vega 1999, Kumar 2001) has demonstrated time and time again that – although decreasing – the most innovatory activities of MNEs remain concentrated in their home location. Nonetheless, for small open economies the level of foreign R&D is non-trivial – roughly half of R&D expenditures by Dutch MNEs are undertaken outside the Netherlands (van Hoesel and Narula 1999).

Thus when one dissects the dynamics of industrial development one can only ignore the cross-border issues at one's peril. I remind the reader that I use the term 'cross-border' in the broadest possible sense to signify *de facto* boundaries, rather than *de jure* ones.

2.2 The basic concepts underlying systems of innovation

Innovation involves complex interactions between a firm and its environment. The environment consists first of interactions between firms – especially between a firm and its network of customers and suppliers. Second, the environment involves broader factors shaping the behaviour of firms: the social and perhaps cultural context; the institutional and organizational framework; infrastructures; the processes which create and distribute scientific knowledge, and so on. This has led to a systems approach to understanding innovation. I should emphasize that systems are not unique to innovatory activities. Indeed, all human endeavour is constrained by its environment: it is only reasonable for economic activity also to reflect this tendency.

The use of the word 'system' does not necessarily mean that the various influences that underpin the generation of industrial innovation are systematically organized (van Hoesel and Narula 1999). To put it in simplistic terms, 'system' is taken to mean 'a regularly interacting or interdependent group forming a unified whole'. It is probably more accurate to say that an innovation system in most cases represents the serendipitous intertwining of institutions and economic actors within industry which defined the stock of knowledge in a given location (Etzkowitz and Leydesdorff 2000). Changes in, say, the educational priorities of a new government are likely to affect other institutions, and eventually the nature of innovatory activities of firms within given industries, thereby influencing the process and extent of technological learning in future periods.

By institutions I mean the 'sets of common habits, routines, established practices, rules, or laws that regulate the interaction between individuals and groups' (Edquist and Johnson 1997). Institutions create the milieu within which innovation is undertaken and establishes the ground rules for interaction between the various economic actors, and represents a sort of a 'culture'. Institutions are associated with public-sector organizations, but not exclusively.

By economic actors I refer to two groups. The first group comprises firms – private and public – engaged in innovatory activity, and the second consists of non-firms that determine the knowledge infrastructure that supplements and supports firm-specific innovation. I define 'knowledge infrastructure' in the sense proposed by Smith (1997) as being 'generic, multi-user and indivisible' and consisting of public research institutes, universities, organizations for standards, intellectual property protection, etc. that enables and promotes science and technology development.

Innovation systems are built upon a relationship of trust, iteration and interaction between firms and the knowledge infrastructure, within the framework of institutions based on experience and familiarity of each other over relatively long periods. It is certainly true that institutions are often associated with spatial proximity (Freeman 1992). This is not unusual, given the concentration of most firms' production and R&D activities close to, or in, their home location, and the long periods over which this has been so. Besides, knowledge diffuses more rapidly when actors are geographically concentrated (Ehrnberg and Jacobsson 1997). This partly accounts for the tendency of firms to locate R&D (or at least the most strategically significant elements) closer to headquarters.

Nonetheless, as firms respond to demand conditions, and because there is increasing need to seek complementary assets in multi-technology, knowledge-based sectors, firms have spread out spatially and sought to relocate some of their activities in host locations. Foreign operations in new locations have gradually become embedded in the host environment. It is germane to this discussion to note that the routines and institutions associated with systems of production in a particular location are related but not identical to systems of innovation. That is, networks associated with production in a location are not quite the same for R&D.

I think it is worth re-emphasizing that systems of innovation are not systematically organized, and are not necessarily confined to political and social borders. The unit of analysis varies considerably by industry, by country and by region. It is perhaps for this reason that this rather large and rapidly burgeoning literature has failed to develop a standardized and definitive road map to the constituent elements of a system of innovation. Lundvall (1992) in his pioneering work on *national* systems of innovation describes the fundamental elements as being:

- the internal organizations of firms;
- inter-firm relationships;
- role of the public sector;
- institutional set-up of the financial sector;
- R&D intensity and R&D organization.

Figure 2.1 gives a stylized version of the primary knowledge sources and institutions that exist within a *national* innovation system. Note that it focuses on purely domestic or local sources, and excludes the international and cross-border element. Indeed, a large component of research has focused on national systems (see e.g., Nelson 1993, Lundvall 1992).

The work of Porter and associates, based on Porter's (1990) diamond, can also be seen as studies on national systems, although

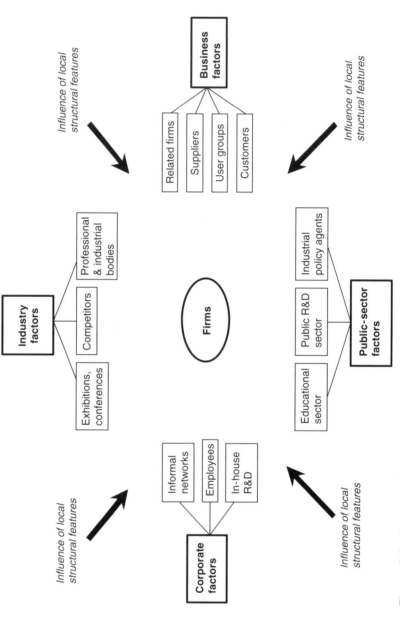

Figure 2.1 Institutional set-up in terms of potential knowledge sources of companies
Source: adapted from Wibe and Narula (2002).

the focus is much broader than systems of innovation. Rather, this body of work examines national systems of competitiveness, but the concept remains the same. Porter's original analysis as well as the strictly national model on which most national systems of innovation literature is based tends to examine competitive and technological advantage with little of no analysis of the MNE/FDI aspect, while Porter also largely ignores the dynamics of technological accumulation. Several variations of the Porter framework exist in the literature that seek to overcome the limitations of the Porter model. Most notably, the work by Dunning (1992) sought to correct this oversight. Rugman and associates (see e.g., Rugman 1991, Rugman and Verbeke 1993, Rugman and D'Cruz 1993) and Barclay (2000) use a 'double diamond' approach which takes into account the cross-border aspect of national systems. Another derivative of the Porter framework which explicitly takes an innovation system view is Narula (1993), which examines the role of technology and economic development.

There is a large literature from the economic geography school examining systems of innovation from a regional, sub-national level (e.g., Cooke 1998, Asheim and Isaksen 1997, 2002 and also contributions to Braczyk et al. 1998). See also Howells (1999). Others have discussed regional systems from a multi-country perspective. This includes regions that span parts of several countries, and in other instances systems of innovation that include components of several countries (see e.g., Bartholomew 1997, McKelvey 2000, SPRU 2001).

2.3 Understanding learning processes

Innovation is attributed to the utilization of economically relevant knowledge (Lundvall 1992). This is done either by recombining existing data, or by the creation of something completely unknown. Following this line of thought, innovation is not merely conceived as a new product of economic significance, but also as the process of knowledge creation, or learning, that generates it. Vital for this understanding of learning processes in the economy is Polanyi's distinction between tacit and explicit knowledge (Polanyi 1967). Tacit knowledge refers to intuitive knowledge that is based on a person's many experiences and cannot easily be put into words. Tacit knowledge is thus context-specific and restricted to the person who controls it. Moreover, it is created though experience-based learning processes such as *learning-by-doing* (Arrow 1962a) and *learning-by-using* (Rosenberg 1982). Explicit knowledge, on the other hand, is possible to codify, standardize and record, and is thus easier to diffuse. What makes tacit knowledge so vital in this connection is that tacit knowledge is a prerequisite to understand and use codified knowledge, while itself possible to obtain unaided by codified knowledge (Polanyi 1969). Nevertheless, the partition between the two kinds of knowledge is not always obvious; rather they are mutually dependent, giving economic knowledge the character of being compound by both tacit and explicit elements (Lundvall and Johnson 1994, Nonaka and Takeuchi 1995, Cowan et al. 2000, Lam 2000). This quality of knowledge suggests that it is better communicated in face-to-face interaction between people and that a social context is essential for constructive knowledge diffusion by way of *learning-by-interaction* (Lundvall and Johnson 1994). Another important distinction to be made in this connection is between individual and collective knowledge, both of which consist of a blend between tacit and codified knowledge (McKelvey 1998, Lam 2000, Antonelli and Calderini 1999). Individual knowledge represents knowledge that is restricted to the individual, and which is accumulated through formal education and other experiences of training or work. Collective knowledge, on the other hand, signifies the common knowledge of, for instance, employees in an organization. Examples of collective knowledge are company routines, norms and puzzle-solving activities. Depending on the effectiveness of the knowledge-creation activities, the collective knowledge in a company constitutes more or less than the aggregate of the individual knowledge within the firm (Lam 2000).

In a company there are various kinds of knowledge, which altogether constitute the knowledge base of the firm. The company knowledge base is a compound of knowledge that exists on different levels of aggregation: company-specific, generic, or industry-specific, and universal, and involves both individual and collective knowledge, as well as various degrees of tacit and explicit knowledge (Smith 2000). Furthermore, as new knowledge in a firm is created through the interaction between tacit and codified knowledge, knowledge bases of firms and industries are in constant evolution. Firms learn, and by doing so increase their knowledge base by incorporating new knowledge, which often implies that some of the old knowledge is no longer applicable. This necessitates an additional process of 'creative forgetting' (Lundvall and Johnson 1994). The two processes of learning and forgetting make up the concept of *interactive learning*, which includes imitation, searching, exploring and any other activity that will lead to the increase of economically significant knowledge (Johnson 1992, Nelson and Rosenberg 1993).

Like innovation, interactive learning is a ubiquitous phenomenon that takes place on every level of the economy. It may be intentionally promoted, or occur as unintentional by-products of routine activities (Lundvall 1992). In addition, a distinction can be made between firm-specific internal learning activities and those that involve interaction with external knowledge suppliers. *Learning-by-doing*, *learning-by-using* and *learning-by-interacting* describe different learning processes, which have in common that they occur in a production-related setting of the firm and are not the result of organized company learning activities (see figure 2.2) (Lundvall and Johnson 1994). On the other hand, there are firm-specific learning processes which are initiated, promoted and accomplished on purpose. Nonaka and Takeuchi (1995) highlight that the success of Japanese firms may be ascribed to the management's focus on the importance of tacit knowledge in the knowledge-creating processes in the company. Thus, successful knowledge creation in organizations seems most efficiently to develop through a multifaceted process of *creating common contexts of experience* amongst the company employees for them to convert their individual tacit knowledge to explicit knowledge (Nonaka et al. 2000). This kind of learning may be translated into *learning-by-social interaction*, a notion which emphasizes the importance of a social context for collective learning. *Learning-by-searching* is yet another important kind of learning, when it comes to technological development and innovation (Lundvall and Johnson 1994). Examples of learning-by-searching include R&D activities in universities and research institutions and in-house R&D in firms. These all intentionally aim for the discovery of new knowledge, and tend to be very structured, involving complex modes of interactive communication. As mentioned above, interactive learning may also be used to communicate knowledge amongst firms and between firms and other relevant institutions that may serve as knowledge suppliers to an innovation system. A typical example of this is the so-called *user–producer relationships*, which are vertical linkages of relatively close interactive learning associations between users and producers in different fractions of the value chain (Lundvall 1988, 1992, Lundvall and Johnson 1994). These may occur as joint development projects on a strategic level, or as regular customer relations and licensing agreements. In addition, as globalization has come to be an ever more characteristic feature of the present economy, a growing

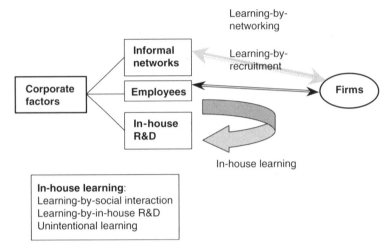

Figure 2.2   Corporate learning processes
Source: adapted from Wibe and Narula (2002).

network of firms thus shares the same generic knowledge base. This has fuelled the motivation for, and importance of, foreign direct investment (FDI) activities, since getting access to interaction with the 'right' kind of knowledge is vital in the global competition. In most industries, a growing inter-firm and cross-national alliance building activity has occurred over the past decades. Of course, not all of these activities are undertaken purely for knowledge-enhancing purposes (Narula and Hagedoorn 1999). Technological collaboration such as strategically motivated joint ventures or joint R&D agreements represent increasingly important processes in the current globalizing learning economy. Thus, learning-by-alliances must be regarded as a significant constituent of the concept of interactive learning. These issues are discussed in much greater detail in chapter 4.

2.4 Understanding the growing international dimension of learning

As has been mentioned before, some systems have a greater cross-border aspect than others. The learning processes described in the previous section are not just limited to intra-national interaction, but increasingly include international interaction. The pervasive role of MNEs in a globalizing world, and their ability to utilize technological resources located elsewhere, makes the use of a purely national systems of innovation approach rather limiting. Broadly speaking, individual national systems remain distinct: Technological specialization patterns are distinct across countries, despite the economic and technological convergence associated with economic globalization (Archibugi and Pianta 1992, Narula 1996a). Studies have shown that these patterns of technological specialization are fairly stable over long periods (see Cantwell 1989, Zander 1995) and change only very gradually, as do the technological profiles of firms (Fai and von Tunzelmann 2001, Fai 2002). The kinds of technology across countries have been shown to have converged because of, *inter alia*, increasing cross-border competition and the increasing interdependence of economic actors in different locations. Cantwell and Sanna-Randaccio (1990) have shown, for instance, that firms seek to emulate the technological advantages of leading competitors in the same industry, regardless of their national location.

The cross-fertilization of technologies – whether through arm's-length means, cooperative agreements or equity-based affiliates – means that few countries have truly 'national' systems. Of course, some innovation systems are more 'national' than others, and the term is indicative rather than definitive. Furthermore, firms need a broader portfolio of technological competences than they have in the past (Fai and Cantwell 1999). The exact causes of the growing role of MNEs and FDI are not germane to the present discussion. It suffices to say that it is so, and the degree is varying. In this section, I want to expand the discussion on the role of the MNE in national systems, introduced earlier.

As discussed earlier, the sources of knowledge available in a typical 'national' system are a complex blend of domestic and foreign ones, as illustrated in a simplified (and stylized) framework depicted in figure 2.3.

In a purely domestic innovation system, the path of technological development is determined primarily by domestic elements. The technological development trajectory is driven largely by the changing demand of local customers. Likewise, domestic governmental organizations determine domestic industrial policy, which in turn determines domestic industrial structure. National non-firm sources of knowledge and national universities also determine the kinds of skill that engineers and scientists possess, and the kinds of technology that these individuals have appropriate expertise in, the kinds of technology in which basic and applied research is conducted in, and thereby the industrial specialization and competitive advantages of the firm sector.

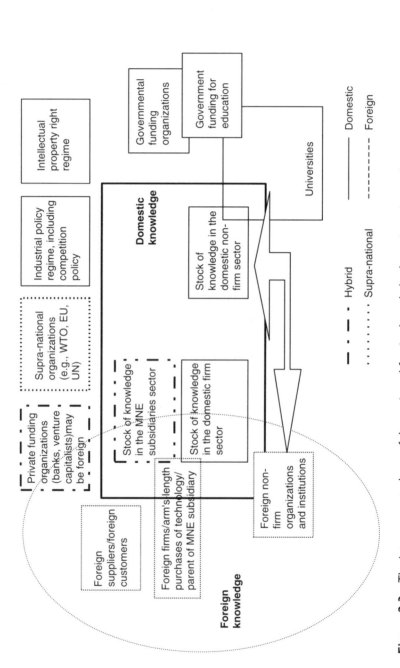

Figure 2.3 The inter-connectedness of domestic and foreign knowledge bases in an innovation system

However few (if any) such purely national systems exist, and have not done so for the last two centuries. The wave of protectionism during the mid- and late nineteenth century and again in the inter-war years in the twentieth century were largely attempts to create national champions, but even here few countries developed purely in isolation. Almost every Western nation undertook industrial espionage at some level, or by encouraging 'immigration' of skilled artisans (Harris 1998). Emigration of skilled workers from Britain was illegal for most of the eighteenth century, while exports of British machinery was prohibited until 1843 (although not steam engines and some other machines[3]). Sweden's metallurgical industries were transformed by Dutch immigrants such as Louis de Geer in the early seventeenth century (Zander and Zander 1996). De Geer is regarded by some academics as the founder of Swedish industry (de Goey 1999). Further waves of (somewhat selective) immigration of entrepreneurs and artisans in the early nineteenth century led to the transfer of British manufacturing capabilities in mechanical engineering to several countries, including Sweden, Norway, the US. The Dutch refused to recognize international patenting laws during the period 1869–1910, which allowed domestic firms to develop ownership advantages through pirated technologies. Likewise, British power looms and the technology behind high-speed spinning were highly sought after. There are numerous other cases of 'technology transfer' and of the development of domestic knowledge bases through arm's-length 'loans' from foreign sources (see e.g., Bruland 1989, 1991). During the first half of the twentieth century borders became less porous and such technology transfer became less evident as most Western economies focused on building up domestic capacity. This eventually extended to the developing world in the post-World War II era, when almost every developing country attempted to nurture a domestic sector by excluding or limiting foreign involvement to arm's-length transfers, with few exceptions such as Singapore and Taiwan. These achieved some limited success: Korean industrial development was achieved largely through excluding active participation of MNEs in its domestic milieu, as in China, Brazil and India.

Such largely domestic systems are artefacts of the past. Some countries have voluntarily accepted the limitations of an isolationist industrial development model based on import-substitution and an inward-looking orientation; others have done so more reluctantly, as part of World Bank instituted structural adjustment programmes. Policies are oriented towards export-led growth and increased cross-border specialization and competition, and most countries are now trying to promote economic growth through FDI and international trade – what has been referred to as the 'New Economic Model' (Reinhardt and Peres 2000). This wave of liberalization is part of the new received wisdom that is focused on tackling the deep-rooted causes that underlie market distortions.

Liberalization is an important force in economic globalization since it requires a multilateral view on hitherto-domestic issues and promotes interdependence of economies. It is implicit within this view that FDI and MNE activity can be undertaken with much greater ease than previously. This view is enforced because countries have explicitly sought to encourage MNE activity as a source of much-needed capital and technology. In addition to financial crises, the general warming of the attitudes towards FDI emanate from an accelerating pace of technical change and the emergence of integrated production networks of MNEs (Lall 2000).

In some countries, it is increasingly difficult to separate foreign knowledge sources from domestic ones. MNE subsidiaries are sometimes so well embedded that they are regarded as part of the domestic environment. This reflects not just the length of time that these subsidiaries have been present (such as ABB in Norway), or that the affiliate is jointly owned (such as Hindustan Lever in India) or has been acquired (such as Nycomed-Amersham, Unilever, Reed Elsevier), but also the nature of the industry, and the growing trend towards consolidation in sectors with low growth and opportunities of global rationalization (for example, metals, banking, automobiles). Nonetheless, the interaction between the domestic firm sector and foreign-owned firm sector varies considerably, either because the domestic sector is largely in different sectors, or because the two have evolved separately. Katrak (2002) shows that, in the case of India, MNEs tend to benefit from knowledge spillovers from other MNEs, rather than to (or from) domestically owned firms. The MNE's degree of embeddedness can differ quite substantially, as explained by Sally (1996: 71):

> At one extreme, MNEs can be weakly embedded in national economies which are still strongly 'disintermediated', that is where MNE relations with external actors are brittle and frequently at arm's length. At the other extreme is strongly national embeddedness, in which MNEs are deeply interwoven in the institutional knitting of the economy in question, committed to organized long-term, usually historically defined, relations with a range of external actors.

Domestic firms, too, seek (and are sought as) partners in international R&D consortia because there is a convergence in technological trajectories across countries, as firms seek the best partners in a given industry regardless of their national origin (Narula and Hagedoorn 1999; see also ch. 4). Learning-by-alliances thus has a large international element, although there is significant variation by country. At 41.3% over the period 1980–94, US firms are the least internationally involved, while the corresponding figure for Japan, Germany, France and the UK are 74.5%, 86.7%, 85.9% and 85.2% respectively. Hagedoorn (2002) points out that there is considerable variation by sector: the ratio of international to domestic partnerships over the period 1960–98 are 0.9 for high tech sectors, 1.5 for medium tech sectors and 0.85 for low tech sectors. It is worth noting that R&D alliances are primarily learning devices. Santangelo (2000) has shown that firms with similar portfolios have a higher propensity to undertake strategic technology partnering, because it is easier to absorb each other's capabilities. This tendency extends to the non-firm sector. Universities and research institutes collaborate – both as organizations and as individual research groups – with other universities and research institutes in other countries, well illustrated by the multi-country task of the Human Genome Project.

Lastly, it is worth noting the role of outward FDI as a means for 'reverse technology transfer', whereby MNEs undertake R&D abroad with the explicit intention of seeking and acquiring technological assets from the host country. This concept is not new: but it has mainly been examined as a means to improve the MNE's portfolio of knowledge and technological assets (that is, intra-firm reverse technology transfer) (see e.g., Mansfield 1984, Cantwell 1995, Pearce and Singh 1992, Frost 1998, Håkanson and Nobel 2000, 2001, Castellani 2001, Lee 2001). However, reverse technology transfer may also have significant effects on the home country, when knowledge and resources are transferred back to the parent firms and spill over to the home economy through its linkages to domestic firms – that is, inter-firm reverse technology transfer (see Pottelsberghe and Lichtenberg 2001, Criscuolo and Narula 2001, 2002). MNEs of any given nationality with subsidiaries in several countries may have links with several different universities in several different countries, and may receive research subsidies from several national funding agencies. Such asset-seeking activity while not new, has until quite recently been a much smaller phenomenon, restricted to the largest firms, or undertaken as a secondary objective alongside the primary objective of modifying and adapting existing products and techniques to host economy conditions (see e.g., Cantwell 1991, Dunning and Narula 1995, Kuemmerle 1996, Patel and Vega 1999, Pottelsberghe and Lichtenberg 2001, Criscuolo et al. 2002).

Reverse technology transfer implies that there is a process of 'feedback' from outward FDI whereby the subsidiary located abroad internalizes concepts and technologies from the host country innovation system, and transfers these back to the MNE's operations in the home country (and over time this body of knowledge becomes available to the home country innovation system).

It is important to note that there is considerable variety in the kinds of activity that can be so defined. First, firms may seek to establish 'listening posts' which essentially monitor the activities of other firms and institutions in a particular environment. Such listening posts have a low R&D intensity, as their role is primarily that of technological reconnaissance, and not R&D *per se*. Such activities seek indirect spillovers, but do so deliberately and tend to be small in size. At the other extreme, firms may engage in R&D in a foreign location to avail themselves of complementary assets that are location-specific (and include those that are firm-specific or institution-specific, which the laboratory in question seeks to use through collaboration). That is, such technological activities aim explicitly to internalize several aspects of the innovation system of the host location, by seeking direct spillovers, in addition to indirect spillovers. Such facilities may be small or big, depending largely on the resources and the objectives of the parent firm.

There is as yet no robust evidence that there are significant spillovers to the home country innovation system at large. The extent to which reverse technology transfer does in fact occur is intermediated by a number of factors, including the industry of affiliate, the size of the parent and its subsidiaries and most importantly the quality and nature of the innovation systems of the host and the home, the technological gap between the host and home, and the level of embeddedness of the parent and the foreign affiliate.

2.5 Limitations of learning

In a globalizing world it seems clear that there are multiple and parallel opportunities for knowledge generation, learning and technological accumulation. Furthermore, learning can occur through a variety of organizational means (both intra-firm and inter-firm).

However, it bears repeating that learning and technological accumulation is not costless or instantaneous. Developing and sustaining a technological or a competitive advantage is slow, reversible and highly uncertain.

Learning takes place at the firm level, but – as I have illustrated through this discussion of innovation systems – the success or failure of individual firms occurs in orchestration with an entire system of firm and non-firm actors. Thus, it is possible to speak of *national* technological or competitive advantages, which is not simply the sum of the innovators, but the synergistic effect of all these players within a given industry within boundaries of a *de facto* region or country.

Learning and the acquisition of knowledge themselves require skills and abilities that are non-obvious. Countries (I have used the term here as a synonym for innovation systems) in any given industry follow a trajectory of technological accumulation. Laggard 'economic units' (be they countries or firms) must possess (*inter alia*) the *social capability*[4] to catch up and converge with economic units at the frontier. Abramovitz (1995) distinguished between two classes of elements. One class includes the 'basic social attitudes and political institutions', the other consists of elements that determine the ability of countries to efficiently absorb and internalize knowledge potentially available at the frontier, that is, from the lead countries. This latter group has been dubbed 'absorptive capacity'. Dahlman and Nelson (1995) define national absorptive capacity as 'the ability to learn and implement the technologies and associated practices of already developed countries'. To put it simplistically, if the institutions and organizations are absent or underdeveloped (a sub-optimal innovation system), economic actors within the system will be unable to absorb and efficiently utilize knowledge that may potentially be made available to them. Absorptive capacity includes the ability to internalize knowledge created by others and modifying it to fit one's own specific applications, processes and routines. It is worth noting that absorptive capacity is a subset of technological capability, which in addition to absorptive capability includes the ability to generate new technologies through *non-imitative* means. This does not imply that absorption is purely about imitation. Firms cannot absorb outside knowledge unless they invest in their own R&D, because it can be highly specific to the originating firm, since it has a partly tacit nature (Cantwell and Santangelo 1999). The extent to which a firm is able to exploit external sources of knowledge thus depends on its absorptive capacity, which is assumed to be a function of its R&D

efforts, and the degree to which outside knowledge corresponds to the firm's needs as well as the general complexity of the knowledge. An important component of absorptive capacity is the availability of an appropriate supply of human capital, which in turn is not always specific to firms, but associated with the capabilities of the non-firm sector. Non-firms determine the knowledge infrastructure that supplements and supports firm-specific innovation. They account for a certain portion of the stock of knowledge at the national level which may be regarded as 'general knowledge' in the sense that it has characteristics of a public good, and is potentially available to all firms that seek to internalize it for rent generation.

There thus exists a relationship between absorptive capacity and the stock of knowledge within any system. However, a cumulative and interactive process between these two variables commences only if a 'threshold' minimum knowledge base is initially present. Furthermore, as Criscuolo and Narula (2002) argue, the accumulation process proceeds at a slower pace as the country approaches the technological frontier.[5]

Thus, even where technological assets at the frontier are made available – either through licensing, or indirectly through spillovers from inward FDI – the domestic system may not be in a position to internalize these assets. Borensztein et al. (1998) and Xu (2000) have both shown that FDI has a positive impact on economic growth only in those developing countries that have attained a certain minimum level of absorptive capacity. Knowledge accumulation is much more rapid once the initial threshold level of absorptive capacity exists. Simply put, technology absorption is easier, once they have 'learned-to-learn' (Criscuolo and Narula 2002). However, at the frontier, technologies are pre-paradigmatic and unproven, and there may be several competing technologies, only a few of which will be adopted, and prove to be commercially viable (Narula 2001b). The cost of imitation increases as the follower closes the gap with the leader and the number of technologies potentially available for imitation reduces. *This implies that there are diminishing returns on marginal increases in absorptive capacity at the upper extreme, at the frontier-sharing stage (that is, for developed and industrializing countries).* Once a country is near the international best practice, a higher level of uncertainty is involved, and it is complicated to identify what is relevant, how to solve problems related to the exploitation of new technology: the task difficulty and the knowledge complexity rapidly increases. Besides, firms at the technological frontier are unwilling to sell state-of-the-art technologies to potential competitors, at least through arm's-length transactions. Firms seeking access often resort to cooperative strategies such as joint ventures and R&D alliances, as markets for nascent and new technologies do not exist (Narula 1999).

Although the New Economic Model promoted by the Washington Consensus regards FDI as a primary – and explicit – means by which growth can be promoted, there are obvious limits to this strategy. The presence of MNEs and FDI is not a *sine qua non* for development (Narula and Dunning 2000, Narula and Portelli 2002, Narula 2002c). The experience of some of the Asian economies has fuelled this belief, and it is now promoted by the Washington Consensus as the cure for many ills. But underlying this view is the assumption that FDI is the same thing as technology imports, and that these technological imports will generate positive externalities and spillovers to domestic firms. But it is by no means clear that this is the case, because there are three other conditions that need to be satisfied (Narula 2002b):

1   The kinds of FDI being attracted should generate significant spillovers.
2   The domestic sector should have the capacity to absorb these spillovers. It is perhaps worth adding that some level of competence level *should exist* in the domestic sector.
3   The FDI that is being attracted should be either a substitute for or complementary to domestic industry.

It is true that the determinants of economic development are similar to the determinants of FDI, but this does not mean that there is a simple cause and effect between them. Particular types of FDI tend to be attracted to countries with certain levels of economic development and appropriate economic structures (see Narula and Dunning 2000 for a review). But simply to 'pump' a country full of FDI will not lead to its catapulting to a higher stage of development. To assume FDI drives economic development is to assume that FDI is about capital, and that the lack of economic growth is about the lack of liquidity.

Indeed, the presence and condition of the domestic sector is crucial. If no domestic sector exists there can be no opportunity to absorb spillovers from FDI: in a perfectly liberalized world, MNEs have no incentive to encourage the development of domestic firms to meet their needs because other MNEs would be able to do so, through either imports or FDI. In an extreme case, there may actually be no FDI inflow, because MNEs will prefer to locate production in a regionally optimal location, and simply import. Thus, FDI in a completely liberalized milieu does not necessarily lead to growth in the domestic sector. The benefits of FDI occur only when there is domestic investment, and where the domestic investment has the ability to internalize the externalities from FDI.

Nonetheless, such an idealized world does not exist, but the point that I want to illustrate is that FDI is not a guarantee of growth. FDI and economic development are highly correlated phenomena, both being strongly dependent on the specific resources, institutions, economic structure, political ideologies and social and cultural fabric of countries. The kind of FDI activity a country might attract (or wish to attract), too, at different stages of development, are different (Narula 1996a). Indeed, these two issues are closely related. Globalization has made the differences between groups of countries more rather than less noticeable, even though simultaneously they are becoming increasingly interdependent. Although every individual investment is a unique event, both the type of investment and the stage of economic development of the host country allow us to generalize that the situation currently faced by the least developed countries is fundamentally different from the catching-up and converging countries (Narula and Dunning 2000). Thus, in the scenario where the necessary absorptive capacity is not present, instead of learning from inward FDI, domestic investment may be 'crowded out' where the domestic innovation system is too weak to compete with the foreign sector (see e.g., Agosin and Mayer 2000). This is also the case for the formerly centrally planned economies of Central and Eastern Europe, although the 'incomplete' aspect of these economies is fundamentally different from that of (say) Africa. Although from a supply aspect of knowledge these countries had considerable technological capabilities, the institutional setting within which knowledge and transactions could be organized efficiently was absent (Gomulka 1990). In other words the competence necessary to organize transactions efficiently, whether intra-firm or intra-market, was unavailable.

There are also complications for firms in using reverse technology transfer. Such growing complex linkages, both of networks internal to the firm, and those between external networks and internal networks, require complex coordination if they are to provide optimal benefits. Such networks are not only difficult to manage, but also require considerable resources (both managerial and financial). It is no surprise, therefore, that external technology development is primarily the domain of larger firms with greater resources, and more experience in trans-national activity.

2.6 Conclusions

An innovation system is not a *systematically* organized group of economic actors, but the *systemic* inter-relationship between the various participants which defines the stock of knowledge. An innovation system is delineated by the concepts of 'the institutional set-up' and 'interactive learning'. The institutional set-up may be understood to constitute the framework conditions that characterize the contextual backdrop of the innovation system. In this perspective, the concept of interactive learning appears to work as a collective concept, describing the many knowledge creation processes that take place within and between the various constituents of the innovation system. The actual *content* of interactive learning seems largely determined *ad hoc* by the knowledge contributors to the different processes, the importance of which, at least in part, is generated by surrounding structural features. Thus, as a means to examine the content of interactive learning, I have attempted to distinguish some general characteristics of the institutional set-up, to outline a theoretical representation of an innovation system. The concept of interactive learning works as a *collective* concept, describing the many knowledge creation processes that take place within and between the various constituents of the innovation system.

I have attempted to argue that technology is not an exogenous variable, nor is it a good: although the acquisition and sale of technology is an instantaneous process, the mastery of this technology so that it may be used in an efficient manner is not. The non-*codified* aspect of technology is accumulated over time, and consists not just of scientific knowledge of processes and products, but of knowledge of the market and its structure. Technology accumulation in the main is an incremental process.

As various scholars have affirmed, economic growth is inextricably linked to technology accumulation, which in turn is a function of market conditions, demand conditions and supply conditions. It has been suggested that economic growth is a function of the rate of innovation and the national technological advantage, and that it is affected by the international trade and investment activities of firms. This also includes the shifting and transfer of resources and technology to and from other countries in the process of structural adjustment as a response to economic growth. Such international activity can act towards consolidating or weakening competitive advantage. Structural adjustment also refers to the acquisition and mastery of new technologies by the firms of a country and this occurs through technology transfer enabled through direct investment or arm's-length technology sales.

I have also highlighted the importance of taking into account the role of non-domestic elements in an innovation system, which is traditionally studied by using the nation-state as the unit of analysis. Learning and knowledge accumulation is often assisted by inward and outward FDI, although this is sometimes overlooked in the study of innovation systems. In addition, foreign-located non-firms also contribute to the domestic innovation system, both directly by collaborating across borders, as well as indirectly by collaborating with MNE affiliates of both domestic MNEs located abroad, and foreign-owned MNEs located in the domestic sector. Learning-by-alliances and learning-by-interaction therefore are much more than just domestic, spatially limited phenomena, and innovation systems are not limited by geographic distance (the complexities of learning-by-alliances is discussed in greater detail in chapter 4). *Indeed, these multi-level, multi-country interactions within a modern knowledge-based economy mean that firms are not just constrained by the limitations of their domestic resources.*

Nonetheless, there are factors that constrain and predetermine what firms can and cannot do. More importantly, they create inertia. Inertia is used here in the sense proposed by Isaac Newton. That is, an object in motion will remain in motion, and an object at rest will remain at rest, until an external force is applied. To paraphrase it for our purposes: *economic units will prefer to maintain existing institutions with competitors, customers and external organizations, produce similar products and remain in similar locations, unless an external force is applied.* That is, they prefer to maintain their current state of equilibrium, if it does not threaten their survival. When an external force is applied – be it because of new technology, change in the industrial or market structure, legal and governmental fiat – economic units will seek to modify their routines to accommodate this change to create a new 'equilibrium', preferably in close proximity to their existing routines. Firms loathe radical change. Radical change is costly and highly risky, and because routines and institutions develop slowly, *radical change that is undertaken rapidly is even more risky.* It is reputed that several years ago Lego (the Danish toy manufacturer) fired its US division manager for achieving revenue growth of 30 per cent in one year, as opposed to a planned 10 per cent, because the subsequent organizational costs of such rapid growth would be hard to handle.

However, every subsequent change becomes less costly, because the knowledge of developing new markets, technologies and institutions can be applied to future scenarios. That is, the economic unit has acquired the 'technologies of learning' – and these can be applied (*ceteris paribus*) to other situations. The experience of developing its first European affiliate by a US firm in (say) Germany makes it relatively easier to enter other similar markets such as Denmark and the Netherlands. This line of reasoning has been demonstrated time and time again for firms of all nationalities (see e.g., Johanson and Vahlne 1977, Hagedoorn and Narula 2001, Hogenbirk 2002).

To reiterate this more technically, within an innovation system framework, it is important to understand the forces that lead to a vicious or virtuous circle of competitiveness, or, in other words, forces that lead to 'positive' or 'negative' inertia and lock-in. Interaction within an innovation system is a self-reinforcing mechanism which may or may not lead to *ex post* efficiency (see e.g., Cowan and Gunby 1996). Lock-in can also occur in a geographical location; particularly, where a cluster of firms exists with a particular specialization, the entire cluster can be 'locked in' technologically to specific paradigms. That is, the self-reinforcing interaction between firms and infrastructure perpetuates the use of a specific technology or technologies, or production of specific products, and/or through specific processes. Increased specialization often results in a systemic lock-in. But I am getting ahead of myself here. Chapter 3 will examine the issues of lock-in and inertia in greater detail.

3

Innovation Systems and 'Inertia' in R&D Location: Norwegian Firms and the Role of Systemic Lock-in

3.1 Introduction

For those of you who have skipped the previous chapter, let me repeat a few points that I made in the introduction to chapter 2. Although it is not necessary to read chapter 2 to make sense of this chapter, these two chapters are sequential in nature. They are naturally related, and form a set. Chapter 2 introduced the reader to the necessity of taking a systems view to understanding innovatory activity, and its choice of location. The primary novelty was to introduce and emphasize the need to include the international aspect of knowledge creation. It attests to the power of globalization in creating fuzzy boundaries. This chapter presents a counterview to this, explaining why boundaries largely remain quite *distinct* despite globalization. This chapter asks why firms have greater reluctance to expand or relocate their R&D operations abroad than their other value-adding activities such as manufacturing, sales and marketing. Empirical work on R&D internationalization has demonstrated time and time again that – although decreasing – the bulk of innovatory activities of MNEs remains concentrated in their home location. Following Gertler et al. (2000), I seek to examine this 'inertia', focusing on the role of systems of innovation (SI) of the *home* country. Although there is considerable literature on the internationalization of R&D, much of it has focused on the firm and strategic perspective (see e.g., Granstrand et al. 1992, Granstrand 1998, Niosi 1999). In particular, I intend to highlight that there are important centripetal forces associated with the SI that lead firms to prefer to innovate at home, even where there are host country-, industry- or firm-specific centrifugal forces at play. I argue that the firm – and its innovative activities – are a part of a network of other firms and institutions that make up SI, and these, *ceteris paribus*, help determine the firm's behaviour.

I focus on the extent to which firms are embedded and interdependent on the external domestic (non-firm) actors that comprise the SI. This process is a self-reinforcing mechanism, and can lead to lock-in. I argue that lock-in can be an efficient outcome under certain circumstances, particularly in sectors where the SI are competitive, and are evolving gradually. However, lock-in can have negative consequences, *inter alia* when radical innovations or technological discontinuities present themselves that are externally generated, and the domestic SI cannot respond to the challenge effectively.

There is undoubtedly an important role for non-firm actors in overcoming lock-in, particularly through government intervention. However, in this chapter I focus on the response of firms to limitations in the SI, and argue that firms can either attempt to modify the SI, or seek alternative SI in other locations to meet their technological needs. I take the example of Norway, using data from interviews with the major private-sector R&D performers in Norwegian industry, and various public-sector institutional actors.

The chapter is organized as follows. Section 3.2 presents the theoretical background, arguing the role of SI in determining inertia in R&D. Section 3.3 discusses the possible responses of firms to systemic lock-in. In section 3.4, I describe the Norwegian SI, and based on interviews with firms and public-sector organizations, I illustrate my theoretical reasoning. Section 3.5 concludes by summarizing the findings and their implications.

3.2 Systems of innovation and inertia in R&D

The literature on R&D internationalization points to a tendency to internationalize for one or two reasons. First, there are demand-driven reasons, as firms increasingly locate production closer to their customers and suppliers. Firms with a higher involvement in foreign production also demonstrate a higher proclivity towards foreign-located R&D. The level of foreign R&D in any given host location is, however, also dependent on the kinds of value-adding activity undertaken there. In general, the more embedded the foreign subsidiary, and the greater the intensity of the value-adding activity, the greater the amount of R&D activity.[1] Such activities lead to a duplication of its home base activities, since the host location is acting as a *substitute* for activities it may have wished, *ceteris paribus*, to undertake at home (Zander 1999), but find that it can undertake these more efficiently elsewhere.

Second, internationalization of R&D may be driven by supply-side factors. In such cases, firms aim to improve their existing assets, or to acquire (and internalize) or create completely new technological assets through foreign-located R&D facilities. The assumption in such cases is that the foreign location provides access to location advantages which are not as easily available in the home base. In many cases the advantages sought are associated with the presence of other firms. The investing firm may seek to acquire access to the ownership advantages of other firms, either through spillovers (in which case the firm seeks benefits that derive from economies of agglomeration), or by direct acquisition (through M&A), or through R&D alliances.

It is important to realize that the nature of technology and innovation plays an important role in the location of R&D. First, knowledge creation, generation and dissemination is highly tacit, difficult to codify and of singular strategic importance to the competitiveness of the firm. This means that firms wish to exert as much control as possible over the process by keeping R&D close to headquarters, or at any rate, in close proximity to a subsidiary which can assure an optimal level of monitoring and control over its activities (see Zanfei 2000 for a discussion). Second, there are also considerable industry-specific differences which encourage or discourage centralization.[2] As Teece (1986) has argued, the maturity of the technology and its characteristics determine the extent to which the innovation process can be internalized. Most mature technologies evolve slowly and demonstrate minor but consistent innovations over time, and can be regarded as post-paradigmatic. The technology is to a great extent codifiable, widely disseminated, and the property rights well defined. Innovation is rarely patentable in these technologies, where applications development accounts for most innovatory activity. Competition shifts towards price, economies of scale, and downstream activities in order to add value, as the original product is priced as a commodity. These sectors tend to have a low R&D intensity. These sectors, generally what Lall (1979) refers to as process industries, do not require outputs to be tailored to customers to the same extent, or as quickly. This means that constant and close interaction with customers is not an important determinant of their R&D. Profits of firms are highly dependent on the costs of inputs, and proximity to the source of these inputs is often more significant than that of customers. On the other extreme, rapidity of technological change in 'newer' technologies, or what Lall (1979) refers to as engineering industries, requires a closer interaction between production and R&D. Technologies have a higher tacit, uncodifiable element, and this requires a closer coordination between users and producers of innovation.

The case of demand-driven R&D is straightforward, being shaped more by host country, technology and firm-specific determinants. These arguments are well developed, and I intend to adopt a complementary view by taking a systems-related approach. My interest here is on the centripetal issues that result in the *non-internationalization* of R&D activities. I argue that the firm – and its innovative activities – are a part of a network of other economic actors that make up the SI, and these, *ceteris paribus*, help determine the firm's behaviour and competitiveness.

That there is a fundamental interdependence between the home country national systems and the technological competitiveness of their firms is relatively uncontroversial. The innovation system concept suggests that there exist certain structural influences (scientific, political, and socio-economic) within any nation-state that help to define the pattern, nature and extent of knowledge accumulation within a given industry, and which also define the extent and nature of industrial innovation within its borders.

The use of the word 'system' does not necessarily mean that the various influences that underpin the generation of industrial innovation are systematically organized (Nelson and Rosenberg 1993). Indeed, it is probably more accurate to say that the SI in most cases represent the serendipitous intertwining of institutions and economic actors within industry which defined the stock of knowledge in a given location (Etzkowitz and Leydesdorff 2000). Changes in, say, the educational priorities of a new government, are likely to affect other institutions, and eventually the nature of innovatory activities of firms within given industries, thereby influencing the process and extent of technological learning in future periods.

Broadly speaking, individual national systems remain distinct: technological specialization patterns are distinct across countries, despite the economic and technological convergence associated with economic globalization (Archibugi and Pianta 1992, Narula 1996a).[3] Other studies have shown that these patterns of technological specialization are fairly stable over long periods (see Cantwell 1989, Zander 1995) and change only very gradually. The kinds of technology across countries have been shown to have converged because of, *inter alia*, increasing cross-border competition and the increasing interdependence of economic actors in different locations. Cantwell and Sanna-Randaccio (1990) have shown, for instance, that firms seek to emulate the technological advantages of leading competitors in the same industry, regardless of their national location.

A majority of the activities of firms – and in particular their innovative activities – tend to be concentrated in their home location. Since the SI of the home country are idiosyncratic, path-dependent and stable, the specialization of their firm's activities is also broadly speaking specialized in these same sectors, despite their increasing international involvement through overseas value-adding activities (Narula 1996a). Firms tend to search for innovation close to their existing base of competences. We know from the literature that firms are often slow in changing their dominant designs because they are path-dependent and technologically locked in.

Institutions create the milieu within which innovation is undertaken and establishes the ground rules for interaction between the various economic actors, and represents a sort of a 'culture'. Institutions are associated with public-sector organizations, but not exclusively.

By economic actors I refer to two groups. The first group are firms – private and public – engaged in innovatory activity, and the second consists of non-firms that determine the knowledge infrastructure that supplements and supports firm-specific innovation. I define 'knowledge infrastructure' in the sense proposed by Smith (1997) as being 'generic, multi-user and indivisible' and consisting of public research institutes, universities, organizations for standards, intellectual property protection, etc. that enable and promote science and technology development.

SI are built upon a relationship of trust, iteration and interaction between firms and the knowledge infrastructure, within the framework of institutions based on experience and familiarity of each other over relatively long periods. It is certainly true that institutions are often associated with spatial proximity (Freeman 1992). This is not unusual, given the concentration of most firms' production and R&D activities close to, or in, their home location, and the long periods over which this has been so. Besides, knowledge diffuses more rapidly when actors are geographically concentrated (Ehrnberg and Jacobsson 1997). This partly accounts for the tendency of firms to locate R&D (or at least the most strategically significant elements) close to headquarters.

Nonetheless, as firms respond to demand conditions, and because there is increasing need to seek complementary assets in multi-technology, knowledge-based sectors, firms have spread out spatially and sought to relocate some of their activities in host locations. In engaging in foreign operations in new locations, these operations have gradually become embedded in the host environment. It is germane to this discussion to note that the routines and institutions associated with systems of production in a particular location are related but not identical to systems of innovation. That is, networks associated with production in a location are not quite the same for R&D.

But the need to create durable linkages with the SI of a host location – especially where the firm is seeking mainly to duplicate its technological profile overseas – is tempered by a high level of integration with the SI in the home location. Such linkages are both formal and informal, and will probably have taken years – if not decades – to create and sustain. At the risk of oversimplifying, firms and the knowledge infrastructure interact to innovate through institutions: the concept of interactive learning (see chapter 2) underpins the concept of SI. Frequently, the most significant issues are the 'know-who'. Government funding agencies, suppliers, professors, private research teams and informal networks of like-minded researchers take considerable effort to create, and once developed, have a low marginal cost of maintaining. Even where the host location is potentially superior to the home location – and where previous experience exists in terms of other value-adding activities – the high costs of becoming familiar with and integrating into the SI of a new location may be prohibitive. Keep in mind that firms are constrained by resource limitations, and that some minimum threshold size of R&D activities exists in every distinct location. Therefore to maintain more than one facility with a threshold level of researchers must mean that the new (host) location must offer significantly superior spillover opportunities, or provide access to complementary resources that are simply not available anywhere else, and which cannot be acquired by less risky means more efficiently. Where firms simply seek to duplicate their home activities abroad, the decentralization imperative is still less powerful.

However, interaction within an SI is a self-reinforcing mechanism which may or may not lead to *ex post* efficiency. This may happen at the level of a given technology or product and lead to technology lock-in. That is, when several technological trajectories are possible, a single dominant technology may prevail which is not necessarily the superior one (see e.g. Cowan and Gunby 1996). However, such lock-in occurs within an industry across firms and across countries. Lock-in can also occur in a geographical location; particularly where a cluster of firms exists with a particular specialization, the entire cluster can be 'locked in' technologically to specific paradigms. That is, the self-reinforcing interaction between firms and infrastructure perpetuates the use of a specific technology or technologies, or production of specific products, and/or through specific processes. Increased specialization often results in a systemic lock-in, because of structural inertia (Hannan and Freeman 1984).

Inertia (as with lock-in) can be a 'good thing' if a virtuous relationship that sustains or improves the competitiveness of firms exists between parties within the SI. This may be because the SI provide the best resources and opportunities on a global level, or because the industry is purely a domestic one. Whatever the reason, a virtuous circle of technological accumulation can be created (Cantwell 1987), increasing geographical specialization may occur, and even more specialized clusters develop. That is, institutions develop that support and reinforce the interwoven relationship between firms and the knowledge infrastructure through positive feedback.

However, a negative outcome from lock-in is also possible where there is systemic lock-in such that the SI cannot respond to, or adopt, extra-SI innovations, creating a vicious circle. The SI may be unable to respond to a technological discontinuity, or a radical innovation that has occurred elsewhere. This is an unfortunate feature of innovation and cross-border competition: firms need to improve on the last-best dominant design, which may or may not be theirs. New or complementary technologies may fundamentally affect a firm's portfolio of technological competences, although this varies by the nature of the product, and how central the new technologies are to their competences.

Over-specialization of knowledge infrastructure to meet the specific needs of a specialized cluster can also lead to *ex post* inefficiencies. Firm–infrastructure relations can be so closely interdependent that the boundaries and functions of firms and the various components of the knowledge infrastructure are unclear, and *de facto* operate as one large unit. Grabher (1993) illustrates how the myopia generated by systemic lock-ins led to the decline of the Ruhr area in Germany.[4]

The point I am leading to is that institutions change very slowly, and I refer to this tendency as 'inertia'. Inertia implies a lethargy towards change, and that a state of affairs continues to be so, unless an exogenous force is applied to change it. Inertia in R&D simply implies that firms will prefer to maintain the status quo in terms of location and type of R&D activity at home, until a change in circumstances requires the firm to act. Firms by definition loathe radical change, and will always prefer to maintain the status quo if it does not endanger their competitiveness. By their very nature all innovation systems have some degree of inertia, and this may lead to lock-in.

Lock-in – or inertia – may not be recognized as such until an exogenous disturbance occurs, and until institutional change is attempted. Institutional restructuring is not an instantaneous or costless process (Hannan and Freeman 1984). It is slow, and not without its trade-offs. Institutions developed for, or specialized around, an industrial cluster are not efficient in responding to the needs of another. This is all the more so where the new technology represents a fundamentally new paradigm, or systemically affects the extant competences of the firm.

The role of a reinforcing SI is crucial in overcoming radical innovations and technological discontinuities (e.g., Freeman 1992, Edquist and Johnson 1997, Smith 2000). Rigidities due to inertia of institutions and the knowledge infrastructure can seriously affect the ability of an economy to introduce and diffuse new technologies. If inertia persists over a long period the firms will not survive (McKelvey 1997), unless external agencies (typically government policy-determined organizations) or firms themselves seek to address these constraints and are able to overcome the lock-in. However, often the external agencies are themselves involved in the SI, and suffer from cognitive inertia, or are constrained by politics from radically modifying the system.

Besides, the old SI may in fact meet the needs of other industries and firms not affected (as severely) by the radical innovation. For example, shipbuilding has only recently been affected by radical advances in computer technologies (and even then, marginally), although its influence has been much greater (and more pervasive) for automobile firms. This is particularly so in multi-technology products.[5] Thus, lock-in may be 'good' for one sector, while simultaneously being 'bad' for another.

Ceteris paribus, the knowledge infrastructure plays a crucial role as a shock absorber, minimizing the disturbances from the environment (Johnson 1992). By establishing standards, subsidizing basic research, and improving the available human resources needed for new sectors, the non-firm sector within the SI can reduce the costs of market failure and lock-in (Smith 2000). However, government intervention is conditional on available resources. Small countries, for instance, simply do not have the resources to sustain world-class competences in as wide a variety of technologies as the economy may require. Thus, the knowledge infrastructure may be unable to overcome lock-in as rapidly as firms need to sustain their competitiveness. Furthermore, there is always a question of how much governments should intervene. Both excessive and insufficient intervention can lead to an uncompetitive firm sector. It is also not obvious whether the non-firm sector can successfully 'pick winners', particularly at the technology frontier, or evolving rapidly (Narula and Dunning 1998). Fortunately, firms also have an incentive to respond to environmental changes. As McKelvey (1997) notes, firms actively attempt to anticipate change and to shape the environment. Carlsson and Jacobsson (1997) and Ehrnberg (1996) illustrate well how a combination of both firm and non-firm intervention can respond to new technological challenges. Using the example of Ericsson, McKelvey and Texier (2000) illustrate how, combined with considerable long-term investment in R&D, its flexibility in scanning the larger environment, and developing extensive linkages beyond Sweden, allowed Ericsson to bridge technological discontinuities.

3.3 Responses to inertia from a firm perspective

As illustrated in figure 3.1, firms can respond to lock-in by 'voice' or 'exit' strategies or simply by not responding (the 'loyalty' strategy) (Hirschman 1970). Firms (or groups of firms within an industry association) can use a 'voice' strategy to overcome the deficiencies of the SI, and can seek to modify it by direct action: for instance, establishing a collective R&D facility, or by political lobbying. Firms are inclined towards voice strategies, because these may have lower costs, especially where demand forces are not powerful, or where the weakness of the SI is only a small part of their overall portfolio.

But voice strategies have costs, and are not necessarily realistic for smaller firms, which have limited resources and political clout. Where the inertia does not threaten their survival, they may pursue Hirschman's third response of 'loyalty', relying instead on institutions to evolve, or seeking to free-ride on the voice strategy of industry collectives, or larger firms.

Where firms choose an exit strategy, they may seek to re-locate all or parts of their innovative activity to exploit a more optimal SI

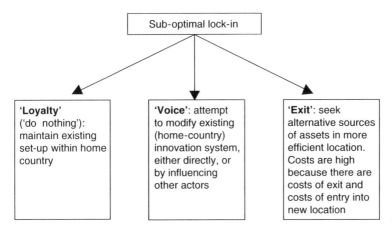

Figure 3.1 Firms' response options to sub-optimal lock-in

elsewhere. When Astra decided to establish a genetic engineering laboratory, it was simply not possible to find sufficient numbers of suitably qualified scientists in Sweden, and it opted instead to establish a new facility in India. Almost all the other Swedish pharmaceutical companies followed a similar strategy, either through greenfield labs or through M&A (Carlsson and Jacobsson 1997).

There are, of course, costs associated with an exit strategy. First, developing alternative linkages and becoming embedded in a non-domestic SI from scratch takes considerable time and effort. Gertler et al (2000) show that in the case of Ontario the home base of foreign subsidiaries remains the primary site for interactive learning. Research communities are often small and parochial, and new entrants may find it hard to join the 'club'. Firms that are 'in the club' have evolved with the SI. The rules of membership for the 'club' are non-codifiable and non-transferable. That is, experience acquired in one country is not necessarily applicable to another. Thus, when a firm chooses an exit strategy, it must suffer the costs of entry in another location (in terms of effort, capital and time), and firms may minimize this through a cooperative strategy with a local firm. This may also explain, in part, the growing use of M&A activity with regards to R&D as some (but not all) of the benefits of membership may be inherited through M&A. An acquired laboratory short-circuits the time taken to develop such linkages vis- à-vis a greenfield laboratory, as they come with ready-made networks and linkages (Narula 1999). However, acquired laboratories bring with them the difficulty of integrating them efficiently into the internal network of the firm, such that their efficiency may be limited, at least initially (Belderbos 2003). But it is not always possible to acquire an R&D unit by itself, without going to the considerable expense of acquiring the entire company (Narula 2001a).

Nonetheless, exit strategies are in fact essential to the survival of the knowledge-intensive firm, simply as a means to maintain diversity, if nothing else. The internationalization of Japanese R&D illustrates this well (Belderbos 2001, 2003). The majority of R&D activity is conducted by large MNEs which are 'core' members of the *keiretsu*. These firms are deeply embedded in the Japanese science and technology base, and this century-long interdependence between these firms and non-firm actors has created an inertia, a consequent bias towards home-base activities, and – until quite recently – a preference to augment technological assets overseas through external or quasi-external means.[6]

While greater internationalization has occurred over the last few decades, the difficulties and costs associated with becoming an 'insider' in a new location impede a geographical spread. This is more so in the case of innovation, because of the partly public-good and tacit nature of such activities, which makes coordination across large geographical distances more difficult. Blanc and Sierra (1999) point out that *internal* proximity between overseas R&D and the rest of the MNE is an equally important issue. A dispersion of R&D activities across the globe also requires extensive coordination between them – and particularly with headquarters – if they are to function in an efficient manner with regard to the collection and dissemination of information.

Second, internationalization requires very specific and specialized intangible knowledge from a managerial perspective, and the costs associated with these are non-trivial. In addition, the costs are even higher for R&D activities than for production or sales. Thus, there are significant barriers to initial exit, although the marginal costs of sequential overseas expansion decline rapidly. That is, once routines associated with identifying suitable foreign collaborators, suppliers, and the appropriate non-firm actors have been developed, it is easier to expand in that location, or to consider locating in another, third location. In other words, once inertia of non-internationalization is overcome, firms have an *inertia to internationalize*. It is no surprise, therefore, that overseas R&D activities tend to be undertaken by larger firms.[7]

It is self-evident that either strategy has considerable costs and limitations in the real world, and that firms may prefer to wait and see ('loyalty'). Firms often prefer to undertake voice and exit simultaneously, although Hirschman (1970) and Helper (1993) have pointed out that firms that exploit exit can reduce the efficacy of voice. However, as I have illustrated, from a systems perspective the costs of either exit or voice on their own may be considerable. Besides, in the case of R&D, demand and supply factors play a role in encouraging exit. Furthermore, the domestic SI may be sub-optimal only in a single technological area which may represent only part of the firm's technological portfolio.

Applying the work of Hannan and Freeman (1984) on an organizational level to the question of R&D, they argue that, faced with structural inertia, firms prefer not to change, because change increases the immediate hazard of mortality. However, if change is successful, then firms have a higher survival rate than in their former state.

3.4 The evidence: R&D activities of Norwegian firms

3.4.1 Data collection

The survey of Norwegian R&D was based on a questionnaire that was developed in cooperation with Robert Pearce of the University of Reading. Although secondary data for Norway indicate that about 600 firms comprise the industrial R&D performing sector, a large proportion of these firms are SMEs (Hauknes 1996). I selected Norwegian industrial firms with R&D expenditures greater than NOK 10 million[8] and/or more than ten R&D employees, which gave me a sample of fewer than fifty firms. Firms that had been acquired by foreign investors, but remain autonomous (and therefore Norwegian-controlled) were included. By excluding all foreign-controlled firms I was left with approximately thirty-five firms. Given the relatively small group of firms that meet the criteria, it was decided to conduct the survey through interviews, conducted with the head of the R&D department or equivalent. No information that provides specific evidence of *individual* company strategy has been revealed in this study.[9]

3.4.2 Firm and industry specific issues

There are two aspects of the economic structure of Norway that are instrumental in defining the nature and extent of R&D activity in

Norway. First, Norway has traditionally competed on resource endowments (see Stonehill 1965, Hodne 1993, Reve et al. 1992). Indeed, much of the industrial activity in Norway has evolved around upstream activity and value adding to resource-based sectors, particularly petroleum, pulp and paper, hydropower, metals and maritime-related industries.[10]

Second, there has been significant government intervention in the structure of Norwegian industry. These have aimed at explicitly creating new areas of industrial specialization and have led to the creation of other incomplete clusters, such as telecommunications, pharmaceutical and information technologies. Such interventions have occurred consistently over the post-war period (and possibly even longer) through several means, which I discuss briefly below:

1   The state has promoted the development of energy-intensive sectors, through the provision of cheap (and subsidized) hydro-electric energy. Although these subsidies have been drastically reduced, the consistent use of this subsidy is partly responsible for the competitive advantages of some of the traditional industrial firms (Kvinge and Narula 2001).

2   There have been several waves of restrictions on the activities of foreign-owned firms in Norway, both through entry barriers to FDI, and through tariff and non-tariff barriers to imports.[11] These have served to keep the role of FDI in Norway to a low level for much of the twentieth century. Since the 1990s both government subsidies and restrictions on FDI and imports have drastically been reduced, and in many cases eliminated, owing to both the GATT and EEA agreements.[12] The restrictions on FDI and trade have been abetted by the high level of state ownership in Norway. Although some privatization has occurred, this has been rather minor, and mainly in sectors no longer considered strategic, such as in former defence-related firms.

3   During much of the post-World War II era, and up to the late 1980s, the Norwegian government has intervened in Norwegian industrial development through some level of import-substitution industrial policy, at different times targeting the development of certain sectors, as well as moulding particular firms into 'national champions'.[13] During each wave, fundamental components of industrial policy were: state-ownership, technology transfer by foreign MNEs, and preferential treatment for Norwegian firms, firms with Norwegian partners, or firms that had transferred significant components of their technological activities to Norwegian locations.

These developments have had a significant effect on the industrial structure of Norway, creating what is essentially a dichotomous industrial structure. The data suggest the classification of firms into two main groups, which are discussed below.

Group A: traditional industries and formerly protected firms   Group A consists of what might appear to be two quite different sub-categories, but they share several important characteristics. The first sub-category is firms in traditional, raw materials-based sectors. Many of these may be described as 'national champions', and have traditionally received a considerable amount of state aid. Indeed, the Norwegian state has considerable ownership in some of these firms, most notably, Norsk Hydro (43.8 per cent) and Statoil (100 per cent). The second sub-category still operates with a competitive advantage that derives partly as a result of protected markets (a result of former infant industry protection programmes), or hitherto-protected sectors where foreign investment has either been discouraged and/or are (or were) nationally owned monopolies.

Group B: specialized and technology-intensive companies   The second group consists of firms that are engaged in more knowledge-intensive sectors, and can be regarded as science-based ('non-traditional') firms. Although some of these firms have evolved from supportive or related sectors to these natural resource-based sectors, they have gradually diversified or specialized into higher value-adding activities. Others are firms which have always operated in specialized science-based sectors.

3.4.3 Trends in R&D and production

Broadly speaking, the survey has observed that there is considerable difference in the way in which firms from these two groups undertake both their domestic R&D activities, and the propensity to undertake international R&D activities. Group A accounts for 63.5 per cent of the R&D expenditure of the sample, and Group B represents 36.5 per cent of the total R&D expenditure of the sample. In general, Group A is also less internationalized in terms of sales, with foreign sales representing (on average) 59.4 per cent of total sales, compared to group B where overseas sales account for 88.1 per cent (table 3.1).

Table 3.2 gives details of the distribution of the sample in terms of R&D expenditure. Two things are obvious from this table. First, that the sample accounts for a large percentage of the formal R&D

Table 3.1 Selected indicators for sample, split into two groups

	Group A	Group B
Total employees worldwide	52,000	10,300
Revenues worldwide (MNOK)	13,385	1,549
Overseas sales (%)	59.4	88.1
Employees in R&D (% of total employees)	3.2	9.4
Employees in R&D outside Norway (as % of total employees worldwide)	0.2	2.7
Employees in R&D outside Norway (as % of total R&D employees worldwide)	5.0	28.9
NFR subsidies as % of R&D budget	3.0	1.2

Table 3.2 Distribution of R&D expenditures of surveyed firms

million NOK	no. of firms	(%) of total firms
<5		34.6
5–9.99		23.1
10–30		11.5
30–50		23.1
> 50		7.7
total		100.0
n (Total) number of firms in survey	26	
Mean R&D expenditure of sample	208	
Total R&D expenditures of surveyed firms [A]	5,415	
Total business expenditure on R&D, all Norwegian firms [B] in million NOK (1997)	8,600	
A ÷ B		63
Estimated share of total Norwegian-controlled R&D (%)		70–80

activities undertaken by private companies. Although the total R&D expenditures of the firms in the sample represents 63 per cent of national business expenditures on R&D (BERD) I estimate that approximately 10 per cent of BERD is accounted for by foreign-controlled firms.[14] In addition, one of the largest Norwegian MNEs was unable to provide data on its total R&D expenditure because it was undergoing massive restructuring, and thus was partly excluded (only one of its subsidiaries was included). I estimate that this firm alone may account for 3–5 per cent of BERD. Thus, I estimate that the sample accounts for anywhere between 70 and 80 per cent of all Norwegian-controlled BERD.[15]

Indeed, as table 3.2 shows, a very large percentage of the R&D activities of Norwegian firms is undertaken at a rather small scale, even within the sample. Over 50 per cent of the sample has annual R&D expenditure of less than NOK 10 million. In terms of R&D employees, there was a similar distribution: 56 per cent of the sample had fewer than fifty R&D employees, and 76 per cent had fewer than seventy-five R&D employees. Only 12 per cent of the R&D facilities had more than 200 R&D employees.

In terms of industrial distribution, 38.5 per cent of the firms could be classified as being engaged in low-technology sectors, and 30 per cent in electronics and IT sectors (table 3.3). Low-technology sectors include food and beverages, wood and wood products, paper and paper products, and fishery equipment. The 'electronics-based sectors' include several specialist companies that manufacture control equipment for ships, and specialized fishing equipment such as sonars, in addition to consumer electronics, telecommunications and medical diagnosis equipment.

Although Groups A and B are roughly equal in the number of firms, corresponding shares of total worldwide sales are 93 per cent and 7 per cent respectively, and in terms of employment, the figures are 84 per cent and 16 per cent. However, in terms of domestic R&D employment, Group A accounts for 70 per cent and Group B for about 30 per cent. Table 3.3 also illustrates that a majority of firms (88.5 per cent) in Group A operate in the low-tech sectors, while only 46.1 per cent of Group B can be so classified.

These data make the following points. Group A consists of firms which are large, which account for a large share of the sales and employment in Norwegian industry, despite representing a small percentage of the total firms in Norway, and are concentrated in more mature (and low R&D-intensive) sectors. They also tend to be less internationally oriented in terms of sales. Group B firms are by and large SMEs, and have a higher propensity to be in more R&D-intensive sectors, but are more active in terms of overseas sales than Group A. In terms of R&D, Group A firms have on average only 5.0 per cent of their R&D employees outside Norway, compared to 28.9 per cent for Group B, despite the fact that Group A firms are on average several times larger in terms of their total operations (table 3.1). These differences not only reflect the extent to which these traditional and protected firms are embedded into the local economy, but also that most of these companies are engaged in low R&D-intensive sectors, while Group B firms are engaged in more R&D-intensive sectors. In addition, the differences are even greater in terms of overseas activities: the ratio of R&D employees to total

Table 3.3 Distribution of surveyed firms, number of firms and worldwide revenues

Sector	% of all firms	Sales worldwide (%)		
		All firms	Group A	Group B
Chemicals, pharmaceuticals and biotech	26.9	5.8	3.6	33.3
Mechanical equipment	0.0	0.0	0.0	0.0
Metals and fabricated metals	15.4	51.5	55.5	0
Other low-tech sectors	23.1	37.0	36.3	46.1
Aerospace + transport eqpt	3.8	0.7	0.8	0.0
Control and measuring eqpt	15.4	1.0	0.0	13.4
Electronic, office and telecoms eqpt	15.4	4.0	3.8	7.2
TOTAL	100.0	100.0	100.0	100.0
Low-tech including metals	38.5	88.5	91.8	46.1
Electronics-based sectors	30.8	5.0	3.8	20.6

worldwide employees is three times higher for Group B than Group A, while the ratio of foreign R&D employees to total worldwide R&D employees is six times greater for Group B than Group A. Indeed, even in terms of absolute number of overseas R&D employees, Group B has almost three times as many employees as Group A, despite the fact that in terms of revenues, they account for slightly over 10 per cent of the total revenues of the sample.

To what extent do these differences in R&D internationalization reflect differences in the internationalization of production and sales? Table 3.4 gives details of the activities of the sample of firms as regards these three elements. These percentages reflect the number of regions in which firms have sales, production or R&D, and not the intensity or the value of these activities.[16] The evidence indicates the following. First, that there is no significant difference in the extent of overseas sales and production, apart from the fact that several of the Group A firms had no overseas activities. However, on the whole, Group B firms were more evenly involved across regions. 85.7 per cent of Group B firms can be regarded as being 'global' in terms of their sales activities, with sales in at least five of the six non-home regions, compared with just 45.5 per cent of Group A firms. A larger percentage of Group A firms were involved in production in the EU compared with Group B, but the difference was marginal. Firms in Group A generally regarded themselves as 'Eurocentric'.[17] In contrast

Table 3.4 Extent of internationalization of sales, production and R&D (%)

	Group A			Group B		
	Firms with sales in region	Firms with production in region	Firms with R&D in region	Firms with sales in region	Firms with production in region	Firms with R&D in region
EU	90.9	72.7	27.3	100	64.3	42.9
North America	54.5	45.5	9.1	100	64.3	42.9
Latin America	72.7	45.5	0.0	85.7	7.1	0.0
Japan	45.5	18.2	0.0	78.6	7.1	0.0
Other Asia	92.9	35.7	9.1	92.9	35.7	14.3
Rest of world	91.2	72.7	9.1	78.5	14.3	0.0
	Sales	**Production**	**R&D**	**Sales**	**Production**	**R&D**
% of firms with 'global' presence[a]	45.5	18.2	0	85.7	7.1	0.0
% of firms with multinational presence[b]	45.5	63.6	9.1	14.3	50.0	35.7

[a]Firms with presence in at least 5 of the 6 non-home regions.
[b]Firms with presence in 2 to 4 non-home regions.

Group B firms took a more global view of their competitiveness. In terms of production, Group B firms were more highly concentrated in three regions: the EU, North America and Asia, but only 7.1 per cent could be regarded as 'global', and only 50 per cent had 'multinational' operations. Group B firms undertook production in many more locations, and 18.2 per cent of the respondents were 'global' in their geographic spread, and 63.6 per cent 'multinational' in scope.

As regards R&D, however, Group B firms had a higher overseas presence, with 42.9 per cent of firms with R&D in both the EU and North America. Corresponding figures for Group A are 27.3 per cent and 9.1 per cent (table 3.4). Of Group B firms 35.7 per cent could be regarded as 'multinational' in terms of geographic spread of R&D compared with 9.1 per cent for Group A.

As I have discussed in a previous section, a large proportion of R&D activities (both home-based and international) primarily support production activities. Norwegian industry is relatively a newcomer to internationalization, having begun to invest abroad in earnest only in the 1970s (Hodne 1993). Thus, although there is a high dependence on overseas sales, production has begun to be relocated only much more recently. Likewise, the level of foreign R&D intensity was also low. In the case of Group A (and especially traditional industries), FDI was undertaken to access lower cost resource inputs as the cost of domestic inputs rose in the 1970s. Many of these companies' products are commodities in nature, and the increasing cost of such activities has led to a dispersion of their production. As one manager said, 'It is important to be close to our markets. . . . we have to think about the breakeven point between transportation and the benefits of consolidation of our market units . . . we are a cost-driven industry, so it is important to be near our customers.'

However, such resource-seeking FDI tends to have very low R&D activity associated with it, if any, and the nature of the industry means that R&D can continue to be done primarily at home. In the case of Group B firms, their small size has also limited their international activities.

Taking tables 3.1 and 3.4 together, it is possible to say that Group A firms have decentralized their production activities but continue to concentrate their R&D activities, while Group B firms have a more centralized production, but more geographically dispersed R&D activities. It is important to note that Norwegian-controlled overseas R&D activities are quite small in terms of absolute size. The largest R&D facility outside Norway has fewer than sixty-five R&D employees (Group A, laboratory located in the EU). In North America and the EU, the two regions with the largest number of

R&D facilities, the total number of R&D employees is 163 and 130 respectively. In other words, these facilities are limited in resources and the intensity of activities they can undertake.

Thus, the differences in industrial structure of the Norwegian environment faced by the two groups of firms play a significant role in determining their domestic R&D activities, and their international involvement. One of the primary questions in the survey was 'how important are the following factors to your decision to maintain R&D laboratories in Norway?', based on a five-point scale. These tendencies are apparent from table 3.5, which gives details of responses by both groups of firms.

Group A firms clearly consider proximity to production units/ customers as an important determinant of the location of their R&D activities in Norway, with 66 per cent indicating that it was of major or crucial importance. As discussed above, a majority of their strategic value-adding facilities remain concentrated in Norway, and it is reasonable to expect that this plays an important role in keeping their R&D centralized at home. In addition, a high concentration in process industries makes decentralization less important. By contrast, only 28.6 per cent of Group B firms felt it was a significant factor, despite the fact that most of these firms also maintain a significant (and major share) of their production activities at home. As I have shown in the theoretical discussion, their technology-intensive nature means that their need to seek complementary assets and specialized resources increases their need to internationalize.

For similar reasons, access to raw materials and inputs is a much more significant factor for firms in Group A, with 33.3 per cent of firms regarding it of major or crucial importance to maintaining R&D facilities in Norway (table 3.5). This reflects, once again, the importance of input costs to commodity-based industries. In addition, former import-substituting firms have enjoyed ownership advantages which are location-specific, and not as easily duplicated in overseas locations. With reduced or withdrawn state protection, these firms are more conscious of the input costs, since profit margins have been considerably affected by competition (most of which comes from inward FDI).[18] As for Group B firms, only 7.1 per cent considered Norway as an important location for R&D because of easy access to inputs. In some cases, as much as 80 per cent of their inputs are imported from other parts of Europe, and the Far East. They are engaged in high value-added sectors, and the transportation costs are negligible in relation to their costs. In general though, for both groups (but particularly for Group B) in terms of R&D activities, inputs are a very small cost of innovatory activity.

Table 3.5 'How important are the following factors and considerations to your decision to maintain R&D laboratories in Norway?'

	Group A		Group B	
	mean	% of respondents 'major or crucial importance'	mean	% of respondents 'major or crucial importance'
Availability of researchers	4.6	91.6	4.3	85.7
Low cost of researchers	2.0	8.3	2.5	21.4
Proximity of production units/customers	3.6	66.6	2.5	28.6
Presence of technical & scientific infrastructure	3.4	50.0	3.6	57.1
Access to raw materials & other inputs	2.3	33.3	1.4	7.1
Monitoring the technology of competitors	1.8	16.6	1.6	14.2
Presence of important suppliers	2.3	33.3	2.4	35.7
Demands/wishes of government	1.9	26.7	1.1	0.0

Norwegian firms do not, in general, consider Norway to be a useful place from which to monitor the technological activities of competitors (table 3.5). Indeed, when asked to list their major competitors, none of the firms in the survey included any firms located in Norway.[19]

Both groups of firms showed a strikingly similar response regarding the proximity of suppliers to the location of R&D (table 3.5). Despite the similarity, the reasons for undertaking outsourcing of the two groups are considerably different and reflect technology-specific characteristics (see Narula 2001b and chapter 5 for a discussion). In the case of traditional industry firms, for instance, because of the maturity of their sectors, and the fact that competition is not based on access to unique technologies, a higher level of external technological outsourcing is feasible. Competitive advantage in these industries generally derives not from technology *per se,* where the products are 'generic', but from marketing and economies of scale. Indeed, one firm explained:

We have nothing to hide. We believe in sharing all our technologies, because we don't really have anything special. There isn't much that our competitors don't already have, and it's really a small circle – everyone knows everyone else – we have all been in this industry a long time. Things change very slowly, and we make most of our profits from downstream activities. Maybe our core asset is our marketing and logistics department.

The results suggest there are distinctive differences between the two groups. Group A firms operate in process-type industries and based on traditional commodity-type inputs, in which Norway has traditionally had a comparative advantage, and in which clusters exist, and for which the domestic SI are more comprehensive.[20] Although changing factor costs, and the high costs of transportation relative to value added, have promoted international production, R&D is by and large concentrated at home. This is in part a function of the industry of these firms. Firms have less need to be geographically proximate to their production activities compared to more R&D-intensive, rapidly evolving industries. In addition, though, because of these technological characteristics, firms can seek to acquire assets through outsourcing: more so than Group B firms.

As for Group B firms, they are engaged in more technology-intensive sectors, and are predominantly SMEs. These are sectors where Norway has no comparative advantage. However, a number of them operate in industries or operated in sectors in which clusters and/or competitive advantages existed in the past, or which were targeted sectors in previous industrial policy. Fragments of clusters or 'incomplete' domestic SI exist and thus they have sought to internationalize R&D relatively more since they need access to a larger variety of technologies. In addition, important demand factors exist, as in many cases they act as suppliers to larger firms, many of which are not based in Norway. However, they demonstrate a low level of overseas production in terms of geographic spread. This may be a result of one of two factors. First, by virtue of their smaller size, they simply cannot afford to internationalize to the extent that they might prefer. Second, because of the more knowledge-intensive nature of their activities and their dominant market positions, transportation costs do not play as critical a role in their location decisions.

3.5 'Systemic' lock-in: dependence on the innovation system

The last section examined the industrial structure of Norway and its effect on, and general trends in, the internationalization of

Norwegian firms. In this section, I more explicitly explore the Norwegian SI to understand the tendency for lock-in and under-lying inertia of R&D. It is clear from the preceding discussion that, although there are differences between the two groups, even Group B firms are also home-country focused in their R&D activities. In order to demonstrate my thesis regarding lock-in, inertia and R&D, I first describe the salient features of the Norwegian SI, paying particular attention to identifying the main actors. I must necessarily simplify the description, as it is not my intention to make a thorough analysis of Norwegian SI.

As in all countries, the primary participants in the Norwegian R&D system comprise three players: private-sector firms, the higher education sector, and the institute sector (Hauknes 1996). Although there are other aspects of the innovation systems that have some bearing on the location of R&D, these will suffice in illustrating my arguments. These institute and universities sectors (the non-firm sector of the SI) together undertake roughly the same level of R&D activities in terms of R&D expenditure as the industry sector.[21] The institutes and universities form the primary means by which the state – directly and indirectly – subsidizes R&D activities: 62 per cent of the funding of the institutes and 88 per cent of that of the universities comes from public sources (NIFU 1999).

The level of subsidies are by themselves not exceptional, but the state has had an active and central role in determining how these funds are spent, and whom they are directed towards. As I have highlighted before, the state has always played a strong interventionist role in Norwegian industry.[22] The importance of government intervention was evident from the interviews, although neither group of firms considered government pressure as a primary factor in maintaining R&D facilities in Norway (table 3.5). However, Group A firms regard government pressure to maintain R&D activity as a much more important factor than Group B, with a quarter of the respondents regarding it as being of major or crucial importance – unsurprising given that many of these firms are either state-owned or national champions.

The different attitudes towards R&D may also partly be a result of the way in which public subsidies are provided to industry. A large share (42 per cent in 1997) of R&D expenditure is provided by the public sources. Until 1992, funding of R&D was undertaken by a variety of research councils, each controlled by different ministries. The Norwegian Research Council (NFR) was established as an attempt to bring together under one umbrella all the various R&D funding and policy making agencies (Skoie 1997), thereby improving coordination, and increasing efficiency. At the same time, the object-ive was to improve the links between basic and applied research. However, ministries still approve and fund projects independently of the NFR – this is indicated by the fact that the direct funding of industry by the NFR is only about 25 per cent of the total public funding of industry R&D (NIFU 1999).[23] The structure of funding towards the larger 'national champions' is evident. The objectives of various programmes is steered by committees where managers from these companies have a significant presence, and they are thus able to influence the design of research themes. Smaller companies tend to have more difficulty in accessing funding directly, partly because of the lack of transparency of NFR programmes, and the large amount of bureaucracy.[24] A manager of one of the larger firms said,

> NFR should cut down on bureaucracy and paperwork – big com-panies like [ours] can handle the amount of effort it requires. But companies which really need the funding are not able to handle this ... it pays to have professional people who are very [skilled] in seeking money ... big companies can always make your proposal directed to [what is advertised in the programme descriptions], because they helped to design the programmes ... small companies do not have these possibilities.

Another firm said that, 'All the paperwork [for the NFR] makes [the funding we get from the NFR] almost not worth it. But we have to, because we must be "invited to the party". It's a club, and we can't afford not to be a member of this club.'

The survey enquired about the average level of NFR funding made available to these firms during the last five years. As table 3.1 shows, firms in Group A received a larger share of public R&D funding than Group B: 3.0 per cent vs. 1.2 per cent, on a weighted average basis.[25] These figures exclude direct and indirect subsidies channelled through other agencies. It should also be noted that Group A includes a number of former monopolies, which have had a drastic reduction in their subsidies in line with conditions imposed by the EEA and WTO agreements and which have a weighted average NFR subsidy of just 0.6 per cent.

The Norwegian higher education sector consists of four univer-sities and a number of 'scientific colleges' which provide tertiary education at a university level. Although all perform R&D-type activities, only one university dominates postgraduate engineering and technology-related education: the Norwegian University of Sci-ence and Technology (NTNU). It graduates upwards of 1,000 engin-eers with masters-level education, and 130 PhDs in engineering every year. These provide the backbone of R&D personnel in Norwegian research establishments. The University of Oslo plays a role in providing R&D personnel in basic and natural sciences, as well as information technologies, but its contribution is clearly secondary to that of NTNU. NTNU, which is located in Trondheim, is also intimately linked with Stiftelser for Industriell og Teknisk Forskning ved NTH (SINTEF), the crown jewel of the institute sector, providing a considerable part of the laboratory facilities for SINTEF. In addition, about 180 NTNU professors are employed as scientific advisers to SINTEF. NTNU's links with industry are unparalleled by any other university in Norway, accounting for an estimated 15 per cent of the total amount of R&D outsourced (in terms of expenditure) by the sample. This figure does not include funding which comes through projects undertaken jointly by SINTEF and NTNU.

The institute sector consists of approximately fifteen techno-logical research institutes and thirty social research institutes, and reflects the various stages of industrial policy over the post-World War II years. They can be classified into four main groups. First, there are the 'collective' industry-specific research institutes. These are based around particular sectoral interests. For instance, the pulp and paper industry sponsors the pulp and paper institute. Second, there are the 'modernization' institutes which were estab-lished as a part of the policy strategy to upgrade and develop particular industries which were deemed essential to create a modern industrial sector, beginning in the 1950s, the most promin-ent of these being the Norwegian Defence Research Institute (FFI), the Central Institute for Industrial Research (SI), Telenor (TF) and the Institute for Atomic Energy (IFA). The third group are the regional institutes which are linked to local university-level col-leges with the intention of developing and supporting local indus-try in the various regions of Norway, and linking them to the regional tertiary-level colleges. The fourth group of institutes evolved in response to new targeted industries (in particular pet-roleum, and later electronics), but over time have evolved and merged, and are now based around what is essentially now SIN-TEF. The SINTEF group was established by the Norwegian Insti-tute of Technology (NTH), the predecessor to NTNU, in 1950 in response to the government's decision to establish SI (Hauknes 1996). By the 1970s, a number of the institutes had lost their *raison d'être*, for a variety of reasons. A decline in defence spending and the end of the Cold War have reduced the strategic importance of IFA and FFI, while TF became part of Telenor, the state-owned telecom former monopoly. Other institutions from the first and second group also merged with SINTEF. The SINTEF group has evolved to what is arguably the largest R&D laboratory in Northern Europe (Skoie 1997), with over 1,800 employees (84 per cent of whom are technicians, engineers and scientists) and a turnover of almost NOK 1.5 billion. It is by far the largest R&D performer in Norway.[26] It undertakes roughly 60 per cent of the R&D out-sourced by the sample, whereas all the other institutes and universities (excluding NTNU) combined undertake less than 15 per cent of total research outsourced by the sample, and probably closer to 10 per cent. Foreign institutes account for approximately 5 per cent. The link between SINTEF and NTNU is a strong one, and it is practical to view them as a single entity, sometimes referred to here as the SINTEF–NTNU axis, given their joint R&D facilities and shared staff, and the historical link. SINTEF and NTNU both undertake a high share of industry-oriented R&D activities (between 70 and 80 per cent). The primary rationale for the very strong, centralized (and concentrated) nature of the institute sector in Norway has been to create economies of scale and scope in research. This reasoning is still in vogue today. As a manager at SINTEF explained,

> There are a large number of SMEs in Norway that cannot afford to maintain dedicated R&D facilities of the scale and scope that is required to compete with their international competitors. [In addition] doing so would mean that facilities and resources would be under-utilized. SINTEF can undertake similar activities for many firms at the same time, and thus be cost and resource efficient.

This policy of centralization of research was meant to allow firms to maintain a smaller amount of internal R&D, and rely on external (domestic) sources of research, in particular, SMEs. Indeed, funding by the NFR to firms is largely provided with the understanding that these funds will be utilized at one of the Norwegian research institutes, and not abroad. This means that broadly speaking, smaller firms undertake only market-related development activities, leaving the applied research and development to the institutes.[27]

This high centralization of activities also has a very important centripetal effect on R&D. Almost all the technical personnel engaged in R&D are graduates of NTNU. Of the managers in the interviews (both firms and institutes) 70 per cent were also graduates from NTNU. This creates a sort of informal network between firms, as most of the personnel know each other, or know of each other, allowing for a greater flow of knowledge between firms and between firms and institutes.

Firms (or more accurately, technical personnel in these firms) are likely to recruit other engineers and scientists who come from this network. In addition, the larger firms have considerable influence on the curriculum and nature of the educational system within NTNU, and are thus able to influence the quality of people. One manager put it nicely,

> Norway is very important to us, not because Norwegians are smarter than other people, but because we know the culture here, and we know where to get people...it's a practical issue...we can put pressure on the universities to change their profile. We could not do this elsewhere without considerable time and effort.

However, it should be noted that the ability to influence the curriculum is something that only Group A-type firms have, given their larger size and economic clout. Larger firms tend not only to get graduates tailored to their specifications, but also are able to recruit the best students. Large firms also invested in sponsoring visiting professors and researchers from other countries in research themes that they felt needed to be developed, something which SMEs could not afford to do. One firm explained that the main reason for having R&D facilities in Trondheim was to be close to NTNU:

> Trondheim is the capital of research in technology...we have found that we can recruit from the top shelf [because we are located in Trondheim]. We find the best candidates before they finish. We finance [the dissertation work of] individuals whose research interests match ours...[Because we know the professors] we know who are the best [candidates], and establish [a] connection with them early. It is a major responsibility [of mine] to handpick the best people every year.

Indeed, both groups regarded Norway very highly in terms of availability of high-quality research professionals, with 91.6 per cent of firms in Group A, and 85.7 per cent of firms in Group B regarding it as of major or crucial importance (table 3.5).

The evidence would suggest that Norwegian firms are 'locked-in' to the SI, and this restricts their activities, both in a technological and an organizational sense. On an organizational level, firms are heavily dependent on the Norwegian system, since they have traditionally relied on these assets, and are reluctant to try new options.

Inter alia, this is because the search procedure to find an optimal alternative source is expensive, and the high costs and considerable time required to develop new linkages with alternative research institutions makes such an attempt out of reach of all except the largest firms.[28] An *a priori* familiarity with outside sources does, of course, help. Several of the R&D managers interviewed who had studied in other countries were more inclined to using non-Norwegian institutes. One of the Swedish-trained managers of an SME (which no longer undertakes any work with the SINTEF–NTNU axis) said, 'When I first took over we spent NOK 10 million in [Norway], but we didn't get anything out of it, so we now use research institutes in Sweden and [other countries] where I know...[where to go], and where we will get what we need.'

Firms from both groups that have more international experience in terms of production activities and are larger are also more likely to use alternative (non-Norwegian) sources of R&D suppliers and new employees. They have learnt about alternative SI and are more familiar with operating in the host environments, because they are linked with them, and have the resources to develop these linkages further. However, the organizational lock-in with Norwegian systems is not necessarily forsaken:

> we are currently establishing a technical centre in the US – but we are trying always to strengthen with SINTEF and NTNU. We sponsor people from Trondheim to go abroad to do joint research, give lectures, and attract professors and researchers to come from [these other institutes]. We sponsor Norwegian students to study [at other institutions abroad where we have identified competences that we need].

> In terms of costs, SINTEF, NTNU are worth it – if you can keep them on track.... but they have more competition – we have found more and more institutes outside [Norway] with competence. But of course [SINTEF–NTNU] are Norwegian and they are close by... nonetheless, we are not increasing their share [of our R&D outsourcing efforts], but increasing [our purchases from] outside Norway.

The second aspect of lock-in creates a 'technological inertia'. Norway has over a period of almost a century focused on low-technology, resource-based sectors. Although knowledge-intensive sectors have received considerable government attention, these sectors (in particular those associated with electronics-based sectors) have not developed into a big enough agglomeration, and are largely incomplete clusters, nor has the government succeeded in creating any large national champions. This situation has probably not been helped by the change of emphasis in policy over the decades. For instance, the most recent shift since the 1980s has been from telecommunications and electronics to software. Many of the companies that have survived these 'reshuffles' have either become associated with one of the more complete clusters, or they have been acquired by larger major international players in their industry. The following observations by Group B companies illustrate the unevenness of the system:

> [the quality of] education is very bad, particularly in our areas of technology. Research funding in [our] industry has been reduced to 40 per cent, universities are lacking resources, and professor salaries are so low that recruitment is impossible in universities. Many of the students...don't meet the standards for taking up technical education.

> There is...far too much raw material-based focus [in the way research is funded]. As a small country, with a high level of education, we should be competing much more on competence base than raw material base. The only so-called competence-based areas [in Norway are traditional sectors] like shipping...we are really pumping that oil, digging that mine...not adding value to the resources...it's the wrong way of using the resources.

> The government needs to promote reasons to stay – if not for our history [our company] would be better off somewhere else. The lack of competence level...is coming from the [low quality of] education. It won't help to pour in more money [to subsidize R&D], if the [human resources] to receive it are not competent to deal with it. [In R&D we] need to start with the people, that there is someone professional to do the thing. Of course there are good professionals [in our area] in Norway, but this is in spite of the government.

In addition though, because of significantly large players in the traditional industries, competitiveness built over a long period, and they are able to shape the Norwegian SI to their needs. Firms in these sectors are locked in to superior (or at least state-of-the-art) technologies.

While the outcome of 'technological inertia' may be positive, it may just as easily lead to a vicious circle. Where clusters exist and the threshold level of support and synergies exist from (and between) firms and the knowledge infrastructure, thereby establishing state-of-the-art technology, then the outcome is superior and optimal. Where these factors are incomplete, or interact in a suboptimal way, then the technological level in the location may be locked into inferior (or lagging, non-state-of-the-art) technologies. This is enhanced in the case of new technologies. By virtue of being a small country with one (albeit large) technological university, there are a fewer number of professors, and the research themes and approaches of their research groups are constrained. The same, rather small group of professors will, simply by the path dependence of their specialization, tend to generate new PhDs with roughly the same interests and skills. In other words, the lack of diversity by virtue of a small group of researchers limits the diversity of new ideas and technologies, even where a high competence level exists.[29] Where the system is supported by inward technology transfer by MNEs which sponsor cooperation between foreign sources of knowledge and the domestic sources, this problem is minimized. It helps, of course, that these areas are relatively slow-evolving, mature sectors. Where technological change is rapid, and firms do not have the resources to help augment the domestic technological base, firms will necessarily seek external sources directly, without improving the domestic scientific infrastructure. In the Norwegian case, doing so involves two related challenges. First, getting access to the right people is not as easy. As one manager explained, it's not just educational levels that count, but experience: 'It's easy to get people from universities, but we prefer people who have been working one to two years after their PhD, because it takes two to three years before they are really producing ...It's becoming more difficult to find people with experience...we are increasingly appointing people from outside Norway.'

Some companies have tried to resolve this matter by seeking to bring in expatriate researchers, but this option has had limited success. In certain areas like biotechnology, there are simply not enough domestic researchers available. One firm recently advertised repeatedly for new scientists in Norway and abroad, but produced only one applicant from abroad, who is of Norwegian background, and no responses from within Norway. The second connected challenge is associated with the relatively low salaries (in purchasing power terms, and relative to salaries offered to similarly qualified researchers in other countries), the climate and the remoteness of Norway. Several Norwegian laboratories have, nonetheless, several expatriate researchers. To have the right people, we have to pay the market price...Norwegian salaries are lower...it is easier to move to London or Paris or Rome where we [would be] much closer to sources of educated and experienced people.

3.6 Summary and policy implications

While accepting that strategic and other firm-specific factors are central to explaining the internationalization of innovatory activities, I have argued here that the industrial specialization of firms and the location of their technological activities are heavily influenced by country-specific factors. This is part of a wider phenomenon: firms of all nationalities display an 'inertia' in R&D internationalization and are more reluctant to internationalize R&D than other aspects of their value-adding activity, such as sales and production. The level of internationalization is also industry- and technology-specific: certain sectors require greater interaction and closer monitoring of customers, suppliers and competitors than others.

I have argued that inertia is associated with the nature of the SI of their home countries, and the level to which these firms are embedded. Institutions and routines have evolved over time which govern the interaction between firm and non-firm actors in the SI. Firms are interdependent and co-dependent on other domestic economic actors which determine institutions and policies which have not only formed them – and with which they are most familiar – but which they have also helped create. This process can be a self-reinforcing mechanism that perpetuates the use of certain technologies through specific processes. SI change only very slowly – what Hannan and Freeman (1984) describe as structural inertia – and this can lead to systemic and technological lock-in. The need for alliances and other more formal interactions between the various actors is considerably reduced, since a high level of trust and interdependence already exists, and in a small community, costs of reneging on agreements are very high. Where lock-in maintains a high level of competitiveness of firms, the outcome is superior and optimal. Where technological discontinuities or radical innovations are introduced from outside the SI, lock-in may have dire consequences, since the domestic SI will not be able to respond rapidly enough to modify institutions to meet the needs of either newer firms or older firms that need access to new competences. Firms may choose to respond directly, by either using a 'voice' or 'exit' strategy. Of course, non-internationalization due to SI-related centripetal forces is countered by industry- and host-country centrifugal forces encouraging internationalization, but I am concerned here with the *net effect*.

The case of Norway illustrates this well. Norwegian industry can be viewed as broadly consisting of two groups of firms. Group A consists primarily of national champions and firms tend to be large, engaged in traditional, more mature, resource-intensive sectors in which Norway has had a historical comparative advantage. They enjoy a certain amount of government patronage, and are highly embedded in Norway. It can be argued that the SI *has been built around these firms*. The Norwegian SI meets their needs quite well, and where it does not, because of their economic and political significance they are able to exercise 'voice' to make the necessary modifications.

Group B firms operate in more technology-intensive, science-based sectors which are nascent and rapidly evolving, and tend to be SMEs. These firms have evolved in part as a result of various industrial policy initiatives over the post-war era to create clusters in more knowledge-intensive sectors, but which – as industrial clusters – failed to achieve sufficient impetus. Group B firms, however, do not have the same close-knit relationship with the SI, which does not meet their needs, being locked-in around 'traditional' sectors. Having fewer resources, and as relative outsiders, they have tended to supplement their less successful attempts at 'voice' with an 'exit' strategy. Nonetheless, Group B firms also suffer from inertia in R&D, partly because there are also high initial costs of exit, although there are decreasing costs of sequential overseas expansion. In addition, even if they find the home SI sub-optimal, they are nonetheless members of the 'club' and have developed informal relationships which cannot be as easily duplicated elsewhere.

I need to emphasize here that my analysis of inertia in R&D is not to suggest whether it is 'good' or 'bad' *per se:* certain sectors are more amenable to internationalization than others, and as long as the SI meet the needs of home-based firms, there is nothing 'wrong' with a systemic interdependence between actors within the SI, and a consequent home-bias. However, when firms exhibit systemic lock-in to SI and it retards or hinders firms' attempts to compensate for weaknesses in the domestic SI by tapping other locations' SI, it can be 'bad'.

I have suggested that SI can be locked in to a vicious circle of technological accumulation. No country can possibly expect to provide world-class competences in all technological fields. Even the largest, most technologically advanced countries cannot provide strong innovation systems to all their industries, and world-class competences in all technological fields. The cross-border flow of ideas is something that has always been fundamental to firms, and this imperative has increased with growing cross-border competition and international production.

However, some countries have regarded imported technologies as a sign of national weakness, and have sought to maintain and develop in-country competences, often regardless of the cost. The strategy of technological self-sufficiency is increasingly untenable. Norway, again, illustrates this well. Relying solely on in-country competences may lead to a sub-optimal strategy, especially in this age of multi-technology products. Nonetheless, in an increasingly internationalized world, and as firms expand their geographical focus, many firms are beginning to rely on more internationalized systems that incorporate actors located in different locations. The dangers of such country-specific lock-ins seem destined eventually to become a thing of the past.

4

Cross-border Interdependence between Firms: The Growth of Strategic Technology Partnering

4.1 Introduction

The second major theme of this book is the growing cross-border interdependence of firms in the creation and diffusion of innovation. The last two chapters have taken a locational view of innovation, arguing how locations are interdependent, yet exhibit tendencies of inertia. This applies to firms too, because they have an embeddedness or familiarity with a given innovation system associated with a location. Nonetheless, supply and demand factors can outweigh institutional inertia. Firms are not restricted just to a dichotomy of choices – either staying at home or relocating to acquire immobile sources of knowledge. There are a variety of 'in-between' options available to access location-specific resources, and these include cooperative agreements. Such agreements are also a useful organizational mode when firms seek technologies that are specific to other firms.

It should be apparent even to the most casual observer of business news that cooperative agreements are being signed continually, and in ever-greater numbers with every passing year. This is a phenomenon that has sparked the attention of managers, national and supra-national regulators, policy makers and academics alike. It is argued by some that this phenomenon is the death knell of the traditional firm, that firms will become increasingly 'virtual'. One of the main points that the next few chapters will highlight is that there are limits to the extent to which firms can use cooperative agreements as a substitute for in-house activity. To paraphrase Samuel Clemens, I believe that the death of the firm is greatly exaggerated. While it is true that there is a growing amount of cooperative activity, I feel that there are a great many misconceptions about cooperative agreements, some of which I shall seek to address in the course of the next three chapters.

The growth of collaborative agreements is undoubtedly hugely influenced by the process of globalization. As with globalization, the effect varies across industries, and is particularly acute in sectors where consumption patterns are increasingly homogeneous across countries, and which are capital-intensive as well as knowledge-intensive, in terms of (1) investment in innovation and technology, (2) requiring large plant scales, and (3) dependence on new and fast-evolving technologies. These are sectors where firms have expanded internationally fastest, as they are thus able not just to compete in the various markets simultaneously, but also to exploit and acquire assets and technology that may be specific to particular locations.

It is axiomatic that firms in some sectors need to innovate in order to survive, which, in this day and age, implies being present in all the major international markets where competitors are present. This is not just to meet demand, but also to overcome supply constraints – companies wish to exploit the particular characteristics of given countries that represent inputs to the innovative process, required to generate new competitive advantages. Unfortunately, given the capital-intensity of these activities and the inherent risk of innovation, firms cannot afford to be omnipresent. Internalizing and undertaking all (or even most) aspects of value-adding activity through wholly owned subsidiaries in every location is no longer possible, and in many instances not even desirable. Over the past two decades, firms have increasingly sought to undertake activities through collaborative efforts. Although collaborative activity is not a new practice, it is undeniable that there has clearly been a process of evolution whereby there is an increasing use of alliances explicitly for strategic purposes. Its novelty is not as an organizational form – economic units have collaborated for millennia. Intricate linkages between economic entities that create informal and formal networks to undertake value-added activity date back to before the seventeenth century, when production of goods was undertaken by 'putting out'. Rapid Japanese industrial growth over the last century has been partly attributed to the cooperation between interlinked firms with limited equity cross-holdings within industrial groups referred to in the post-World War II era as *keiretsu* (see e.g., Gerlach 1992, Nakamura 1981). Dunning (1995, 1997) and others suggest that this represents a new 'age of alliance capitalism' whereby flexible economic arrangements find increasing favour, shifting away from the older paradigm of hierarchical capitalism where hierarchies represented the primary mode through which economic activity was undertaken. What is unique about 'the age of alliance capitalism' is its widespread use by firms of all sizes and nationalities, and its use in a growing variety of activities which have hitherto been centralized and internalized, such as R&D. Furthermore, cooperative activity has a growing international element, and is not just limited to related firms but is often undertaken with international competitors. In addition, even within international strategic technology partnering (STP), there has been a gradual shift away from equity-based partnering to non-equity forms of agreement.

The rest of this chapter focuses on evaluating some of these trends. First, I will clarify some definitional issues. The fact is that there is a wide variety of such agreements, all of which have fundamental differences in their structure and objectives, but are often referred to interchangeably as strategic alliances, collaborative agreements, or networks or outsourcing. I intend to clarify this issue. My primary objective is to focus on R&D alliances, but in the process I intend also to deal with more general aspects that apply to all kinds of cooperative agreements.

Second, cooperative agreements have different objectives, depending on what aspect of the value-added chain we are dealing with. This chapter focuses on the narrow area of collaborative R&D activity. I intend to explain what role cooperative agreements play in technological competence development, in light of the growth of what is best described as the multi-technology corporation. I propose that these trends can be explained by combining a resource-based view of the firm, in addition to traditional economic rationale, and by acknowledging the special nature of innovative activity, which has certain unique characteristics that separate it from production activities, as well as the strategic nature of firm-decision making. I will illustrate my arguments with particular reference to some data on EU strategic technology partnering, explaining why alliances have become increasingly important to firms.

4.2 The characteristics of ownership advantages and technology

Although there are many motives for undertaking R&D alliances which Hagedoorn (1993) classifies into those relating to general characteristics of technological development; those relating to the innovation process; and those relating to market access and opportunities. One of the primary objectives of R&D collaborative ventures is to learn, for the basic reason that the ability of firms to compete effectively for market share is a function of their ability to maintain and renew firm-specific assets. These assets are commonly referred to as ownership advantages. An important distinction needs to be made about the nature of ownership advantages of companies, which, in knowledge-intensive firms, comprise different forms of knowledge. There are two types of knowledge that comprise the ownership advantage of firms. First there is technical knowledge which is made up of what might traditionally be defined as technology, embodied in plant and equipment (and to a large extent codifiable), as well as the employee-specific knowledge that is only to a limited degree non-tacit. Second, there is organizational knowledge, which comprises knowledge of transactions, both *intra-firm* and *inter-firm*. In general, throughout the current chapter, we focus on R&D alliances whose primary purpose is to acquire technical knowledge and to generate innovations. Although innovations can (and frequently do) occur through the acquisition of organizational improvements, and/or the ability to undertake inter-firm transactions more efficiently, we limit ourselves here to study only alliances to undertake *overt* R&D.[1]

There are different ways of classifying innovatory activities. In this chapter I view innovation along a continuum between basic research to development, with the determining factors being (1) the generic nature of the innovation and (2) the distance from market. By generic nature, I refer to a distinction introduced originally by Kuznets (1962) and used in a modified way by Arora and Gambardella (1994) and Trajtenberg et al. (1997). Figure 4.1 summarizes the basic argument. Knowledge that is 'basic', or 'generic' represents knowledge that is not country- or demand-specific, and is less appropriable than 'applied' or 'specific' ('Applied D' in figure 4.1). It is important to highlight that we are speaking of *research outcomes*, since laboratories are often engaged in several similar (and often related) projects simultaneously, and since technological development is an uncertain process, it is not always possible to say *ex ante* whether a certain project is applied or basic research. Nonetheless, a distinction can be made between the extremes. On the one hand, firms can explicitly engage in projects that are more 'blue sky', or pursue scientific research that has no clear market value in the short run, aim to change the technological paradigm, or have a major impact in defining general laws rather than solving particular problems. On the other hand, demand-specific modifications or

Technology is tacit, and property rights undeveloped – alliance possible, but depending on speed and uncertainty.
Object is to invent and share costs and risks of innovation – R&D alliance likely only if technology likely to have systemic influence of background or main technological competence; in-house R&D will be preferred.

Technology is more codifiable – possible to subcontract – objective is to 'sell' innovation, and share cost of making product saleable – R&D outsourcing more likely: if technology is part of core competences, then R&D alliance likely, but probably equity-type agreement.

Figure 4.1   'Distance-to-market' issues in the innovation process

adaptations can be explicitly undertaken, which are more context-specific and are clearly 'applied D'. It is worth noting that regardless of the basic-ness or generic nature of the knowledge, there is always some extent of context specificity. Even codifiable technology is context-specific to at least some extent (Cantwell 1991). Because technology is the cumulative sum of innovations and proceeds incrementally based on 'localized search' patterns centred on the technology possessed by the firm in previous periods, the technology of any given firm is unique, such that no two firms can have exactly the same kind of technology.

4.3 Explaining strategic technology partnering: some definitions

It is germane to begin this discussion with some fundamental definitions of terms as used throughout the next three chapters. Before proceeding further, we need to distinguish between the following three terms which are often mistakenly used as synonyms: cooperative (or collaborative) agreements, networks and strategic alliances. Cooperative agreements include all inter-firm cooperative activity, while strategic alliances and networks represent two different (though related) subsets of inter-firm cooperation.[2]

By strategic alliances I refer to inter-firm cooperative agreements which are intended to affect the long-term product-market positioning of at least one partner (Hagedoorn 1993). I am specifically interested in strategic technology alliances where innovative activity is at least part of the agreement. What differentiates a strategic alliance from a network is the underlying motive of the cooperation (figure 4.2). This differentiation has its roots in an ongoing debate within the management literature on the relative merits of various underlying theories explaining the behaviour of firms in using markets and hierarchies (see Madhok 1997 for a more in-depth analysis of the various aspects of this debate). On the one hand, there is the transaction costs/internalization perspective, which has its roots in the work of Williamson (e.g., 1975) and Coase (1937) which explains the behaviour and organizational mode and the mode of entry of firms based on their need to *minimize net transaction costs* faced by the firm. This body of literature has been expanded by others including Buckley and Casson (e.g., 1976), Hennart (e.g., 1993) and Rugman (e.g., 1980). On the other hand, there is also the organizational capability and technology-based view of the firm developed in parallel by several schools, including behavioural theory (Cyert and March 1963) and the economics of technological change (e.g., Nelson and Winter 1982). Other work includes Kogut and Zander (1993) and Hill et al. (1990), and Cantwell (1991) who have highlighted the fact that firms undertake decisions based on the need to enhance their technological and organizational capabilities because they need to *enhance the value* of the firm. Underlying the difference between these two perspectives is a fundamentally different view of the way firms make decisions, since the transactions cost school assumes that firms are driven by opportunism while the technology/knowledge view assumes that firms are boundedly rational. We do not intend to debate the views here, but accept Madhok's (1997) perspective that the two schools may be regarded as complementary to each other, although an organizational learning- and technology-based view underlies our understanding of strategic technology partnering.

The approach favoured here is that both transaction cost minimizing and value-enhancing reasons underlie most of the behaviour of firms. Firms would *prefer* to increase short-term profits through cost-economizing as well as long-term profit maximizing through value enhancement, but this is not always possible. It is important to emphasize that very few agreements are distinctly driven by one motivation or the other. What I am trying to show here is that

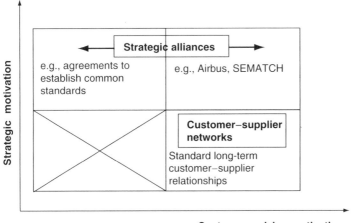

Figure 4.2   Explaining the underlying differences between strategic alliances and customer–supplier networks
Source: Narula and Hagedoorn (1999).

agreements that are established with primarily short-term cost efficiencies in mind are generally customer–supplier networks, while agreements where a long-term value enhancement is the primary objective are strategic alliances. Figure 4.2 illustrates my basic argument with a few examples.

Decisions to conduct a vertical alliance may tend to be primarily cost-economizing, but also have a strategic element to them, in that by collaborating with the supplier firm you may have pre-empted a similar move by a competitor. The behaviour of firms within Japanese *keiretsu*, to a greater extent, tend to have cost-based benefits. Collaborations such as these are primarily cost-economizing and may be defined as *networks*. On the other hand, cooperative agreements such as between Sony and Philips to develop DVD technology, or the Sematech partnership, are clearly aimed at improving the future value of the various partnering firms and are thus more strategically motivated than cost-economizing. As such they represent strategic alliances rather than networks. It should be noted that it is particularly difficult to delineate strategic alliances from networks clearly, given that firms have no incentive to reveal their true motives to the public, and more importantly to their partner firm, especially where these might prove detrimental to the proposed relationship.

Box 4.1   Networks vs. alliances

Strategic alliances are essentially *peer* alliances, between competitors, where both partners have a largely equal relationship. Customer–supplier agreements are outsourcing agreements, and are *subordinated partnerships*. By subordinated, we mean that there is a customer and a contractor, whereby the customer is dominant, and the nature of the cooperation is determined by the customer. The customer gives specifications in the contract about the nature of the product or service that the contractor supplies. The level of cooperation is much lower, because the contractor is dependent on the needs and requirements of the customer.

Competitive partnerships are more interactive (but not necessarily more stable) than subordinated ones, because both partners have assets that the other partner needs. In subordinated partnerships, the customer often has multiple contractors providing the same or similar services and products, so the bargaining power in the alliance is with the customer.

Collaborative agreements of all sorts have been undertaken for strategic, economic and diplomatic reasons since the beginning of history. However, what differentiates their current popularity is that until recently they represented a second-best option, utilized only where full internalization was not possible. It was conventional wisdom that firms preferred, wherever possible, to establish wholly owned subsidiaries, and where this was not possible for whatever reason, to maintain a controlling (which generally implied majority) stake in its affiliate. In general, firms preferred to maximize their equity stake in all their activities, particularly when entering or expanding in foreign markets. Over the past two decades or so, alliances and networks have come to represent a *first-best* option. Indeed, there are four primary characteristics that differentiate collaborative activity in the era of alliance capitalism from those in earlier periods (Narula and Dunning 1998). First, agreements are not primarily made to overcome market failure. Second, alliances are increasingly made to achieve not just vertical integration, but also horizontal integration. Third, alliance activity is no longer a phenomenon peculiar to certain countries such as Japan (see Gerlach 1992), but typical of most advanced industrialized economies (see chapter 6 for a discussion on developing country alliances). Fourth, while agreements were primarily made to enhance or achieve market entry or presence (that is, asset-exploitation), an increasing number of alliances are now made to protect or enhance the technological assets of firms (that is, asset-creation or acquisition). It is worth noting that alliances involving marketing and sales are, more often than not, cost-economizing in nature, while R&D alliances are more strategic in character. Two independent surveys of alliances (Culpan and Costelac 1993, Gugler and Pasquier 1997) found that sales and marketing accounted for 41 per cent and 38 per cent of all alliances surveyed, while R&D alliances accounted for 10.8 per cent and 13 per cent respectively. One of these studies noted, however, that R&D alliances tripled in relative importance since the 1980s.

Box 4.2   Vertical vs. horizontal alliances

Horizontal alliances are those among enterprises operating in the same industry, engaged in roughly the same kinds and types of value-adding activity. The opportunities for economies of scale and scope are here maximized, but also provide the possibilities for conflict and leakage of intellectual property from one partner to the other. The cooperation between two biotechnology enterprises or between a human biotechnology enterprise and a pharmaceutical manufacturer would be considered a horizontal alliance.

   Vertical alliances occur among enterprises operating in related industries *along the same value chain*, where one partner produces inputs for the other. The latter may be a larger enterprise assembling or sub-assembling products from parts and components acquired from different suppliers, including SMEs. It may also be a small systems integrator close to markets and obtaining equipment from larger suppliers. Vertical collaborations are less problematic, as the partners possess complementary but not competing capabilities and opportunities.

4.3.1   Organizational modes of alliance

Figure 4.3 describes the range of inter-firm organizational modes generally utilized in collaborative agreement activity. There is a wide range of types of agreements, reflecting various degrees of inter-organizational interdependency and levels of internalization. These range from wholly owned subsidiaries, which represent complete interdependency between the firms, and full internalization. At the other extreme lie spot-market transactions, where totally independent firms engage in arm's-length transactions in which either firm remains completely independent of the other. As figure 4.3 illustrates, we include within the rubric of collaborative agreements two broad groupings of agreements that can be

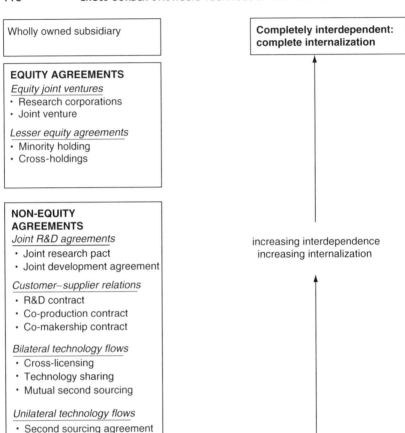

Figure 4.3 Organizational modes of inter-firm cooperation and extent of internalization and interdependence
Source: Narula and Hagedoorn (1999).

regarded as representing different extents of internalization, or what may succinctly be described as quasi-internalization. Although it is difficult to be specific and concrete regarding the ordinal ranking, it is safe to say that equity-based agreements represent a higher level of internalization and inter-organizational interdependence than non-equity agreements.

Box 4.3 Why joint ventures are not always strategic alliances

Not all equity cooperative arrangements are alliances. For instance, joint ventures have always been a popular means for undertaking business activity in developing countries, but this was often because of government restrictions on the ownership of domestic companies by foreign investors. In other words, these joint ventures were undertaken only because government restrictions prevented the establishment of majority or wholly owned subsidiaries. Very often, the partner would be a government corporation or ministry, which would act as a silent partner. Thus, these so-called joint ventures actually represent a subsidiary of a multinational rather than a true joint venture, since the local partner is not sharing managerial control and providing a proportional input in a strategic sense. In addition traditional joint ventures were generally undertaken across several activities, often including marketing and production. Newer joint ventures are increasingly single-activity: joint ventures that are formed primarily to conduct R&D are often referred to as research corporations.

4.4 The growth of alliance activity

There is little doubt that the growth of R&D alliances mirrors the globalization process. Although there was some growth in R&D alliances in the 1960s and 1970s, inter-firm agreements have begun to grow exponentially since the 1980s (Hagedoorn 2002). Figure 4.4 illustrates this trend with data from 1980 onwards.

As discussed in chapter 1, the growth of partnerships is associated in part with economic imperatives. Nonetheless, simply by invoking globalization one cannot explain the growth of this form of economic activity. I intend to shed some light on the determinants of this sustained interest in cooperative agreements in R&D.

One of the fundamental reasons for the growth in alliances lies in the reduction of transaction costs. These have occurred due to, *inter alia*, (1) the introduction of new space-shrinking technologies (particularly information and computer technologies), which have reduced cross-border communication, information and organizational costs; (2) the harmonization of regulations and barriers as a result of growing economic liberalization. These have been further enhanced by the establishment of supra-national regional and inter-regional agreements such as NAFTA and the EU, as well as multilateral protocols and agreements under the auspices of the WTO, WIPO, etc. These agreements have, *ceteris paribus*, reduced

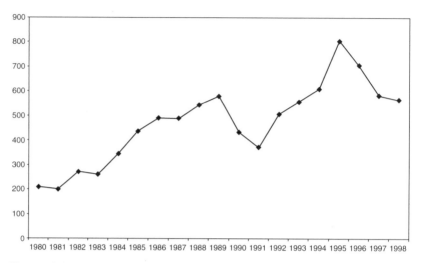

Figure 4.4 Growth of strategic technology partnering, 1980–1998
Source: MERIT-CATI database.

the risks of shirking contractual responsibilities as the costs of monitoring and enforcing cross-border alliances have fallen. The case of the EU is particularly useful in illustrating the growth of alliances because the EU is not only at a rather advanced stage of economic integration achieved over the last fifty years, but EU firms are at the technological cutting edge, and some EU locations are important centres of agglomeration (see e.g., Cantwell and Iammarino 2003). From a transactions costs perspective, the harmonization of regulations within the Single European Market (SEM) initiative, in such a view represents a more advanced version of this activity, and further lowers transaction costs for firms within the Union. As Narula and Hagedoorn (1999) have shown, there are no significant country-specific differences in the propensity to engage in alliances. Therefore the benefits of integration have resulted in lower costs for all firms regardless of nationality. However, there continues to be a considerable bias of MNEs towards the home country in terms of the concentration of value-adding activity: it can thus also be argued that, *ceteris paribus*, greater absolute cost reductions might occur for EU firms since the extent of their European value-added activity is generally higher and the significance of their European operations much larger to their total worldwide activity. This reasoning might suggest that, *ceteris paribus*, EU firms should derive a larger benefit when engaging in collaboration

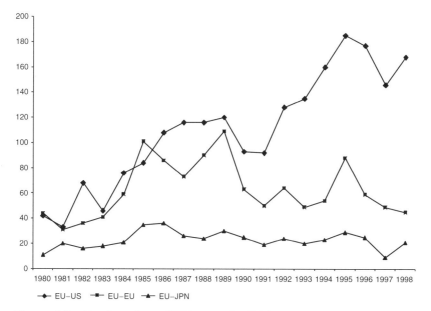

Figure 4.5 Number of new STP by year for EU firms

with other EU firms as a result of European integration relative to *collaboration* involving non-European firms. As figure 4.5 shows, intra-European cooperation did gain briefly in popularity relative to EU–Japanese and EU–US alliances, but this growth was not sustained for long, as predicted by Kay (1991).

It is important to remember that the decline in transaction costs due to the SEM have also reduced costs for other organizational modes (Kay 1991, 1997). The costs associated with full internalization will have also proportionally fallen, and if all else were equal, alliances would still be a second-best option. Certainly, reduced transaction costs might lead firms which otherwise might have considered full internalization to undertake collaborative agreements. Firms that might not have had the resources to expand (whether domestically or internationally) on their own would now also be able to consider it, since a collaboration could require fewer resources than it might otherwise have done before European integration. In other words, this line of reasoning would suggest, *ceteris paribus*, the number of firms undertaking alliances within the EU would have increased since the 1980s in response to integration.

However, transaction costs provide only a partial explanation for the growth in alliances, and suggests only why one group may derive greater benefits from collaboration than other groups. It does not completely answer why firms increasingly prefer quasi-hierarchical arrangements to fully internalized ones. If transaction cost theory were to provide a complete explanation, the decline in costs due to either globalization or integration should lead to at least the similar extent of benefits for traditional hierarchical arrangements. To understand the non-transaction cost-based reasons for alliances, it is useful to return to the motives for alliances as discussed in figure 4.2, and reflect on the word 'strategic' in strategic alliances. What differentiates a strategic alliance from a customer–supplier network is the underlying motive of the cooperation. The primary motivation for a customer–supplier network is that it is primarily cost-economizing in nature, while strategic alliances embody a second motivation, which is strategic in nature. By 'strategic' they suggest that such agreements are aimed at *long-term profit-optimizing* objectives by attempting to enhance the value of the firm's assets.

Several reasons exist for the growth in popularity of cooperative agreements which embody a strategic element. One explanation is based on the increased competition due to liberalization of markets and the globalized nature of the operations of firms. Such increased competition has led to a low-growth scenario over the past two decades or so, and firms need to seek cheaper sources of inputs or divert sales from slow or negative growth markets (Buckley and Casson 1998). Such changes often need to be undertaken with rapidity. Declining transaction costs associated with contractual or quasi-internalized relationships in addition to falling profits margins have led to a *dis-integration* of certain firms in particular industries, as they seek flexibility and lower risk, which have hitherto preferred vertical integration. Indeed, some notice has been taken of the process of dis-investment, that, coincidentally or not, appears to have become quite commonplace during the last decade (Benito 1997).

In addition, though, the emergence of new technological sectors (such as biotechnology) and the growing technological convergence between sectors (such as computers and automobiles, or new materials with transportation) have also played an important role. The cross-fertilization of technological areas has meant that firms need to have an increasing range of competences (Granstrand et al. 1997). This encourages the use of alliances to seek complementary assets. As has been emphasized by others (e.g., Kogut 1988), the use of M&A is not a viable option where the technology being sought is a small part of the total value of the firm. Greenfield investment does not represent a viable option either, in most instances, as the time and costs of building new competences from scratch may be prohibitive. It should be noted that in some instances alliances are used as a precursor to M&A (Hagedoorn and Sadowski 1999). In connection with this, there has also been a growing cost of development, and of acquiring the resources and skills necessary to bring new products and services to market. Increasing the market size, and the sharing of costs and risks associated with staying on the cutting edge of technology creates strong motivation to undertake alliances, no matter how much firms may prefer to go it alone.

Last but not least, there are the game-theoretic considerations. As Kay (1997) explains, 'it is necessary to engage in networks with certain firms not because they trust their partners, but *in order* to trust their partners' (Kay 1997: 215). In addition, there is the follow-my-leader strategy, as originally highlighted by Knickerbocker (1973). Firms seek partnerships in response to similar moves made by other firms in the same industry, not always because there is sound economic rationale in doing so, but in imitation of their competitors.

If firms were to go it alone, they would forgo the opportunity to observe what the other firms in the same industry are up to. This goes for firms that have proven abilities in a given area of specialization, as well as firms that do not. In addition, where new technologies are concerned, there is an increasing need to seek a broad range of competences in unrelated fields. Firms generally have limited resources and cannot possibly engage in vertical and horizontal integration to internalize all their needs. As I have noted earlier, there is a growing tendency to focus on a few selected core technologies rather than vertically integrate. By engaging in alliance activity rather than internalization, as Buckley and Casson (1998) have noted, firms are thus able to be more flexible, and can respond to low growth scenarios and, at the same time, optimize returns. In addition to the benefits of flexibility, the need for complementary assets, market power and economies of scale, there are other reasons which are peculiar to strategic technology partnering which I will discuss in the next section.

4.5 The special case of strategic alliances to conduct R&D

R&D alliances are of a different and special nature: this is the one aspect of value-adding activity that continues to be highly centralized and internalized, even in a domestic scenario. In general, while production activities have gradually been increasingly internation-alized, R&D tends to stay 'at home' (see discussion in chapters 1, 2 and 3). Nonetheless, it is worth noting that there has been some growth in the technological development activities of MNEs rela-tive to their level twenty years ago, and these changes indicate two trends worthy of note. First, in addition to overseas R&D activities associated with demand-side factors, there has been a growing extent of foreign R&D activities by firms in response to supply-side factors (Florida 1997, Kuemmerle 1996). Second, there has been a growing use of external or quasi-external technological sources. Tidd and Trewhella (1997) suggest that the most important external sources of technology are: universities, consortia, licensing, custom-ers and suppliers, acquisitions, joint ventures and alliances and commercial research organizations. Although there is little system-atic and thorough analysis of this process, companies such as Philips and Akzo-Nobel are currently attempting to source 20 per cent of their technology needs externally (van Hoesel and Narula 1999). Indeed, there is a direct relationship between how much R&D a firm does internally, and its external acquisition of technol-ogy – Veugelers (1997) demonstrates that there is a positive rela-tionship between external technology sourcing and internal R&D. Indications are that collaborative arrangements to undertake R&D are becoming ever more popular, having tripled in significance since the early 1980s (Gugler and Pasquier 1997).

Its special characteristics require certain important caveats to be noted. To begin with, there is a fundamental difference in the definition of R&D alliances and non-R&D alliances. Traditionally alliances have been defined as agreements which have a long-term and formal aspect which link aspects of their businesses (Porter and Fuller 1986). Strategic technology partnering, as used here, refers to agreements that are intended to undertake specific tasks and are generally terminated at the completion of these tasks, and are by definition short- (and often fixed-) term in nature.

There are other important considerations due to the special nature of R&D alliances. First, it is important to note that there is a strong causality between size and the propensity to engage in STP, given the need to have sufficient resources to undertake R&D (Hagedoorn and Schakenraad 1994). Second, trade barriers have not played a major role in inhibiting the relocation of R&D, except where such R&D is associated with production (that is, adaptive R&D). Stand-alone R&D facilities, which are common in know-ledge-intensive sectors, are often located according to supply-related considerations. Such activities have not necessarily been affected by the decline in transaction costs due to the SEM initiative – skilled human capital and knowledge (in either tacit or non-tacit form) has long enjoyed relatively restriction-free freedom of movement across borders. Although certain improvements such as the common patenting system, and the harmonization of regulations may have lowered costs in general, the benefits of lowered communication costs (due *inter alia* to ICTs) have occurred on a global level.

Although the reduction in trade barriers may affect both exporting and foreign direct investment through wholly owned subsidiaries, R&D alliances are largely unaffected by these. While it is true that firms engaged in asset-exploiting activities such as production or sales have a broader choice of options that include wholly owned subsidiaries and arm's-length technology acquisition, some of these options are simply not available to firms that are seeking to undertake R&D. First, because technology is tacit by nature, and as far as technology development is concerned, even more so. Arm's-length transactions are simply not as effective, particularly in technology-intensive sectors or new, 'emerging' sectors, even if markets for these technologies were to exist. The further away these technologies are from the market (that is, more research-oriented than development-oriented) the less likely that technology can be obtained through market mechanisms. Besides, its partly public good nature prevents prospective selling firms from making technologies available for evaluation, and without doing so, the prospective buyer is unable to determine its worth. Markets, therefore, are liable to fail, or at least will function inefficiently. It is no surprise, therefore, that technology partnering has grown fastest in high-technology sectors where market options are less well developed, while partnering activity in low- and medium-technology sectors has steadily declined as a percentage of all agreements (Hagedoorn 2002).

The choice of partner in R&D alliances can be international or domestic. There has been considerable variation in the international aspect of R&D alliances over time, although broadly speaking this reflects the gradual internationalization of firms and competition. Country size differences persist: small countries tend to engage in more alliances than large countries – the US has the smallest level of international partnerships with less than 50 per cent being international, while Switzerland has an international share greater than 90 per cent. There are also considerable differences by industry (Hagedoorn 2002). Why do firms prefer in certain instances to partner with a foreign firm rather than a domestic firm? This is related to the question of why firms do not undertake all the R&D at their home location in the first place. The literature suggests that this is due to both supply and demand issues. The demand issues are well known, and are generally associated with adaptive R&D in response to specific market conditions. More recently attention has been drawn to the supply issues. Firms are seeking to utilize immobile assets, which may be either firm-specific or location-specific. In the case where they are firm-specific, they are often associated with clusters of firms, and country-specific characteristics. It is well acknowledged that location advantages are idiosyncratic and path-dependent, and the nature of innovatory activities in a given location is associated with the national systems of innovation (Edquist 1997, Lundvall 1992). The nature of the benefits arising from a non-cooperative arrangement requires physical proximity to the firm or cluster, in order to seek indirect technology spillovers, which can be a highly costly, uncertain and random procedure that requires a long-term horizon. In the case of basic research, for instance, this might occur through the hiring of researchers that hitherto worked for a competitor. Where such immobile assets are country- but not firm-specific, they may be embodied in aspects of the national systems of innovation. Whether the advantage being sought is firm- or country-specific, the establishment of a greenfield laboratory is a feasible option, but involves high costs of start-up, and considerable time. In fields where innovation is rapid, it may not provide a fast enough response. The use of M&A is even less attractive where the area where the complementary resources are sought covers only a small area of the firm's interests. Even where a firm wishes to acquire an R&D facility, it is generally not possible to do so, except in rare circumstances.

It is true, nonetheless, that there are also strategic *limitations* to the use of alliances. First, there is a danger that an alliance may represent a precursor to M&A. Indeed, Hagedoorn and Sadowski (1999) show that 2.6 per cent of strategic technology alliances lead to M&A, a figure that is quite significant given the high percentage (estimates vary between 50 and 70 per cent) of alliances that are terminated before completing their stated objective (see Inkpen and Beamish 1997).

Why would a potential partner wish to collaborate with another which has limited or as-yet-undemonstrated resources to offer? First, because of the nature of innovation, the only way to determine the nature of a potential partner's research efforts is to examine them. One way it can do so is by engaging in some form of mutual hostage exchange, which an alliance provides. Second, even where the partner's resources prove to be of a limited or inappropriate nature, and the alliance is terminated prematurely, information about its former partner's competences are then available to either firm in future periods, should it require competences similar to those on offer by its ex-partner. Third, as Hagedoorn and Duysters (2002) have argued, while selecting partners that are well-established players in existing technologies may represent a profit-maximizing situation, it is optimal only in a static environment. In a dynamic environment, where there is a possibility of technological change (or even a change in technological trajectories), having ties to a wide group of companies, including companies that have yet to demonstrate their value, represents a higher learning potential.

Strategic technology alliances are not undertaken only by firms seeking complementarity of resources. As Narula and Dunning (1998) note, firms may also engage in alliances in order to co-opt the competition. Take the situation where two firms in the same industry are pursuing an important new breakthrough. Neither can be certain that it will win the race to innovate. Therefore it may be in their best interest to collaborate, thus ensuring that they are both jointly 'first': half a pie may be considered better in conditions of uncertainty while there is a probability that there may be none at all.

The evidence on strategic technology partnering points to the fact that the need for complementary assets and the reduction of risk have become increasingly important as these are global phenomena, while open markets may have aggravated the need to co-opt and block competitors, since firms are obliged to restructure to strengthen or even maintain their competitive position, through either aggressive or defensive means. Indeed, such a restructuring of EU industry has occurred since the early 1980s in response to the impending single market agreement (Dunning 1997). Much of the EU-subsidized R&D programmes were aimed at achieving this renewed competitiveness, and indeed, were undertaken in earnest by most firms with a view to being able to compete on equal terms with other EU firms as well as US and Japanese firms by 1993. As Peterson (1991) has pointed out, although technological collaboration has constantly remained high on the agenda of European policy makers, pan-European R&D activities have only systematically been developed by policy makers since the 1980s. Several initiatives by the European Commission have been implemented over the past two decades in an attempt to bolster the competitiveness of European firms, particularly in high-technology sectors. Indeed, Hagedoorn and Schakenraad (1993) show that there was a concurrent rise in non-subsidized and subsidized R&D during the latter half of the 1980s. Nonetheless, in a study of non-subsidized R&D collaboration by European firms, Narula (1999) shows that while intra-EU cooperation did in fact increase during the second half of the 1980s, this level was not sustained through the 1990s (as illustrated in figure 4.5). The initial rise in intra-EU alliances reflected the fact that European industry began to undertake a much more serious view of alliances in the mid-1980s, with a doubling of activity over a short period. This can in part be attributed to three things. First, that the process of economic integration had by this time been seen to be a reality. Second, European firms had begun to realize by the mid-1980s that they were technologically lagging in new core high-technology sectors such as information technology, and leading European firms had begun to cooperate by this period (Mytelka and Delapierre 1987, Mytelka 1995). By the end of the 1980s this growth in intra-EU activity declined, but EU firms showed a continued propensity to undertake EU–US and EU–Japanese R&D collaboration, particularly in the information technology, biotechnology and new-materials sectors. The subsequent decline of the number of new alliances in the 1990s is quite dramatic. Narula (1999) postulated that this reflected the result of restructuring of European industry, in part through the series of M&A that occurred in the run-up to the single market (for example, Nixdorf by Siemens, ICL by Fujitsu, Plessey by Siemens-GEC) as well as the re-positioning of firms' technological profiles (for example, the exit of Philips from computers, its entry into the telecommunications sector with AT&T) (Mytelka 1995).

The second reason for the decline in intra-EU alliances may have to do with the growth of extra-EU alliances. As figure 4.5 shows, the propensity for EU firms to engage in alliances with Japanese and US firms also increased in the mid-1980s. This reflects in part the desire for Japanese and US firms to seek strategic positions within European industry prior to 1992 to avoid any question of being excluded from 'fortress Europe'. In addition, there had been some attempt to spur transatlantic R&D cooperation though the strategic defence initiative (SDI) programme of the US government in the mid-1980s (Carton 1987). Perhaps most significantly of all, however, was that EU firms were primarily spurred to partner with US and Japanese firms given the technological lead that US firms possessed, in information technology and biotechnology, and to a lesser extent, new materials, while Japanese firms had a technological lead in information technology and new materials. In other words, EU firms would be interested in partnering with firms regardless of nationality, depending primarily on their relative competitive positions in the industry, or the presence of significant clusters at given locations.

It is important to note that the definition of strategic technology alliances includes both equity and non-equity agreements, as discussed in an earlier section. Thus, while we have made general comments about the choice between markets, hierarchies and quasi-hierarchies, there is a significant difference between various organizational modes of STP. Broadly speaking, though, it is possible to consider these as being of two major groups – equity-based agreements and contractual, non-equity based agreements. It is significant to note that the choice of alliance mode is determined by the technological characteristics of sectors of industry (Hagedoorn and Narula 1996). Equity agreements are preferred in relatively mature industries while contractual alliances are more common in so-called high-tech industries.

There is, however, another dimension that is worth noting. There has been a decline in the use of equity agreements on a global basis, whereby the percentage of equity STP has fallen steadily from 46.9 per cent in 1980–4 to 26.7 per cent during the period 1990–4 (Narula and Hagedoorn 1999). A similar tendency has been noted for all alliance groupings by region. This points to an important issue which relates to the process of learning. Given the novelty of R&D alliances, it can be hypothesized that firms prefer to undertake more hierarchical arrangements, but as they have acquired experience with this form of technological innovation, they have gradually switched to more flexible, but inherently riskier agreements.

European R&D alliances have demonstrated a similar tendency, and indeed the fact that these patterns demonstrate industry-wide trends rather than national suggests that the same process of learning about the mechanics of alliance formation and management apply to all firms regardless of nationality. It also highlights the need of firms, again regardless of nationality, to partner with the most appropriate firms regardless of national origin.

4.6 Conclusions

Our admittedly simplistic analysis lends support to, and confirms, some of the trends and patterns observed by the technology partnering literature. First, that strategic technology partnering as a phenomenon is best explained using an organizational learning framework. Recent theoretical studies have suggested that firms' decisions regarding what extent to internalize value-adding activity is determined not just by a cost-minimization strategy driven by short-term profit optimization, but also by an interest to enhance the value of the firm in a more long-term horizon. It does so by improving the nature and types of technological/knowledge-based assets it possesses. Given the firm's bounded rationality, however, this decision is more of a strategic one. This is what determines the primary difference between networks and alliances.

There has clearly been an explosion in the use of alliances to undertake innovative activity, and this trend is closely related to the process of globalization. Globalization has affected the need of firms to collaborate, in that firms now *seek* opportunities to cooperate, rather than identify situations where they can achieve majority control. In addition, the increasing similarity of technologies across countries and cross-fertilization of technology between sectors, coupled with the increasing costs and risks associated with innovation has led to firms utilizing STP as a *first-best* option. STP, as with most forms of innovative activity, is primarily concentrated in the Triad countries. However, the propensity of firms of a given nationality to engage in STP varies according to the characteristics of the country. This is because small and technologically less advanced countries tend to be focused in fewer sectors than large countries, due, *inter alia*, to the differences in economic structure and demand. We also see that strategic alliances are dominated by large firms, and there is indeed a positive relationship between firm size and STP levels by firm. We also observe a high percentage of STP utilized on a cross-border basis. That is, a considerable share of STP seems to be undertaken with partners of other nationalities. There seems to be some suggestion that while some firms undertake STP as a means to complement their existing R&D activity, others seek to use STP as a substitute.

There seems to be no clear relationship between the extents to which firms engage in international production and engage in technology partnering. This difference is not mediated, as might have been expected, by nationality of ownership or by R&D expenditures, but preliminary indications suggest that its differences exist on a sectoral basis, suggesting that it is an industry-specific phenomenon.

There is also a clear shift of alliance activity towards non-equity forms of agreements, and this has occurred more or less uniformly across countries, and we attribute this change partly to the improved enforceability of contracts and intellectual property protection, and partly to the increasing knowledge and familiarity firms now have in conducting international business activity. At firm level, the propensity to use equity agreements is associated with industry-specific differences, rather than country-specific differences.

It would seem that countries are increasingly engaged in promoting the competitiveness of their domestic firms, in what can loosely be described as 'techno-nationalism' (Ostry and Nelson 1995), with the intention of developing 'national champions'. Most of the major industrial economies practise some sort of government intervention to boost the ownership advantages of their firms. While some governments do so through indirect means that improve the quality of location-bound resources and capabilities to attract mobile ownership advantages of domestic and foreign owned firms, others attempt more direct intervention by participating in ownership advantage-generating activities.

Much of this intervention was originally as a response to globalization, with the desire of protecting weak domestic firms from international competition. Ironically, this has led to a greater use of alliance and network-forming activity. Therefore techno-nationalism is doomed to failure, as the question of 'who is us' and 'who is them' makes such policies increasingly redundant (Reich 1990, Strange 1998). National champions are equally willing to act as free agents, and are in some instances receiving national treatment (and support) from several governments, both national and regional. The example of IBM being involved in several research consortia funded by both the EU and the US governments best illustrates this point. The role of governments in promoting alliances is taken up at length in chapter 7.

As for the underlying motive of improving levels of R&D activity, this too would seem to be in doubt. It should be noted that R&D alliances are even more footloose than traditional majority-owned production or R&D activities; nor, it must be stressed, do R&D alliances provide significant levels of spillovers to the host economies where they might be located. Funds invested in joint research by governments are notoriously hard to track down, in terms of their application, in both a geographic and a technical (project-specific) sense. Furthermore, firms are more interested in establishing themselves near centres of agglomeration, regardless of where these might be located. This indicates a very real danger of entering into an incentive war, with so many countries willing to subsidize R&D (Niosi 1995), and with so little obvious spillovers therefrom. Chapter 7 delves deeper into the policy implications of the growth of R&D alliances.

I have focused my attention primarily on discussing on a rather 'macro' scale the reasons why firms of a given nationality tend to engage in R&D alliances. Within this discussion I have dealt fairly superficially with some of the firm-level issues that determine why firms prefer alliances to full internalization. Furthermore – as I have suggested here – there are other modes for organizing non-internal R&D such as outsourcing. In the next chapter I will examine some of the technological and economic factors that determine when, how and under what circumstances firms decide to undertake different modes of innovatory activity.

5

In-house R&D, Outsourcing or Alliances? Some Strategic and Economic Considerations

5.1 Introduction

Although this is by no means a new development, there is evidence to suggest that firms have reduced their dependence on internal R&D activities at an increased pace over the last decade. This has been highlighted most recently by Veugelers (1997), Veugelers and Cassiman (1999), Hagedoorn (1996, 2002), Narula and Hagedoorn (1999) and Archibugi and Iammarino (1999), among others. This development, it has been argued, in part reflects techno- and economic globalization, whereby there is an increasing similarity (and growing capital intensity) in the types of technologies across countries of the Triad. This is a result, *inter alia*, of growing cross-border competition, which has also led to reduced opportunities for profits, in the face of higher costs in maintaining technological assets to remain globally competitive (Archibugi and Michie 1998).

My use of the term 'non-internal' is a deliberate one, and is intended to include both external activities: arm's-length relationships such as licensing, R&D contracts, outsourcing and other customer–supplier relationships; and quasi-external activity, such as strategic alliances, which are taken to include a myriad of organizational modes (see chapter 4).

My starting point in this chapter is a synthesis of the seminal work of *inter alia* Teece (1986, 1996) and Granstrand et al. (1997). I develop an understanding of some of the most significant technological factors that determine the kinds of non-internal R&D activity undertaken by multi-technology manufacturing firms. The choice between internal and non-internal R&D activities is determined by (1) distribution and kinds of competences that the firm possesses, (2) the evolution of individual technologies, and the changing characteristics of the technology as it progresses from a new technology to a mature one, (3) strategic and economic issues relating to the competitive environment.

Although I primarily describe a conceptual framework to understand how a firm decides between internal, external and quasi-external technology development, it has been refined and synthesized on the basis of a number of interviews with thirty-two senior R&D managers of European-based technology-intensive firms. I have illustrated my arguments with anecdotal evidence based on these interviews. Appendix A (p. 162) gives details of the interview methodology and limitations of the data.

Understanding the reasons for the success and failure of cooperative activities has far-reaching implications from both a managerial and a policy perspective. The 'right' mix of internal and non-internal R&D activities can prevent firms not only from over- or under-investing in R&D, but also help to maintain their long-term competitive position.

The next section discusses some of the relationships between the multi-technology firm and the growth of non-internal R&D. The third section attempts to differentiate between alliances and outsourcing. The fourth section examines the static issues underlying the choice of mode and the distribution of competences. I then discuss the evolution of technologies, and the dynamic choices that firms must make. The final section develops some conclusions, highlights the caveats, and develops an agenda for future research.

5.2 The growth of the multi-technology firm and non-internal R&D

The growing need for firms – particularly in technology-intensive sectors – to have multiple technological competences is by now axiomatic. Several contributions, notably by Granstrand and associates (see e.g., Granstrand 1998, Granstrand et al. 1997) have noted the growing technological diversification of companies and, more recently, that this is associated with a reduction in product diversification over time. Even where products are mono-technology-based, the processes used to manufacture them often utilize several technologies. Furthermore, within a given technology, there are several technological paradigms at play, as firms base products on the current dominant design, yet develop nascent technologies with the long-term intention of replacing the current technology with a new dominant design.

The increasing cross-fertilization of technologies across disciplines and resultant broader portfolio of competences has become fundamental to the competitiveness of technology-based firms. There has also, however, been a concurrent increase in competition, due, *inter alia*, to the liberalization of markets, and the reduction of transaction and transportation costs. This has led to a decline in the profit margins due to increased cross-border competition and barriers to entry (Buckley and Casson 1998). Therefore the increased cost of requiring more technological competences is not offset by greater profits, but quite the opposite. In addition, R&D in new technologies has been seen to be increasingly capital-intensive. So, the need to reduce costs (and maintain profits) while maintaining the firm's technological assets has become an important managerial balancing act.

The attempt to understand the reasons behind a firm's choice between external and internal technological development is not new. The work of Teece (1986) presents a pioneering analysis of this issue, which builds on work by Abernathy and Utterback (1978), and Dosi (1982) among others, and further developed by Pisano (1990), Arora and Gambardella (1990) and Henderson and Clark (1990). More recent work includes Granstrand et al. (1997),

---

Box 5.1   The importance of in-house capabilities for multi-technology products

Despite the growing opportunities to outsource technologies, firms need to have considerable in-house capabilities. This is for several reasons. First, firms need to be able to specify very clearly what they wish to outsource. Second, they need to be able to integrate the externally produced technologies and components with other technologies and components produced in-house as well as by other contractors. Brusoni et al. (2001) analyse this issue in great detail, using evidence from the aircraft engine industry. They argue that 'lead' firms in such multi-technology industries act as systems integrators. They need to maintain in-house capabilities because various technologies evolve at differing and uneven rates, and with unpredictable product level dependencies. The firms within such networks can be loosely coupled only because of the presence of a dominant stabilizing systems integrator, with in-depth competences in a wide variety of sectors. Modular products may allow some level of non-internal technological development, but there are clearly limits to how far this can be extended. Networks of suppliers built around a powerful systems integrator are not always loosely coupled (for example, mobile phone systems), and in other cases are decoupled (for example, the PC industry).

Granstrand (1998), Nagarajan and Mitchell (1998), Veugelers and Cassiman (1999), Croisier (1998), Lowe and Taylor (1998), Tidd and Trehwalla (1997) and Gambardella and Torrisi (1998).

One of the reasons attributed to the growth of non-internal activity has been the decline in transaction costs for external or quasi-externalized relationships, relative to complete internalization, not just for R&D, but for most aspects of value-adding activity. As firms have responded to this new scenario, there has been a *dis-integration* of certain firms in particular industries, as they seek flexibility and lower risk, which have hitherto preferred vertical integration. Some observation has been made of the process of dis-investment, which appears to have become quite commonplace during the last decade (Benito 1997). However, this has happened only to a limited extent in the case of R&D (estimates suggest that between 10 and 15 per cent of agreements involve R&D, although this figure has increased three-fold since the 1980s).[1] Why do firms demonstrate a lower propensity to use non-internal sourcing for R&D? The reasons for its relative lack of popularity have to do with the nature of the innovation process. First, because the innovation process is highly uncertain, and there are considerable costs in negotiating and enforcing contracts. Second, the large tacit component of innovation means that through external sourcing, firms are only able to get codified results, not the accumulated, person-embodied skills. Third, the partially public good nature of technology also means that there is considerable opportunity for technological leakage and/or opportunistic behaviour by collaborators (Veugelers and Cassiman 1999). Fourth, appropriability of innovation varies widely, both by country and by industry, which further increases the possibility of loss of key assets. In other words, the uncertainty of the process, the high costs of transaction and risk of losing strategic assets crucial to the survival of the firm inhibit non-internal activity. As Nagarajan and Mitchell (1998) point out, the advantages of internal R&D activity are also its limitations. Firms are path-dependent, and find it costly to break away from existing routines towards radically new or different concepts. There are additional costs involved in switching trajectories which may impede organizational change and exacerbate the level of uncertainty and therefore economic risk.[2]

Can the growth of non-internal R&D activity be explained simply by imperfections in the strategic and economic organization of internal R&D? The answer is complex, and is associated with our use of the term 'non-internal' to include both external activities (arm's-length relationships such as licensing, R&D contracts, outsourcing and other customer–supplier relationships) and quasi-external activity (such as strategic alliances, which are most often undertaken between competitors). Non-internal activities, apart from the obvious benefits of exploring new areas and instigating radical change, have the advantage of being a 'reversible' form of investment (Gambardella and Torrisi 1998). The capital needed is smaller, and the risks are substantially reduced, and in case of failure or organizational crisis, limited damage is inflicted on the primary operations of the firm.

Fully external activities are not novel – it has, for instance, been accepted for quite some time that universities and state-subsidized institutes represent an important source of basic research for commercial firms. Indeed, it is the development of horizontal collaboration between competitors that is relatively new, particularly in strategic technology partnering, where the growth has been almost exponential (see chapter 4). Nonetheless, as the survey by Tidd and Trehwalla (1997) illustrates, external sourcing of technology remains a larger phenomenon than strategic alliances. However, it is difficult to quantify the differences in growth between external and quasi-external R&D, because it is hard, if not impossible, to estimate the potential value of quasi-external agreements to the firms involved (Narula 1999). First, because R&D is tacit, and has a long-term horizon: the value of the research cannot be estimated *ex-ante*. Even where there is a short-term horizon and the objective is non-tacit (say, establishing technological standards), and the resulting output is patentable or licensable, technologies cannot always be correlated with products (and thus sales). Second, even where firms can place a value on an agreement, they have no incentive to make such information available, either to each other, or to the public. The evidence from our interviews indicates that in terms of expenditures, firms spend between 15 and 25 per cent of the R&D budget in technology outsourcing, and 5 to 10 per cent in collaboration, although the *value* of the latter may well be greater, because of the strategic importance of the areas where alliances are undertaken. At the same time, as discussed below, it is relatively easy to determine the value of outsourcing. It is important to note that alliances are a complex organizational form and require considerable resources to maintain collaborative activity, compared with more arm's-length agreements such as outsourcing. Tidd and Trehwalla (1997), for instance, note in their survey of Japanese and British technology acquisition strategies, that only 13 per cent of their firms considered alliances as a significant technology source. It is worth noting, too, that horizontal alliances, in the sense of collaboration between competitors, are a relatively small phenomenon. Firms partner with competitors only with the greatest of caution, and only on specific and carefully defined projects.

5.3 Standardization, cost and industrial organization

The growth of non-internal activity has in part occurred because of a redefinition of the boundaries of the firm (in the Coasian sense) such that it is increasingly cheaper to undertake such activities outside the firm. Clearly this has not happened on an equal basis for quasi-external and fully external agreements, particularly for R&D activities. As I have highlighted earlier, firms in our sample engage in three times as many outsourcing agreements than they do alliances. The answer to this discrepancy lies in a simple fact: standardization of technologies across borders due to technological convergence has led to a decline in the production costs of *clearly defined inputs* to the value-adding process, *as well as* the transaction costs associated with their acquisition. By 'clearly defined' I refer to codifiable, non-tacit inputs to the production process.

Here it is cogent to distinguish between vertical-chain-related activity and horizontal activity. The growth of vertical relationships (essentially customer–supplier agreements) is governed by the ability of firms to monitor the quality of external suppliers due to improved communications. The convergence of technological standards in 'generic' production technologies creates alternatives to direct control, since quality requirements are similar, and if these inputs do not meet specifications the shortcomings can be quickly identified and addressed without costly time delays. Horizontal alliances, particularly with competitors, are generally undertaken for strategic reasons, with cost issues playing a secondary role (Narula and Hagedoorn 1999). The principal reasons for alliance activity is to maintain closer control of the activities of the collaborator, and to enhance and monitor the transfer of technology between the partners. If the knowledge to be transferred is well defined and available from multiple sources, complex organizational cooperation modes such as alliances are unnecessary.[3] It follows, therefore, that R&D alliances take place in diametrically opposed circumstances to outsourcing. The relationships in horizontal agreements tend to reflect a more complex strategic intent, and arm's-length transactions do not in general provide this.

External acquisition of technology is most easily done when the technology behind the product is codifiable and standardized and when *multiple non-distinguishable* sources of these inputs are available. The same argument holds true for R&D activity: since R&D output is partly tacit, externalization of R&D means that the firm gets only the codified results, not the accumulated person-embodied skills. As has been noted elsewhere, even where firms outsource, they maintain a minimum level of in-house capacity in those technologies in order to decipher and utilize them (Veugelers 1997). In other words, R&D outsourcing is only undertaken where doing so is cost-effective *and* does not threaten the competitive advantages of the company. Having a single source or single buyer may prove to be most cost-effective, but it is generally accepted that low costs do not always translate to the best technology. Moreover, dependency on a single supplier (or a single customer) represents a bottleneck, and the problems associated with a monopolistic/monopsonistic pricing. Furthermore, there are positive technological externalities of multiple sources of innovation. Pratt and Whitney, for instance, has several suppliers of turbine intakes, even though it has in-house design and manufacturing facilities. External bids are always sought for new products from all parties, as a way of establishing a benchmark for quality and costs. Innovations from the various suppliers are all absorbed into the final product.

Where either the know-how for the inputs is unique and non-substitutable (either because it is proprietary and firm-specific, or because it is location-specific), or it is tacit and non-codifiable, cost-based issues become less relevant, and strategic (and resource) considerations (such as core competences) take on greater importance. These issues are examined separately.

5.3.1 When the input necessary is unique

If the input is firm-specific (for instance, Windows operating system), the cost becomes less relevant and the resource availability becomes important.[4] The development of new software is generally dependent on the features to be incorporated into the next version of Windows. In these cases, the relationship between the software firm and Microsoft is much more strategic, and requires certain resources to be devoted to the interaction between the two firms. Therefore the software firm is involved in an alliance which determines the long-term product-market positioning of at least one of the firms. Where the resource is not completely internalized by the firm, but is particular to a location or a region, a similar scenario applies, except that this affects production costs more than transaction costs. There is a well-developed literature on the role of national (and regional) systems of innovation and their influence on the location of companies (see chapters 2 and 3). This may either be to benefit from socio-technological inputs such as educational establishments, infrastructure, or simply to exploit economies of agglomeration, and to seek possible spillovers. Where such inputs are unique, that is, the resource is unavailable elsewhere, and proximity to its source is necessary, the choice of location is production-cost-independent (Sachwald 1998). It is to be noted that although the cost issue may be secondary in the case of immobile location-specific factors, that does not mean that it is unimportant.[5] Since these resources are crucial to the survival of the firm, they take on a strategic importance that clearly outweighs any cost-savings that might derive from outsourcing. Where the input is unique, some of this uncertainty can be reduced by considering quasi-hierarchical agreements such as alliances.

5.3.2 Tacit or non-codifiable inputs

Because of their nature, certain inputs to the value-adding process are less clearly defined. This is especially the case with most innovatory activities, and is also true for specialized resources where innovation is not involved, but the final product is tacit in nature. Therefore, it is much more difficult to outsource these aspects of the production process, because it is hard to specify the quality of the resource. Identifying a supplier who would be able to produce it may be difficult, since its nature is difficult to specify.[6] Where the product has a high level of tacitness, property rights will most likely be unclear. In other words, the market for such resources is hard to establish. Where such supplier firms do exist and property rights are well defined, they able to charge monopoly rates, since they have access to unique resources, and price comparisons are thus impossible. In addition though, closer cooperation than might be provided by networks is also necessary, first because the contracting firm is itself unsure of the nature of the resources, and must monitor the activities of the supplier firm more closely. As Cantwell and Santangelo (1999) discuss, greater tacit and uncodified knowledge require closer, face-to-face interaction. Second, the customer would like to avoid the potential loss of his assets to the supplier company. In such cases, outsourcing is the least preferred option.

5.4 Distributed competences and the choice between internal and non-internal activity: a static view

The technological competences and assets of a firm can be classified into several distinct kinds. Not all activities are equally crucial to the competitiveness of the firm. Nagarajan and Mitchell (1998) propose a two-way classification of core and complementary technologies, while Granstrand et al. (1997) view these as being of four types. I have utilized the Granstrand et al. framework in which the competences of technology-based firms can be viewed as being of four types (figure 5.1).

Firms have *distinctive* competences, which command a high share of technical resources of a company. These form the 'core' of the firm, which defines the technological profile of the firm and its competitiveness. Then there are the *niche* sectors, which are technologies in which the firm possesses some level of expertise, but these areas are intrinsically small in terms of their profile, and in terms of the resources they command. These technological fields are generally complementary to their distinctive competences. *Marginal/peripheral* technologies are sectors which were important to the firm in the past, or are expected to become important in the future, in which limited resources are invested, and where the firm has no distinct technological advantages. Finally *background* competences enable firms to coordinate and benefit from technical changes in the supply chain, which are essential to the competitiveness of the firm, and its ability to efficiently utilize its other, more 'crucial' competences. Although these are equally crucial, and significantly determine the competitiveness of a firm, they utilize only a small percentage of the firm's technology resources. They are, however, an important part of the firm's technological *assets*.

I postulate that figure 5.2 shows how the choice between in-house R&D, alliances and outsourcing relate to the four-way classification of figure 5.1 from a *static* perspective. Firms in our interviews were asked to discuss the importance of their technological activities within this four-way classification, in terms of competences and technological assets. Then, their primary internal, external and collaborative efforts were identified according to the areas of in-house R&D, technological collaboration and outsourcing. Figure 5.2 presents the generalized results of the interviews. Firms will, *ceteris paribus*, prefer to undertake innovative activities in their distinctive competences (Quadrant I) through in-house R&D.

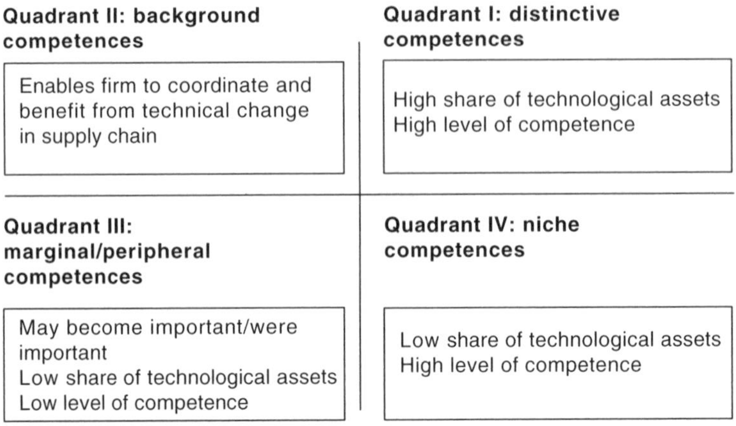

Quadrant II: background competences

Enables firm to coordinate and benefit from technical change in supply chain

Quadrant I: distinctive competences

High share of technological assets
High level of competence

Quadrant III: marginal/peripheral competences

May become important/were important
Low share of technological assets
Low level of competence

Quadrant IV: niche competences

Low share of technological assets
High level of competence

Figure 5.1   The distribution of competences
Source: based on Granstrand et al. (1997).

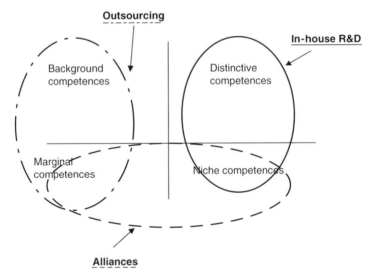

Outsourcing

Background competences

In-house R&D

Distinctive competences

Marginal competences

Niche competences

Alliances

Figure 5.2   The static view: relationship between distributed competences and internal/non-internal R&D

Although there is considerable overlap in the case of Quadrants III and IV (figure 5.2), broadly speaking these competences are strategically less significant, and can be undertaken through alliances. However, the strategic importance of these technologies determines to what extent their development can be externalized. This, in turn, is determined by the extent to which the technology is tacit, the extent to which collaboration is required to utilize it, and to what extent the partner's activities need to be monitored.

Background competences (Quadrant II) are, by and large, the area where outsourcing is primarily used. In general, it would seem firms prefer to undertake research in their distinctive competences in-house as much as possible. There is, however, considerable overlap in the use of in-house R&D and alliances for niche competences, and between outsourcing and alliances in marginal/ peripheral competences. In general, there is considerable idiosyncratic behaviour of firms. Take for instance the case of 'Firm A' (see appendix A, p. 162, for brief description), which considers alliances in their niche sectors unacceptably risky: 'These competences are too important to us. . . . we have spent many years building our strength in these sectors . . . frankly we have world class competences. . . . I am loath to consider letting anyone near our technology. We only use alliances [in these areas] if we have to.'

The differences in propensity varied according to industry and size (discussed further in the next section). The use of alliances in connection with niche sectors was, in general, associated with firms that had limited R&D facilities and/or considered that there was a large technological gap between their technological competences and the market leaders. The issue of size seems to be a very significant one. Firms with limited resources considered alliances as a way of extending their technological competences. For instance, one medical equipment manufacturer ('Firm A') did not have the resources to invest in the next generation of displays. Although LCD technology has become more mature over the last five years, it remains capital-intensive, and proprietary technology at the forefront rests with a handful of companies. It therefore sought an alliance with a US company which is a market leader in medical equipment, many times its size. However, the US firm did not currently compete with it in its particular product segment, and agreed to share the technology and to distribute its products in the US. As a manager pointed out,

> It's a risk [to ally with such a large player], but the cost of developing our own display systems would use up almost our entire R&D budget for a couple of years . . . and our old product range was [beginning to look] old. [They] have the technology lying around, because they have more people in their R&D facilities than we have in our entire company . . . [if they wanted to] they could buy us out, whether we had a partnership with them or not [so it doesn't matter whether or not we partner with them].

Figure 5.3 illustrates the distribution of competences for 'Firm B' which represents an amalgam of the competences of four measuring and control equipment manufacturers. The decision to use alliances is determined by additional issues apart from the protection of competitive advantages. Firm B's scale of production is in the thousands, far below the minimum efficient scale for active component manufacture. The manufacturing and design of specialized active components is therefore an area where it is impractical for the firm to maintain in-house facilities. It makes economic sense, therefore, to provide the performance specifications to a specialized component manufacturer. Nonetheless, because this is an input that is crucial to the competitive advantage of the firm, it is designed in close cooperation with the engineers in Firm B.

The manufacture and design of printed circuit boards (PCBs) was left entirely to external firms, and completely outsourced. Apart from quality control checks when the completed boards were delivered, no attempts were made to monitor or control PCB production and design. Likewise casings, mountings, and the design of power supply units (which have become highly standardized and are now essentially off-the-shelf products) were

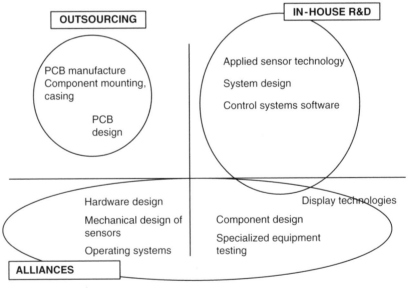

Figure 5.3 Distribution of competences of firm B, based on managers' perceptions
Note: No attempt has been made to locate technologies on a relative basis within any given quadrant.

also completely outsourced. For all these products there were several suppliers available. As a principle,

> we use more than one supplier, our products are based on several boards. Each supplier produces only one board, because we don't want any supplier to have access to our complete product. We might be able to get a lower price, but we don't want to be in a position that the supplier is able to become a competitor. Non-disclosure agreements aren't enough.

As we have earlier suggested, all the managers interviewed agreed that the volume of outsourcing has expanded considerably over the last two decades. They considered that the growth of outsourcing has a lot to do with the process of globalization, particularly in terms of (1) ease of enforcement of contracts and the ability of firms to monitor the activities of suppliers due to ICTs, and (2) the increased competition due to the entry of several emerging Asian economies in technology-intensive sectors: 'The world is a much smaller place... we travel to visit our major suppliers in Taiwan and America at least three or four times each [every year], and they ship us samples by DHL for us to test.'

It is worth noting that not all firms based their decisions on rational economic or strategic issues. One medium-sized firm ('Firm A') had, in the early 1990s, started manufacturing trauma and intensive-care equipment. As its first-generation products reached the end of their life cycle by 1997, the firm was faced with a dilemma. It had continued to maintain a relatively low R&D intensity (and a correspondingly small in-house R&D staff) despite adding more high-tech products, and therefore decided to outsource its new generation of products *completely*, but in order to maintain what it saw as its competitive advantage, the head of R&D decided to outsource the design and manufacture of different sub-assemblies separately, co-ordinated by Firm A's research lab. Partly because the manufacture and the design of the sub-assemblies was done by different contractors, and there was little, if any, direct coordination between the design and manufacturing teams, the final assembled products failed to work within specifications. The product release was delayed by a year, as the in-house R&D had to engineer changes, modification and further testing. Firm A has now responded by establishing a policy against outsourcing of any aspect of the design and manufacture process. It has now established a strategic alliance with a competitor (which has a different geographic focus) to develop its next generation of products.

A cautionary attitude towards alliances is widespread, especially among smaller firms. 'Firm D' outsources almost all aspects of its manufacturing activities, and represents an extreme approach. It has a policy against strategic alliances. It does, however, invest considerable time in selecting supplier firms, so that its customer–supplier relationship is very close-knit. Small supplier firms are selected so that there is little chance of their being able to reverse-engineer their product, and of their becoming a competitor. Long and complex contractual agreements with non-performance penalties and clauses are made with each firm, and the production activity is monitored regularly by visits from the R&D department of Firm D.

As I have earlier emphasized, there is considerable variation between firms, due not just to differences in strategy and history, but also by industry. The next section discusses how technologies evolve, and how this changes the choice of organizational mode over time.

5.5 The dynamic view: the evolution of technological paradigms

I now turn to the dynamics aspects, and in particular the issues relating to the evolution of technologies, and its effect on the decision to internalize innovatory activities. The primary emphasis here is on explaining (1) how the choice of mode is affected by the stage of evolution of the technological paradigm, and (2) how the introduction of new innovations to the existing portfolio of a firm affects its static choices, highlighted in the previous section. The discussion of this evolution is not new, and builds on earlier notions of this process developed by Dosi (1982) among others. Teece (1986, 1996), in particular, has utilized these ideas to build a framework upon which we expand.

As Teece (1986) has argued, the maturity of the technology, and its characteristics, determine the extent to which the innovation process can be internalized. Obviously, every technological trajectory of each individual firm is unique, since the innovation process is path-dependent on previous innovation. In other words, there are cognitive limits on what firms can and cannot do (Pavitt 1998). Nonetheless, once a 'dominant design paradigm' has been established, firms innovate around this paradigm, with the intention of improving it, or replacing it. They therefore are dependent on the *last-best* (that is, state-of-the-art) innovation. If a firm is engaged in developing an innovation in a given technological paradigm, it must strive to improve (or at least take into account) *not* its own last-best innovation, but the last-best innovation that has been patented, or that is the dominant design on the market,[7] even if this was created by another firm. Thus its path-dependency is always tempered by the state-of-the-art, and this means that roughly speaking technological trajectories of different firms within any given technological paradigm are similar. At the risk of over-simplifying, technologies (within a given paradigm) evolve through different stages, and these can be viewed as being deter-mined by two factors: the level of uncertainty in the nature of the technology and the speed of technical change within it. These two factors also determine other issues which affect the internalization or externalization of R&D, such as the level of appropriability. Figure 5.4 places these two dimensions into context, using a 2 × 2 matrix. The arrows indicate the typical time-trend of evolution of a technology, from Quadrants A to D.

The concept of uncertainty within the innovation process is well understood, and we shall not delve into it in detail. In general, the newer the sector, the closer it is to 'basic research' in the sense that the outcome of the research will lead to fundamental changes in knowledge, rather than technology. Such 'blue sky' or pre-paradigmatic research generally has a higher level of uncertainty than research within a defined paradigm. As the technology

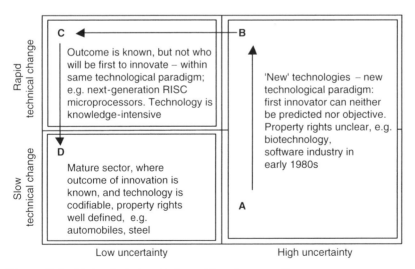

Figure 5.4   Technological evolution with a given paradigm

becomes diffused and codified (and a paradigm defined), the level of uncertainty drops.

The rate of technical change is determined not just by the level of uncertainty of technological change, but the number of possible directions in which it can develop, because there are multiple alternatives to any innovation. Thus, while technological change may not always be perceptible or discrete, it is continuous. It is not, however, determined by one company or idea but by numerous path-dependent solutions being developed independently by several innovators or would-be innovators. In other words, while the innovation being developed by one company is unique to it, it represents one of many possible solutions to a technological hurdle. Whether it belongs to the dominant paradigm is irrelevant, because modifications to the dominant design continue, as well as attempts to supplant it with a new design.

Although the rate of technical change is not linearly related to uncertainty, it is nonetheless determined by the reduction of uncertainty, as a dominant design is established. However, as I have earlier emphasized, in addition to innovation within the dominant design, there are attempts to supplant the dominant paradigm with new paradigms. These may occur directly, or because of changes in complementary technologies. As Teece (1986) observes, complementary technologies may evolve together, and affect each other, depending on whether the technologies are co-specialized, specialized or generic. I illustrate this point by taking the example of the further miniaturization of integrated circuits, and two related technologies: that of fabrication technology and the materials technology, which are co-specialized technologies (developments in one restrict and/or define developments in the other). Within the existing fabrication technological paradigm, the solution is to use lower wavelengths in the etching process. The current technology relies on lens-based tools which use deep ultraviolet light, which may be regarded as generic and paradigmatic. Markets for this innovation already exist, and these markets operate efficiently. The nature of the property rights of innovation are clear. Technological change is rapid, and the dominant paradigm is well established. Such a technology could be classified in Quadrant C in figure 5.1. However, simply reducing the wavelength further to get further miniaturization is a limited option, since traditional optics become opaque below certain wavelengths. There are at least four different technological trajectories being proposed, and being pursued by various consortia. IBM and Canon plan to replace this with X-rays, while Siemens is working on ion-beams. Intel,

Motorola and AMD are working with soft-X-rays.[8] The technology is undefined, but change is rapid, because the technologies are clear, and the outcome desired is a matter of 'when' and 'who' rather than 'if'. It only remains to be seen which of these technological solutions will be dominant. Such a technology is in Quadrant B, and will move rapidly into a paradigmatic state (Quadrant C).

However, technologies do not necessarily evolve endogenously. Complementary and related technologies also evolve, and can change the distribution of a firm's competences, especially where new innovations or completely new technologies are introduced in the market-place. Teece's distinction between systemic and autonomous innovation is critical here. Autonomous innovations fit comfortably into existing technologies and competences, while systemic innovations significantly affect the existing competences of a firm, and the distribution of its competences. For instance, a company engaged in the production of fabricated metal equipment will find an innovation in adhesive technology to be peripherally related to its industry, since improvements in epoxy-based adhesives represent an option to replace welding, and may at best represent a niche competence. It does not, however, systemically affect its operations, nor is it likely to, even if adhesives eventually replace welding.

In the case of integrated circuit fabrication, developments in new materials for insulation materials, semiconductors and micro-wiring represent possible systemic innovations. There are limitations associated with making chips smaller with the current materials, and this requires a complete change of technological paradigm to other materials such as copper, plastics and gels from aluminium and silicon dioxide, but these are unknown (and therefore pre-paradigmatic) areas. Copper-based wiring technologies are also in Quadrant B, because although they have been developed, they are still highly tacit and pre-paradigmatic. Plastics and gels as insulators are in Quadrant A, because they are as yet impractical, and little further than promising concepts.

Differentiating between Quadrants A and B is difficult, because they are 'new' technologies and new trajectories within technologies. These industries share certain characteristics: neither the dominant technological trajectory is known, nor indeed the objective. The technology is highly tacit, and not necessarily commercial. It is important to emphasize that we are speaking of technologies and practical research outcomes, rather than products. Take the case of battery technology. Although there has undoubtedly been vast improvement in the technology, the basic paradigm underlying stored electrical energy has not changed dramatically in the 200 years since Volta. There is slow technical change taking place within the old technological paradigm – that of chemical batteries. It would thus be in Quadrant D. There are new technological trajectories (such as fuel cells), but because they are new and commercially unproven, the outcome of the selection process is unknown, so it is impossible to determine *ex ante* whether the research outcome is in Quadrant A or B. Which of these trajectories will be the commercially successful one is also unknown. So until a trajectory becomes 'established' as a dominant one, it is uncertain whether technical change is rapid or not. What we are trying to suggest here is that technical change and innovation cannot be viewed from an entirely scientific perspective, but must also be assessed according to commercial viability.

At the other extreme of technical change are most metal technologies (steel, aluminium, etc.) – these are slowly evolving and mature technologies which demonstrate minor but consistent innovations over time, and can be regarded as post-paradigmatic. Thus they are located in Quadrant D. The technology is to a great extent codifiable and widely disseminated, and the property rights are well defined. Innovation is rarely patentable in these technologies, where applications development accounts for most innovatory activity. Competition shifts towards price, economies of scale, and downstream activities in order to add value, as the original product is priced as a commodity.

5.6 Dynamic aspects of choosing between in-house R&D, alliances and outsourcing

How does this relate to the use of non-internal modes of technology sourcing? It is clear from the preceding review of fundamental concepts that the choice between non-internal and internal R&D (and within non-internal activities, between outsourcing and alliances) is a complex process. We focus on two main questions. First, how does the use of non-internal sourcing vary by industry? Second, how do technologies change over time, and how does this affect the use of internal and non-internal sources?

The main issue here would seem to be the stage of evolution of the distinctive competences of the firm. This is the reason why there is considerable overlap in figure 5.2 between in-house R&D, outsourcing and alliances. Take the case where the *products* and the distinctive technologies that underlie them are pre-paradigmatic, that is, they are in Quadrants A or B. Technologies that relate to them are likely to be tacit, and competition to create a *de facto* standard and establish a paradigm is high. A firm in such a market segment will try, as much as possible, to keep its niche and distinctive competences in-house, but support these with alliances wherever necessary, particularly for strategic reasons. It will seek to establish alliances with competitors to create standards, as well as with suppliers to establish a dominant design. Even in marginal and peripheral sectors of competence, it is important to develop long-term relationships with firms so as to establish these firms' products as dominant designs. The establishment of a dominant design is also enhanced by the entry of a number of complementary and peripheral products, which depend on compatibility. Take the example of the hand-held computer (HPC) manufacturer Psion. In order to establish its operating system (Symbiant) as the standard, it has established alliances with the four largest mobile telephone manufacturers (Nokia, Ericsson, Motorola and Matsushita). The merger of mobile telephony with computing is as yet (*circa* 2002) a nascent idea, and it represents a peripheral technology to both parties, but one which all concerned believe will dramatically change their distinctive competences. The rival operating systems and designs have each been engaged in the same attempt to create a 'critical mass' of peripheral device manu- facturers and to establish standards.[9] However, the battle is not simply over operating systems, but also between hardware systems.

The preference, however, for in-house R&D for distinctive and niche competences, supported by alliances, is only where radical changes or new technologies might have a systemic effect on their distinct competences. Figure 5.5 gives the decision tree that would ordinarily face a company that has to decide how to allocate re- sources for a new pre-paradigmatic technology. For instance, where the new technology has an autonomous effect on its com- petitiveness – in the case of Psion, say, new battery technology (slow technical change) – and multiple substitutable sources are available, outsourcing is undertaken (see figure 5.5). However, standards for mobile telephony and related technology are central to Psion's competitiveness. This is an area where standards are almost paradigmatic (only two sets of standards remain in conten- tion), but not quite (Quadrant B). It will have a systemic effect on its existing assets, so the firm is obliged to conduct in-house R&D in combination with alliances (figure 5.5).

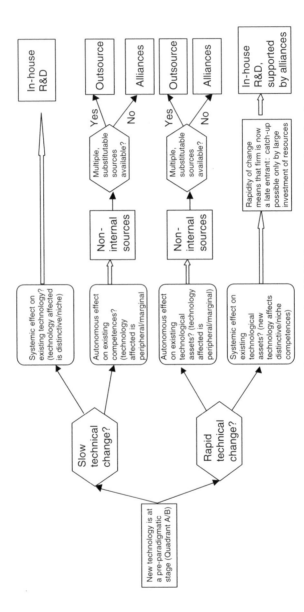

Figure 5.5 Decision tree in selecting mode of R&D for pre-paradigmatic technology

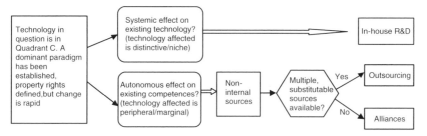

Figure 5.6   Decision tree in selecting mode of R&D for paradigmatic technology

For firms for which core products technology is in Quadrant C, where a dominant paradigm is established, more technologies can be outsourced, and more areas of niche competences can be undertaken though alliances. Figure 5.6 gives the corresponding decision tree that firms face. However, there are two aspects to engaging in alliances in Quadrant C technologies. On the one hand, the technology is fast-evolving, and although nominally property rights protection exists, patenting is often a limited source of competitive advantage given the rapidity of change. Firms do not always have recourse to patenting as a means to protect new and rapidly evolving technologies, and must rely on secrecy, or on lead time,[10] or by co-inventing with a potential competitor (Levin et al. 1987). As noted in a survey of European firms, the propensity to patent new products averaged 35.9 per cent across sectors, and 24.8 per cent in process innovations (Arundel and Kabla 1998). The need for secrecy combined with the rapidity of change means that, where the technology is a niche or distinctive one, *ceteris paribus*, firms will choose in-house R&D. On the other hand, the rapidity of technical change and the high costs of innovation may lead to alliance activity.

Technologies also evolve in their importance to the firm. Figure 5.7 shows several technologies for Firm B which shifted in importance over time, and moved from one kind of competence to another (illustrated by arrows). For instance, until recently, PCB design was done in-house. The design of double-sided printed circuit boards had required a high level of skills, but recent software design products for PCs had become so powerful, and the knowledge to produce them quite diffused, that this was no longer a complex task. Thus, design could now be outsourced.

Once a dominant design establishes itself, a technology that may have been a distinctive competence may in fact be peripheral, or

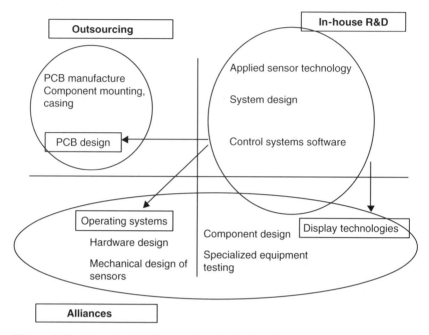

Figure 5.7 How the significance of technologies changes over time
Note: No attempt has been made to locate technologies on a relative basis within
any given quadrant.

even background. For instance, in the case of Firm B, in the early
1980s, the operating system was considered a crucial technology
and a distinctive competence (figure 5.7). This was a technology
that was fiercely guarded, and on which almost 20 per cent of its
R&D resources were invested. By the late 1980s, it had become a
niche sector. It had become easier to hire programmers skilful in
operating system (OS) development, and although the OS was still
seen as crucial, fewer resources (less than 10 per cent) were devoted
to it – essentially a niche sector. By the late 1990s, although the OS
remains crucial to their competitiveness, they no longer have to
maintain a proprietary OS, since a dominant design (Windows)
exists, for which considerable off-the-shelf software is available, a
high level of competence at developing customized versions of the
OS and software can be easily (and cheaply) accessed from consult-
ants. Less than 5 per cent of their resources are spent on software
development as a whole, and most of their requirements were
either outsourced, or developed within an alliance. There are now
no R&D staff that are engaged full-time in software design or

development. PCB design has also demonstrated a similar shift (see figure 5.7), going from a niche technology to a marginal one, while PCB manufacture has progressed from a niche competence to a background one, and is now completely outsourced.

It is important to note that it is not always possible to determine *ex ante* whether an innovation will have a systemic effect or an autonomous one. Take the situation where a new technology may threaten the distinctive competences of a firm, but the area of innovation is pre-paradigmatic (in Quadrant A) and the potential benefits or effects on current competences are still highly uncertain – say gene therapy for a pharmaceuticals company. Such an area of innovation can be pursued independently from other innovations; it will more likely undertake this through non-internal means. Where the expected benefit of the new area of research is still unknown, the firm will not be interested in investing large internal resources, until the potential benefits are more tangible, so a risk-reduction strategy through collaboration is most often viable (Mitchell and Singh 1992). However, complete externalization is impossible, since the nature of the output is unknown. In the case of biotechnology, large pharmaceutical firms resolved this by acquiring a minority stake in small, start-up biotech firms. This gave the large firms an 'option' to acquire (and thus internalize) or otherwise control the research output of the small firm were the technology to develop a practical value to them. If the research outcome proves to be not commercially viable or not the prevailing technological paradigm, the relatively low costs of this strategy are not a matter of great concern. However, this is not an option that presents itself for smaller firms with limited resources. In addition, property rights protection is as yet undetermined – for instance, the question of cloning and gene manipulation research output is still an area of some controversy. Property rights protection is thus achieved through secrecy, and collaborative research therefore is a risky option.

Where property rights are clearly defined, technical change is slow and uncertainty is low (Quadrant D), non-internal R&D options are least risky – completely external technological outsourcing is feasible. Competitive advantage in these industries generally derives not from technology *per se*, where the products are 'generic', but from marketing and economies of scale. Indeed, as Firm E, which is engaged in a natural-resource extracting sector, explained:

> We have nothing to hide. We believe in sharing all our technologies, because we don't really have anything special. There isn't much that our competitors don't already have, and it's really a small circle –

everyone knows everyone else – we have all been in this industry a long time. Things change very slowly, and we make most of our profits from downstream activities.

Indeed, with very low R&D intensities, much of the research by such companies is done with universities, and in collaboration with equipment suppliers. Another Firm E manager explained,

> If there is a new environmental standard, its good for us. We have to design new machinery or adapt existing equipment for our major customers. It means more orders. But it also means we have to make the R&D investment. If we don't, a competitor will, and they will get all the orders. Margins are tight, because we have a long-term relationship, so we never question the wisdom [of subsidizing the R&D of customers].

The need for alliances and more formal interaction between buyers and suppliers, then, is considerably reduced, since a high level of trust and interdependence exists. Likewise, because technology changes only very slowly, quick response alliance modes such as non-equity agreements are not at all popular (Hagedoorn and Narula 1996). Therefore outsourcing is often the most preferred option. Figure 5.8 summarizes the decision tree for Quadrant D industries.

5.6.1 Creating compatible standards

Referring to figure 4.1, we make a distinction between 'front-end cooperation', closer to 'Applied D', and 'back-end cooperation',

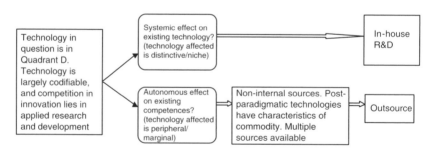

Figure 5.8 Decision tree in selecting mode of R&D for post-paradigmatic technology

which is closer to the 'Basic R'. In the case of front-end cooperation, the objective is to actualize the innovation since the distance-to-market is small. This is an important area for alliance activity, where the innovation is fine-tuned to maximize its market potential. One way to do so is to collaborate with competitors to modify similar technologies so as to create *de facto* industry standards. The selection of partners and the breadth of the partnership tend to be limited, often in response to alternative attempts to create industry standards. Sony, Philips and Sun Microsystems have recently established an alliance to develop software for Home Audio Visual Interoperability (HAVi) architecture so as to allow dissimilar consumer electronics devices to be linked together. This is in response to a similar attempt by Microsoft and Intel to develop Home Application Program Interface.[11] In such alliances, the joint R&D activity is demand-driven, with a view to expanding the market share of the collaborators in the long run. Their success or failure is partly a function of the number of alliance partners that can be drafted into the agreement, and their market power – the success of the UNIX alliance, and its establishment as a *de facto* industry standard, as well as the growing popularity of Java are associated with this. Such alliances also face considerable regulatory scrutiny from anti-trust regulators. Back-end cooperation, on the other hand, tends to be pre-competitive in nature, and is often sanctioned by regulatory authorities.

How does this relate to the question of core-competence considerations and the evolution of technological sectors? It seems clear that technologies that are new (such as in Quadrants A and B in figure 5.3) are unlikely to attract much front-end cooperation. Nonetheless, even though most of the activity might be 'Basic R', there is some variation, with certain alliances being focused in activities closer to the market than others. As figure 5.9 tries to illustrate, as technologies evolve, there is increasing emphasis on front-end cooperation, with the widest range of collaborative opportunities being attempted in Quadrant C.

5.7 Some conclusions, caveats and avenues for future research

This chapter has tried to develop an understanding of *some* of the technological and economic factors that underlie how firms choose between in-house R&D, R&D alliances and outsourcing. We have

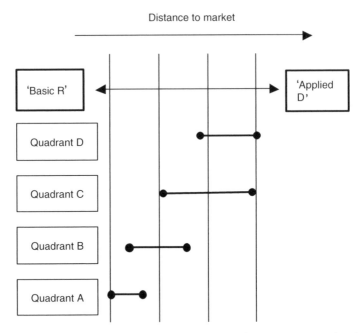

Figure 5.9 Relating distance-to-market considerations to technological evolution

developed our framework along two lines. First, I have examined how firms choose between these three modes in a *static* situation. That is, given a firm's distribution of competences, and the availability of alternatives, it is possible to determine, *ceteris paribus*, which technologies will be undertaken in-house, and for which technologies firms are more likely to use non-internal means. I have used some anecdotal data based on interviews to lend support to our framework. There is, of course, considerable variation between technologies, depending upon whether they are pre-paradigmatic, paradigmatic or post-paradigmatic. In addition, technologies evolve over time, and new innovations external to the firm may have to be absorbed, and utilized within the existing technological portfolio of the firm.

Thus, my second objective has been to develop a framework that examines these *dynamic* issues, based in part on the pioneering efforts of Teece (1986, 1996). I have argued that the choice between these three organizational modes varies with the maturity of the technological paradigm and the distribution of technological competences of the firm. In addition, as changes take place in the maturity of the technology, the choice of mode will change. Furthermore, new technologies may be introduced into the firm's portfolio of competences, and the choice of mode is also determined by its having a systemic or an autonomous effect on the firms existing technologies.

Obviously, firms are path-dependent, and idiosyncratic. I do not claim that my analysis is by any means exhaustive, or necessarily provides more than guidelines about how firms might behave when it comes to decisions about non-internal R&D activities. I would go so far as to say that my analysis and discussion simply points towards some general trends, rather than hard and fast rules about the choices open to firms.

Indeed, in developing my discussion, I am only too aware of the large number of caveats that apply to these models. There are numerous strategic and economic issues that have not been included in my arguments, strongly supported by anecdotal information acquired from the interviews. I shall endeavour to highlight some of these here, which need to be considered in future work.

Perhaps the single most important variable that seems to be ignored in much of the literature is the issue of firm size, and the consequent limited resources these firms are able to invest in R&D. The pressure to innovate and to master multiple technologies applies to firms of all sizes. Clearly, outsourcing and alliances provide an opportunity for small- and medium-sized enterprises (SMEs) to have access to capabilities they ordinarily might not be able to afford, or to justify a higher-than-industry-average R&D intensity to top management. This use of outsourcing to 'smooth out' cyclical variations in demand has been noted also by Buckley and Chapman (1998: 373). As Firm C noted, 'building up [research capacity in a new area] takes time: [up to] one or two years to hire five to six qualified researchers, and to work as a team. It is justifiable when times are good, but we can't just lay researchers off when times are hard. We have to keep them on, or we demoralize the whole department.' This strategy, it should be noted, was used by large companies too. Firm D noted of its customers, 'They use us as a valve. When times are good, they give us more design projects, and more orders. When times are hard, we are told to cut costs [before they do].'

Box 5.2 Opportunities and limitations for SMEs

New technologies and globalization have profoundly affected the Small and Medium Enterprise (SME). These developments have affected SMEs in two ways. On the one hand, SMEs have always sought to specialize in niches, given their limited resources. Therefore their role as specialized suppliers to large firms has increased as larger firms have sought to utilize non-internal means to maintain a sufficient breadth of technological competences. On the other hand, the cross-fertilization of technologies has meant that SMEs also (like their larger counterparts) need to span several competences. This dualistic state of affairs has altered the *raison d'être* of the SME and has created both new opportunities and threats for the SME. Inasmuch as the improvements in communications and the ease of enforceability of contracts has helped the SME, these benefits have accrued to at least the same extent for large firms too, and perhaps to a greater extent. Traditionally, large firms have had material (that is, resource) advantages, while SMEs have had the advantages of flexibility and rapid response to change. ICTs and transaction cost reductions due to economic integration have further increased the flexibility of the large firm, thereby narrowing the competitive advantage of flexibility due to smaller size. Indeed, the disadvantages due to SMEs' absolute size limitations may have been enhanced due to increased cross-border competition, and their need for multiple technological competences. Nowhere is this more obvious than in collaborative activity with regards innovation. It puts pressure on SMEs – already resourceful in their use of collaboration – to be even more efficient. Although alliances may overcome barriers to growth due to size, there are cognitive limits to efficiency gains from non-internal R&D, and the extent to which SMEs can afford to do so without weakening their technological advantages (Narula 2002a).

Indeed, SMEs may utilize non-internal means to a greater extent than large firms, not just because it allows them to have access to and/or master new technologies, but also because they themselves are often dependent on larger firms as customers. Large firms have the resources to commercialize production of products and processes involving new technologies, and can afford the high capital costs needed to achieve the necessary market penetration, since the marginal cost of using their existing facilities is low. Small firms often have no choice to be involved in close-knit alliances with large firms. Although our data are by no means representative, SMEs tend to engage in fewer horizontal alliances with other SMEs.

It should be noted that there is a lower limit to the extent to which any firm (but particularly SMEs) can use non-internal sources as a substitute for internal R&D. Both alliances and outsourcing require complementary resources. Some level of in-house capacity is essential to absorb the externally acquired information. Furthermore, alliances in particular require considerable managerial resources, not just because of the collaborative aspect, but also because alliances tend to be used where technology is tacit.

Firms also determine their R&D strategies based on purely strategic rationale, in order to improve their long-term product-market positioning. I suggest four of the more important reasons. First, as Kay explains, 'it is necessary to engage in networks with certain firms not because they trust their partners, but *in order* to trust their partners' (Kay 1997: 215). When companies decide to seek cost-savings in an innovatory process (or any other high-cost/high-risk project), it makes sense to do so with a partner with whom no free-rider dangers exist. In other words, although it is impossible to be certain about the outcome of an alliance, there is a higher probability that, where trust has been created in a previous alliance, the new alliance will be successful.

Second, there is the follow-the-leader strategy, as originally highlighted by Knickerbocker (1973). Firms seek partnerships in response to similar moves made by other firms in the same industry, not always because there is sound economic rationale in doing so, but in imitation of their competitors.

Third, firms sometimes choose unknown partners with uncertain or unproven technologies rather than successful players, as discussed in section 4.5.

Fourth, the high rate of failure of alliances and their inherent instability (Inkpen and Beamish 1997) means that it is a good idea to have redundant agreements – not all agreements will be successful for all parties concerned, and in addition to allowing firms to discover what cards their competitors have up their sleeves, it permits them to 'learn about learning' and the art of managing alliances.

I have not discussed the differences in types of partner, and how this may affect the choice between internal and external R&D. Universities, for instance, are regarded in a different way in terms of trust than commercial enterprises. Firms often undertake more 'sensitive' research at arm's length with universities than with other firms. However, this may simply reflect the tendency for firms to undertake more basic (and therefore tacit) activity with universities. Tidd and Trehwalla (1997), for instance, observe that universities are the most widely used external source of technology, although this may vary quite considerably across countries (Granstrand 1998), and across industries.

All these issues are important, and deserve far more attention than has been given here. Nonetheless, I feel that the two frameworks developed here allow both firms and policy makers to consider the significance of the options available to them. In addition, they can be useful in assisting in making more rational decisions, and to evaluate the implications of the *type* of R&D investment, in addition to the *amount* of investment, on long-term competitiveness.

Appendix A

The anecdotal evidence cited here derives from a larger ongoing survey being conducted on the internationalization of R&D by European-based MNEs. Currently, over 100 firms have been surveyed, through mailed questionnaire surveys and thirty-two firm interviews. The criteria for selection of these firms has been that they were (1) majority European-owned as of 1998, (2) engaged in manufacturing, (3) had annual R&D expenditures greater than (approximately) US$1 million and/or ten full-time R&D employees. All interviews were conducted with the head of the R&D department or vice-president of technology development, or equivalent. In case of multi-divisional firms, interviews were conducted with several divisions. Detailed information on internal and external activities were not collected through the questionnaire survey, which was undertaken during 1998, and was undertaken only during the interviews conducted after the survey. In all interviews, without exception, the interviewees expressed concern about the sensitive nature of the information provided, and have insisted on confidentiality. Therefore, given the relatively small sample size, the very specific nature of their products and competences, and the small number of firms in each industry, it is difficult to give a statistical overview regarding our sample without breaching confidentiality.

We have used the interview material along the lines of an unorthodox case-study analysis to illustrate our arguments, by amalgamating firms that have similar technological activities into fictitious firms, so as to prevent any single firm from being identified. We give a brief overview of these here. We have attempted to match 'similar' firms together, in terms of technology intensity, primary technologies, size and distribution of international activities, but not nationality, structure of ownership or age of firms. In addition, some amalgamations include a division of a large multinational conglomerate. In such cases, we have excluded certain details which might reveal the identity of the parent firm, and therefore the firm in question.

We use the terms alliances and outsourcing as understood and used in relation to the MERIT-CATI database. By outsourcing we take to mean agreements that are more arm's-length in nature, where active collaboration does not take place. There is generally a clear customer–supplier relationship, and no joint innovative activity takes place, although coordination for systems integration may be undertaken. Alliances are taken to be agreements where there is a clear, significant and systematic interdependence between the parties involved, with both firms undertaking innovative activities.

6

Technological Catch-up and Strategic Technology Partnering in Developing Countries

6.1 Introduction

As discussed in chapter 4, multinational enterprises (MNEs) around the globe have begun to engage in strategic technology alliances at an unprecedented pace. Driven by globalization, which has manifested itself through, *inter alia*, faster technological change and intensified competition, firms have shown a growing propensity to link up with other firms – frequently competitors – in order to survive in an increasingly global market-place. Globalization, as used here, refers to the convergence of incomes and consumption patterns, both across and within countries, rapid technological change and subsequent increased cross-border economic activity.

The reasons for this growth are relatively clear. As firms are faced with limited resources, they have found it convenient to establish collaborative activity with other firms, both in the same sector (through alliances along the same value-added chain as well as horizontal agreements with competitors), as well as those engaged in activities in unrelated sectors, as a means to enhance their competitive advantages. Like their industrialized-country counterparts, firms from developing countries have also engaged in strategic alliances, albeit at a relatively slow pace. In this chapter my intention is to focus on the growth of agreements amongst developing-country firms. I will concentrate on alliances that involve some level of technological interchange and/or innovatory activity which I shall refer to as strategic technology partnering (STP).

The forces of rapid technological change and high uncertainty are especially intense in new and rapidly developing technological sectors. New forms of inter-firm cooperation have been critical in the face of global competition, particularly in innovative activity, where the risks and costs are very high. Indeed, these very sectors have seen the most growth in STP activity given the opportunities for growth, as well as technological leap-frogging. It is not surprising, therefore, that developing-country firms have been actively involved in these sectors (Vonartas and Safioleas 1997). However, the participation of developing countries in these sectors, through both production and R&D activities, as well as through STP, is unevenly distributed across regions and countries. This chapter investigates the extent to which STP by companies in developing countries has been characterized by a similar evolution and equivalent modes of cooperation compared to those utilized by firms in the industrialized world.

This line of research has been explored previously, most notably in the work of Freeman and Hagedoorn (1994). This chapter has four primary objectives. First, I re-evaluate the situation regarding the propensity of developing-country firms to undertake STP, in light of more recent data. Second, I examine, in greater depth than previously, the kinds and types of organizational strategic technology alliance utilized by developing-country firms. Third, I examine the reasons for the growth of strategic alliance activity by developing-country firms, and, in particular, propose explanations for the considerable variation between countries and regions, in terms of both propensity and organizational modes. I propose that while the issue of economic divergence and 'falling behind' remains valid, there are convincing arguments that the failure of developing countries to participate is also a result of fundamental structural differences in the economies of these countries. The analysis will be based on data from the MERIT-CATI data set, which contains information on almost 8,000 cases of strategic technology partnering between 1980 and 1994. It should be noted that the data are based on announcements of an intention to engage in technology partnering in a given year. Thus, the data do not allow us to determine whether in fact agreements are in effect, or were terminated, either successfully or unsuccessfully. Furthermore, this data set has a bias towards new and emerging technologies. Additionally, it should be noted that in this chapter the term 'developing country' includes the formerly centrally planned economies of Eastern Europe. Although I classify them together with 'traditional developing countries', it is important to realize that this qualification is based primarily on income levels.

6.2 Strategic alliances and catching up

Freeman and Hagedoorn (1994) in a pioneering work on this subject, confirmed that most of the strategic technology alliance activity in the 1980s was conducted primarily by firms from the
industrial countries, particularly those from the Triad of North
America, Europe and Japan. Firms from developing countries contributed only insignificantly to strategic alliance formation – less
than 5 per cent of agreements involved developing countries
during the period 1980–9. These results lent support to the argument that the technological and economic catch-up by developing
countries was subdued, and suggested that the vast majority of
developing countries were increasingly lagging behind, particularly in new and emerging technological sectors.

The data show that this trend in newly established alliances in
developing countries apparently continued during the 1990s.
Figure 6.1 shows the trends in STP between 1980 and 1994. Unsur-
prisingly, a majority of agreements between 1980 and 1994 have
been between firms from the Triad. Although there is some variation between years, table 6.1 shows that the number of new agreements in Triad countries signed in a given year saw a steady
growth at an annual average rate of about 6 per cent between
1980 and 1987. The corresponding rate for the period 1987–94 was
about 2 per cent. This suggests that there was a slowdown in the
growth of newly established alliances in the early 1990s. Table 6.1

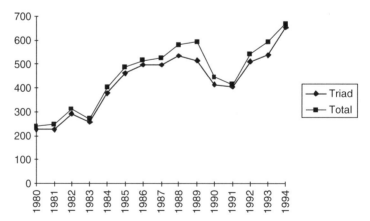

Figure 6.1   Growth of strategic technology partnering, 1980–1994
Source: MERIT-CATI database.

Table 6.1 Newly established strategic technology alliances in Triad and developing countries, 1980–1994

	1980–1994	1980–1987	1987–1994
Percentage of Triad STP (annual average)	93.85	94.51	93.11
Annual average growth rate (%)	4.15	6.05	2.24
Percentage of agreements in developing countries	6.15	5.49	6.89
Annual average growth rate (%)	5.98	7.03	4.93
Percentage of DC STP involving Triad firm	91.24	90.29	92.19

Source: MERIT-CATI database.

also reveals that there are considerable differences between the propensity to engage in STP by Triad firms and by developing-country firms. As the data show, the growth in STP activity in developing countries has been slightly higher than in Triad countries over the whole period from 1980 to 1994. However, although there was a modest decrease in the annual average rate of STP in developing countries in the early 1990s, this rate was still higher than the annual average rate in Triad countries in the same period.

Table 6.1 provides additional data on STP activity during these periods. In general, it can be observed that the percentage of newly established STP agreements by developing countries accounted for 6.15 per cent of all STP between 1980 and 1994, increasing slightly in the early 1990s compared to the early and mid-1980s. It should be remembered that since these represent newly established alliances in a given year, it is difficult to ascertain whether the stock of agreements still in force is smaller or larger than the average for Triad firms. However, there is no reason to suspect that developing-country agreements have a longer life or success rate than Triad alliances, which are believed to have a failure rate of at least 70 per cent (Harrigan 1988). Moreover, as table 6.1 notes, well over 90 per cent of the STP involving developing-country firms involve at least one Triad partner.

It is important to ask why these agreements have started to play an increasingly significant role, especially among firms from the Triad. The growth of alliance activity in general has been attributed in part to globalization. It has done so through three means. First, firms from countries in the Triad have become increasingly similar in the kinds of technology and competitive advantages they possess. The traditional technological gap approaches were proposed during a period when technological innovation was dominated primarily by US MNEs, which enjoyed a technological hegemony, particularly since the end of World War II. Over the past three decades, MNEs from Europe and Japan have been able to catch up technologically with US firms and now are able to compete directly with US firms. Indeed, in many instances these other firms have developed superior technologies to the US firms. One effect is that there are a greater number of competitors with similar products that compete directly, thereby increasing the pressure on individual firms to maximize their market share as well as continually develop new products. Needless to say, this increases the scope for firms to engage in cooperative agreements as a way of minimizing the risks and costs of maintaining or improving their competitive advantages.

Second, there has been an increasing homogeneity in consumer needs and preferences among the countries of the Triad as markets have become global, and income levels have converged amongst the Triad countries. This has encouraged firms to collaborate in order to develop worldwide standards. Even where industry standards are not an issue, cooperative agreements become necessary in order to enter as many new markets as possible, to spread the rising costs of innovation, as well as to defend existing markets, as a defensive measure.

Third, the development of new technologies has greatly accelerated the need and ability of firms to engage in cross-border activity. This has occurred through two primary means. On the one hand, new technologies have affected the structure and trend towards STP because of the improved coordination of cross-border activities. It is a fundamental feature of MNE activity that cross-border market failure exists in the supply of intermediate products, and especially intangible assets. Information and communication technologies have reduced both the costs of acquiring and disseminating information, and the transaction and coordination costs associated with cross-border activity. It has done so on two levels:

1   Information about both input and output markets is more easily accessible. This allows firms which previously could not engage in international business transactions now to do so. Indeed, a UN study (United Nations 1993) has indicated that there is an increasing number of small and medium enterprises engaging in international activity than hitherto.

2   MNEs are better able to integrate the activities of their various
    affiliates through the use of these technologies and to respond
    more quickly to changing conditions in the countries in which
    they operate.

Taken together, these transaction cost-reducing processes have
enabled MNE activity to be much more efficiently organized across
borders. They have also facilitated a shift towards more rationalized and strategic asset-seeking MNE activity, and away from the
more multi-domestic approach which was more prevalent prior to
the 1970s.

While the decline of transactions and coordinating costs has led
to an increased efficiency of *intra-firm* networks, there have also
been substantial cost savings in the coordination and monitoring
costs associated with *inter-firm* networks. Indeed, the growing use
of organizational modalities which permit firms to engage in quasi-
internalized arrangements is attributable, at least in part, to the ease
with which collaborators and competitors may be monitored, and
the extent to which the risks of shirking contractual obligations
have declined (Narula 1999). Larger markets for similar products
and the ability of MNEs to organize production activities on a
rationalized basis has led, *ceteris paribus*, to higher rents, allowing
MNEs to exploit economies of scale, since similar products may be
sold in several countries at the same time.

New technologies have also influenced the world economy because of the emergence of completely new industries, which have
generated entirely new sources of employment in both the manufacturing and services sectors. The difference in the extent to which
these developments have affected the converging and the diverging
countries is not as acute as elsewhere for the simple reason that
because these are new technologies, there is not likely to be as large
a 'gap' between the lead and lag countries. Indeed, developing
countries have attempted a 'niche' strategy in developing created
assets by specializing in particular new technologies as a way of
achieving competitiveness – the often cited example of India's
burgeoning software sector and the focus of other nations in biotechnology is another (Acharya 1996). However, the failure of the
majority of developing countries to exploit these new technologies
has acted as a centripetal force, encouraging centralization of production to within the Triad by MNEs.

New technologies have also led to a shortening of product
life cycles, which has led to new or modified products being
more rapidly developed and brought to market. Firms are able to

undertake technological developments and are able to bring them to market much more rapidly than was previously the case. Computer-aided design (CAD) as well as developments in 'flexible' manufacturing systems and computer-aided manufacturing have further reduced the set-up costs and time taken to bring a new product to market. Although this has led to a reduction in fixed costs associated with new products, these technologies are not costless. First, rapid product life cycles imply a relatively high R&D intensity if firms need to remain competitive. They also suggest that an innovating firm needs to recoup quickly these high fixed costs before its technology becomes redundant, especially so if a rival firm wins the 'race' to innovate the next generation product (Levin et al. 1987).[1] It must therefore

1 sell at a relatively high cost per unit, and/or
2 develop a production process with a low minimum efficient scale and/or
3 recoup its investment by acquiring a large market for its products so as to spread its fixed costs.

However, whichever strategy a firm undertakes, this generally enhances the need for it to seek and expand overseas markets. Once again, target markets tend to be those with similar income and consumption patterns, rather than the diverging developing countries, where multi-domestic strategies still prevail, and where the R&D costs of products for its markets have already been amortized.

It should be remembered that strategic alliances are most often used where collaboration may lead to the potentially improved position of at least one of the partners. In industries where the technology is tangible and codifiable, as in mature, stable sectors, firms will prefer to engage in equity-type wholly or majority-owned subsidiaries (see discussion in chapter 4 as well as the following section). It is a well-known feature of development, that as countries experience growth, they will experience economic restructuring to progressively higher technology levels. At the same time, the modalities with which international transactions are conducted and the organization forms which domestic firms engage in will also become increasingly complex. Indeed, alliances call for a particularly high level of managerial and organizational expertise which is generally not available to developing-country firms.

Therefore, for the most part, the countries where R&D activities by domestic firms and/or affiliates of foreign MNEs is high tend to have a higher propensity to engage in STP (Hagedoorn and Sadowski 1996). These tend to be the Eastern European countries and East Asian economies. Most other developing countries' R&D activities tend to be sparse and concentrated in a few conglomerates which dominate the alliance activity undertaken by these countries.

Despite the fact that the data presented in table 6.1 suggest that developing countries have managed to keep up with the growth of technology partnering at more or less the same growth rate as those of the Triad, not all countries have benefited from globalization to the same extent. The increasing homogeneity of technologies across countries and firms has enabled companies (especially in the newly industrialized countries) to use STP as a means to acquire technological competences and capabilities as well as support export marketing. With every new wave of innovation, a window of opportunity has opened up for companies in developing countries to close the technology gap between themselves and the market leaders. In the newly industrialized countries especially, catch-up development occurred on a firm and industry level based on technological learning. In these countries, technological learning allowed firms to advance slowly from the manufacture of simple goods to the design and development of more complex products for export markets. Indeed, STP with firms from Triad countries played an important part in technological learning (Hobday 1995).

It has been shown (Verspagen 1993, Dowrick 1992, Dowrick and Gemmell 1991, Alam and Naseer 1992, Narula 1996a) that only a handful of developing countries – mainly the Asian NICs (Korea, Taiwan, Hong Kong and Singapore) and some East European economies – are experiencing convergence with the industrialized world, while a majority of developing countries are in fact diverging away from the industrialized world, both as a group and individually. With ten developing host countries accounting for 67 per cent of inward FDI stock and 79 per cent inward FDI flows in 1993 (Narula and Dunning 1999), this suggests that, with the increasing reliance of less developed countries on FDI as a source of capital, technology and knowledge, there is an increasing likelihood that there will be further polarization of the world economy and widening of the gap between the Triad and the bulk of developing countries. In an analysis of the effects of global integration on development, Gray (1996) predicts that the marginal net benefits from international involvement will decline with globalization for the least developed countries, because the benefits of globalization are self-reinforcing.

Table 6.2　Strategic technology alliances in developing countries by region, 1980–1994 (%)

Regions/countries	Alliances (1980–1994)	Alliances (1980–1987)	Alliances (1987–1994)
East Asian NICs	58.41	63.95	55.84
Other Asia and Africa	8.84	17.01	5.05
Latin America	4.31	6.12	3.47
Eastern Europe	28.45	12.93	35.65

Source: MERIT-CATI database.

As table 6.2 amply illustrates, as with FDI, trade, productivity and economic development, the growth of strategic technology partnering has not been even across regions and countries. In the 1980s and early 1990s, the highest proportion of STP has certainly been in the newly industrialized countries in South East Asia. More than half of all STP has taken place in this region but – as the data show – with a decreasing tendency during the late 1980s and 1990s. It seems that companies in other regions in the world increased their importance in strategic technology partnering. Companies in Eastern Europe, in particular, increased remarkably their engagement in STP in the 1990s. There was a proportional decrease in the participation of firms from Latin America and Africa.

6.3 Organizational modes and developing-country STP

Recent theoretical and empirical contributions have highlighted the variation in type of strategic alliance activity, in terms of choice of organizational modes, on both a country and a firm-specific basis (Osborn and Baughn 1990, Hagedoorn and Narula 1996, Narula and Hagedoorn 1999). For developing countries in particular, contributions have been made by Freeman and Hagedoorn (1994) and Vonortas and Safioleas (1997). Following these efforts, in this section I wish to evaluate the propensity to utilize different forms of STP agreement.

Figure 4.3 in chapter 4 illustrates some of the primary options available. There exists a spectrum of organizational modes through which the firm may conduct such international operations. At the one extreme, the firm can establish a wholly owned subsidiary through foreign direct investment (FDI), or an M&A such that it has ownership and control over its subsidiary operations. Such an arrangement would provide it with complete control over the activities of its subsidiary, but it would also involve a degree of risk, given its unfamiliarity with the target market. If it were to engage in a purchase of assets on the open market, there is no expansion of the firm, and it simply engages in an arm's-length (or spot) transaction with separate independent firms, leaving the risks and benefits to another firm. Between these two extremes lie several other options that represent a compromise between a wholly owned subsidiary and a spot transaction. These intermediate options represent varying extents of organizational interdependence between the two firms, and a consequent sharing of the risks and benefits between them.

A strategically motivated agreement is based on improving the position of a firm relative to its competitors. For example, in order to sustain its competitive position vis-à-vis new entrant firms mainly from Western Europe, Videoton, the largest Hungarian-owned electronics company, began to engage in 1992 in a series of subcontracting deals with a number of major Western electronics and engineering firms. The aim of these agreements was to secure market access for Videoton against new entrants in the Hungarian electronics market while sharing the cost of R&D in this rather risky industry (Havas 1996). This sort of agreement is aimed at gaining sufficient market share from the common competitor, so that the increase in sales volume may make up for the loss of profit margin in the long run.

Strategically motivated agreements may be both offensive and defensive. If two firms make a horizontal agreement to protect their market from a large (and more cost-efficient) competitor, they may do so by agreeing to lower their prices to gain market share, or exchanging technologies to become more efficient. Such an action would lower their profitability in the short run, but if they succeed in increasing their joint market share there may be long-term benefits. If the firms participating in an agreement are simply intent on maximizing profits, a cost-economizing motive is more likely to achieve this.

However, thus far I have simply revisited the earlier discussion of the motive underlying collaborative activity. If the motives of developing-country firms and industrialized-country firms were similar, one might expect them to utilize similar organizational modes. From table 6.3, this is clearly not the case. Overall, during the period 1980–94, less than 30 per cent of developing-country STP was non-equity based, while almost 70 per cent of Triad firms' STP was non-equity based. Even amongst developing countries, there

Table 6.3 Equity and non-equity modes of strategic technology alliances in developing countries, 1980–1994

	All STP	Developing country STP	East Asia	Asian NICs	Eastern Europe	Other Asia and Africa	Latin America
1980–1994							
Share of equity modes (%)	32.96	72.45	68.46	49.77	75.76	90.91	72.00
Share of non-equity modes (%)	67.04	27.55	31.54	50.23	24.24	9.09	28.00
1980–1987							
Share of equity modes (%)	40.06	82.05	79.84	77.03	80.00	92.86	71.43
Share of non-equity modes (%)	59.93	17.95	20.16	22.97	20.00	7.14	28.57
1988–1994							
Share of equity modes (%)	31.98	62.94	58.67	49.46	73.91	84.62	72.73
Share of non-equity modes (%)	68.02	37.06	41.33	50.54	26.09	15.38	27.27

For definitions of organizational modes, see figure 4.3 and Narula 1996b.
Source: MERIT-CATI database.

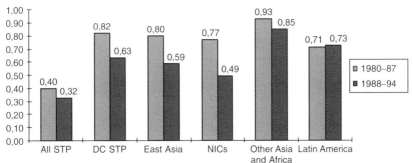

Figure 6.2 Ratio of equity to non-equity strategic technology alliances in developing countries, 1980–1994
Source: MERIT-CATI database.

was considerable variation, with NICs showing the lowest propensity to utilize equity, and 'other Asia and Africa' with the highest propensity.

In terms of changes over time, there would seem to be an across-the-board decline in the use of equity agreements between the two periods, except in Latin America, which remained more or less at the same level. Indeed, as figure 6.2 dramatically illustrates, the ratio of equity to non-equity STP for the NICs has declined considerably, and would seem to be converging with that of the Triad firms. Indeed, when the data are examined on an annual basis for NICs, it is observed that in the most recent years the equity/non-equity ratio is identical to that of the developed countries.

6.4 Differences in the industrial specialization of countries

The above discussion indicates that developing countries are heterogeneous in their STP activity. It also illustrates that certain developing countries are in danger of 'falling behind', but this does not take into account the question of industrial differences. The data presented in table 6.3 would seem to suggest that countries and regions that are 'closer' in terms of economic development to the Triad (that is, have been experiencing convergence) show a similar propensity to engage in non-equity agreements relative to those firms that hail from countries that are further away from the economic development levels of the Triad countries. Nonetheless, it cannot be taken as positive proof from the differences between these groups of countries that the gap is either widening or decreasing, although this might be taken as a simplistic explanation. Indeed, as argued in this section, these differences and the changes over time may find their explanation in structural changes and industry-specific differences. Osborn and Baughn (1990) and Hagedoorn and Narula (1996) have illustrated that there are concrete differences in the choice of organizational mode that derive from the rate and uncertainty of innovatory activity, as well as the technological intensity of sectors. For instance, non-equity forms of agreement are more efficient for undertaking more research-intensive activity. However, where the aim of the alliance is to learn and transfer tacit knowledge to its other operations, equity agreements are often preferred (Osborn and Hagedoorn 1997). Hagedoorn and Narula (1996) showed that equity agreements are preferred in relatively mature sectors, while non-equity agreements are utilized in high-tech sectors. Given the bias of the data set towards core technologies such as biotechnology, new materials and information technology, it is therefore only natural to expect such differences to manifest themselves in the analysis. Indeed, as table 6.4 shows, on a simple disaggregation of data by sectors, there are differences in the choice of organizational mode on a global level, and although there are relative differences between groups of countries, there are also differences between industries. For instance, non-high-tech sectors display a higher preference for equity than any of the core high-tech sectors.

Therefore, some of the differences in the propensity to undertake STP as demonstrated by the data may be due to the fact that some of these developing countries are specialized in other sectors, rather than an indicator of their failure to catch up (on a technological or economic level). In other words, this may simply indicate path-dependent differences in the industrial specialization of countries, or at most, a divergence or 'non-catch-up' scenario in particular sectors.[2]

Table 6.4 Equity to non-equity ratio by major industries and regions, 1980–1994

Ratio of equity to non-equity	All countries	Developing countries	Developing countries excluding NICs	Eastern Europe	NICs
Biotechnology	32.30	62.96	75.00	100.00	51.45
Information technology	8.92	59.13	85.00	88.89	45.33
New materials	39.97	83.33	75.00	66.67	91.66
Non-high tech sectors	53.83	79.20	80.25	100.00	74.65

Source: MERIT-CATI database.

However, the story is not quite as simple as that. The data are very much biased towards new, core technologies, where path-dependent country-specific characteristics do not play a significant role. These are sectors where the stock of knowledge is small, since they are new. These sectors represent an opportunity for leap-frogging for developing countries, since the economic cost of acquiring a competence in state of the art is relatively low. In these situations, strategic technology partnering represents a very important option, as a means both to advance and modify a product developed in a third-world environment to developed-country market conditions and requirements. Alternatively, from a Triad firm perspective, STP with a developing country firm represents a low-cost technology development option.

Nonetheless, despite the decision of countries to target particular sectors within these new technologies, such an overt intention assumes a certain basic competence in the manufacturing sectors and, within manufacturing, prior experience with technology-intensive sub-sectors. What is being suggested here is that the propensity of firms in a given country to be involved in technological activity in a given sector is not solely based on its desire to be in a given sector, but also reflects country-specific differences that are specific to its stage of economic development.

It is well known that the economic structure of a country is a function of its stage of economic development. This thesis has been examined most thoroughly in the work of Chenery and associates (Chenery and Taylor 1968, Chenery 1979, Chenery et al. 1986). This line of research argues that countries' economic structure evolves with their stage of development to reflect the comparative advantage of the country as well as the nature of its natural and created assets. More recently, efforts have been made to relate evolving economic structure to the pattern of foreign investment activities (Narula 1993, Narula 1996a, Ozawa 1995, 1996). These contributions have taken a general view of foreign investment activities to include all forms of MNE activity, whether it be through licensing or wholly owned activity. It is not my intention to discuss this body of research in detail. Instead, I present the salient features from this research through a set of stylized facts:

1 The comparative advantage of countries evolves gradually with development from the primary sector to manufacturing to services.

2 This gradual shift reflects the upgrading of the capabilities and resources of the country in terms of the quality and quantity of

its infrastructure, technological assets and manpower, and the competitive advantage of its firms.

3 There is a systematic relationship between its economic structure and the kind and extent of the exports of its firms, inward investment activity by foreign firms, and the outward FDI activity of its firms.

4 Although this relationship is idiosyncratic and country-specific, depending upon its exogenous and endogenous country-specific characteristics, there is a broad similarity of this relationship across countries.

5 Within the manufacturing sector, there is a general evolution in four phases, which can be linked to the development of particular types of industries:
   (a) labour-intensive light (Hecksher-Ohlin) industries,
   (b) heavy and chemical (undifferentiated Smithian) industries,
   (c) assembly-based industries (differentiated Smithian) and
   (d) innovation-intensive (Schumpeterian) industries.
   In other words, countries and their firms evolve through successively higher levels of skill and technological intensity with economic growth.

6 The motive and extent of inter-firm activity, and the organizational mode utilized by domestic firms in undertaking international activities vary with the stage of development. Likewise, the organizational mode utilized by foreign firms engaged in inward investment in the host developing country will also vary with the motive of their investment, and stage of development of the host (which is itself determined by, *inter alia*, the stock of accumulated technology possessed by it).

Given these stylized facts, it is not reasonable to expect that countries engaged in the first two phases of Ozawa's typology should engage in STP in technology-intensive sectors, and indeed, with some exceptions, that they should be involved until the end of the third phase. In fact, the countries that Ozawa predicts will be engaged in Schumpeterian-type innovation industries are the Asian NICs and the Eastern European countries, although some of the more advanced 'new' NICs are attempting to acquire technological competence in several phases simultaneously (such as China and Malaysia). In relation to this attempt to acquire mastery across a range of sectors, it is important to note that there are fundamentally different motives attributed to developing-country firms which engage in STP. When, say, Samsung enters into a partnering agreement to develop a new memory chip, it is more likely to result in a technology exchange, than, say, a collaborative effort on the Indonesian aircraft project. Therefore, it may be postulated that the kind of knowledge that the developing-country firm brings to the bargaining table considerably affects its ability to acquire additional technology through STP, and indeed, its ability to internalize it.

Therefore, with the exception of some 'white elephant' projects, most STP in high-tech sectors is undertaken by the NICs and Eastern European countries, as the evidence so far has demonstrated. Indeed, as table 6.5 shows, the majority of developing-country STP in the core technologies tends to be dominated by these countries.

A caveat needs to be noted here. The growth of strategic asset-acquiring MNE activity has continued to grow in popularity, particularly given its success as part of the industrial development policy of countries such as Japan, Korea and Taiwan. Nonetheless, there is considerable variation between countries as to the level of intervention and the industrial sectors targeted, as well as the predominant use of particular technology acquisition modes. The economic success of these countries has prompted imitators throughout the developing countries, with varying degrees of success. However, what is clear is that the growing use of STP is an increasingly important tool in the process of structural upgrading.

This is further buttressed by the fact that during the two periods a large number of the STP activities by the NICs tend to be in the medium and non-core technologies in the first period. Table 6.6 gives the breakdown of alliance activity between the two time periods, 1980–7 and 1988–94. It is clear from this that the gradual restructuring that has been experienced by these countries is also

Table 6.5 Distribution of STP activity by regions with developing countries, 1980–1994

Industrial sector	NICs	Eastern Europe	Latin America	Other developing countries
Biotechnology	40.74	18.52	14.81	25.93
Information technology	65.22	7.83	3.48	23.48
New materials	52.17	13.04	8.70	26.09
Other high-tech sectors	37.50	25.00	6.25	31.25
Medium-tech sectors	35.15	6.06	5.45	53.33
Low-tech sectors	6.25	6.25	6.25	81.25

Source: MERIT-CATI database.

Table 6.6   Distribution of STP activity for the Asian NICs, 1980–1994

Newly industrialized countries (NICs)	1980–1987	1988–1994
Information technology	36.49	51.61
Biotechnology	2.70	9.68
Other high-tech	9.46	13.98
Medium-tech	35.14	11.83
Low technology	16.21	12.9
TOTAL	100.00	100.00

Source: MERIT-CATI database.

apparent in their STP activity. For instance, there has been a grad-ual decline in the importance of medium- and low-tech sectors, which in the first period accounted for over 50 per cent of all STP activity. During the second period they accounted for less than one-quarter of all agreements, with much of the growth having taken place in the information technology sectors. It is interesting to note, however, that biotechnology has not as yet seen much growth in STP activity, a sector in which none of these countries has made large development investments.

6.5 Conclusions

Although the analysis conducted here has mainly been qualitative, and the evidence not empirically rigorous, some clear trends have been identified. I succinctly summarize these here.

First, the number of STP activities involving developing-country firms has increased only marginally to approximately 7 per cent of all agreements between 1988 and 1994, up from 5.5 per cent between 1980 and 1987. However, although the increase has been minimal, this does nonetheless reflect marginally faster growth rates, which have been higher than the growth rates of Triad STP.

Second, within the developing countries, there is a clear differ-ence between regions and groups of countries. STP activity is dominated by the East Asian NICs and Eastern Europe, and this dominance has become even more marked. On the surface, this increased dominance can be attributed to the increasing divergence between the countries which have converged from those that are in danger of diverging. It is also, in the case of the Eastern European firms, a result of the entry of these countries in the late 1980s, thus sharply increasing the number of alliances by former socialist states in the second period.

Third, I examined the propensity of developing-country firms to use different organizational modes of strategic technology alliance. The data demonstrate that although developing-country firms have a higher propensity to undertake equity-type agreements, this too varies between groups of countries and regions.

Fourth, there is a gradually declining propensity to use equity-based agreements, and the decline is most noticeable amongst the Asian NICs, with equity to non-equity ratios approaching Triad levels. However, the decline in the use of equity-type agreements does not, apparently, reflect differences in growth rates.

Fifth, although there are differences between countries in the use of equity-based agreements, there remains a clear difference between industrial sectors. However, unlike in the Triad countries, differences do not seem to be completely explicable by industry-specific sectors.

Sixth, I propose that the failure of certain countries to participate in STP cannot be entirely attributed to their economic divergence or their 'falling behind'. Based on scholarly research that has studied the process of structural change and economic development, I suggest that the low levels of participation can be explained by a combination of the 'natural' process of structural upgrading and the nature of the empirical evidence. I elucidate: on the one hand, firms from a large number of developing countries (with the exception of the NICs and Eastern Europe) do not as yet have the competitive advantage to engage in innovative activities in technology-intensive sectors, given their stage of economic development. On the other hand, the data set used here has a strong bias towards technology-intensive, new and emerging sectors, such as information technology, biotechnology and new materials.

The narrow focus here on STP raises questions about the most efficient means to undertake innovative activity, given its costs, particularly in terms of resources. With increased global competition, firms are forced to increase their own R&D activity, which requires capital and access to complementary created assets. Partly as a result of this and partly owing to globalization, there has been an increase in the use of strategic asset-acquiring MNE activity as a means to develop assets. This includes the use of intra- and inter-firm networks, primarily through strategic alliances and other forms of collaborative agreements. A second means has been the use of outward strategic-asset seeking FDI, where MNEs from these countries invest in affiliates located in close proximity to a major competitor in order to maximize the internalization of spillovers and externalities.

As I have emphasized in this chapter, these activities, however, require considerable organizational skills, and are generally associated with firms that already have considerable experience with international operations, and innovative activities. Indeed, the growth of the use of strategic alliances has tended to be primarily associated with the converging economies: the Triad firms, some of the rapidly industrializing Asian economies and more recently the Eastern European Economies in Transition (EET). Most of the developing countries have tended to experience a divergence in growth rates and are focused on relatively low-technology sectors, and have domestic firms which have relatively few competitive advantages.

Indeed, from the discussion here it would seem that technology agreements tend to be the domain of firms from the more advanced 'developing' countries. In general, it would seem that countries with the most advanced technology stocks, and those with firms that have competitive advantages that are world-class, dominate technology alliance activity.

As Ozawa (1995) suggests, the Asian NICs have now entered a stage of industrial restructuring where their competitive advantages are focused in technology-intensive, Schumpeterian-type industries, and away from low- and medium-tech industries. Strategic alliances in these high-tech sectors are more amenable to non-equity agreements given the high costs of R&D and uncertainty in these sectors.

Unfortunately, many developing-country firms do not possess the characteristics described above to be able to operate as 'partners' to relatively sophisticated MNEs from the industrialized world, often becoming 'junior' in any relationship. The technological gap and managerial know-how that is required to manage and sustain a strategic alliance is considerably greater than for international operations. Therefore only countries such as the Asian NICs and the EETs are really in a position to undertake these agreements. The EETs possess technology but not the managerial know-how relative to the NICs, which explains the high failure rate of these alliances (Paliwoda 1995).

Another point that is often forgotten is that one of the most important advantages of strategic alliances is the relatively quick response rate that these provide in developing innovations. Therefore they seem to be used most often in industries which are marked by high uncertainty and/or rapid technological changes. Developing-country government regulations and red tape, however, tend to discourage such quick response rates.

7

Technology, Globalization and Policy Issues: Some Observations

If [a] place was to be a permanent forge of industry, fuel must be constantly added to the fire.

Honoré de Balzac

7.1 The challenges of globalization and fuzziness

Globalization has come to be a universal specific in every sense of the expression. There are as many definitions of globalization as there are hairs on a very hairy dog. Globalization is a synonym for growing world trade, for FDI, the spread of multinational corporations, increasing homogeneity in consumption patterns, to mention just a few. It has been blamed for third-world debt, third-world poverty, the destruction of the ozone layer, unemployment, again, to mention just a few. Likewise, innovation and technology can be as broad and as specific as one wants them to be, as indeed the literature shows.

This book is not meant to be an exhaustive study of technology and globalization, nor is it an attempt to 'prove' or 'test' a single model, theory or framework. However, there has been a consistent and repetitive use of certain ideas, concepts and research themes. I have largely concentrated on the 'big picture', with an unashamed bias to 'macro', policy-related issues, with the exception of chapter 5, where I have examined the issue of non-internal R&D from a firm's perspective. Chapter 5, too, has important policy implications, when one realizes the importance (as discussed in chapter 4) of alliances and outsourcing as a growing organizational form, and the problems of the utilization of national subsidies and resources (which are provided with the ambition of improving domestic capabilities) for cross-border, collaborative activity in a foreign location.

Broadly speaking I have tried to shed light on the somewhat contradictory trend by commentators on globalization to describe its effects as either leading to 'fuzzy' boundaries of economic units, or, as a counterfactual, reaffirming the importance and clear delineation of existing boundaries. What I have tried to show over the course of the various chapters of this book is that, as far as technology development is concerned, both states of nature exist simultaneously. On the one hand, boundaries of economic units remain relatively distinct. Countries remain sovereign; firms can still be identified as such. Knowledge creation, like the control (but perhaps not the ownership) of MNEs, remains concentrated in a few locations and primarily in the home country. The point that I have tried to emphasize is that there remains a high level of inertia in the location of R&D of firms, and this is due to the intricacies of the processes of learning and the extent to which firms are embedded in systems of innovation, as well as the complexities of creating institutions and linkages in a new location.

At the same time, there is a growing indistinctness, not just due to the difficulties of agreeing on the definition of the appropriate terminologies (for example, what constitutes a firm or a region). Boundaries are becoming fuzzy, in the sense that they have become less precise, and in some instances blurred. I have argued that this is not a new phenomenon, because globalization itself is not novel. As chapter 1 has argued, the processes underlying globalization have been unfolding for centuries, if not millennia. Fuzzy borders and the precise boundaries are two sides of the same coin, and are in no way paradoxical. Indeed, the fuzzy boundary problem is in part *because* of the distinctness of boundaries, and the existence of inertia. There are cognitive limits to the capabilities and resources of any economic unit. The limits on resources and capabilities are partly determined by history. These resources and capabilities have a particular character unique to the economic unit, and the nature of these resources cannot be changed rapidly, if at all (*inter alia* because of technological or structural inertia). Ergo, an economic unit must seek some means of acquiring complementary resources it does not have (but needs) within the limits of its existing assets. Countries therefore seek to utilize the capabilities of other countries (whether through immigration, or by encouraging inward and outward FDI), and firms may seek to use other firms' capabilities (by locating in proximity to other firms, or by developing strategic alliances).

The cognitive limits to the capabilities and resources of any economic unit also mean that growth and development are not unidirectional and linear. Society and civilization (the bedrock upon which economic activity of any type is anchored) is in a constant state of flux, and any long-term view of economic, social and political events will demonstrate that fuzziness and clarity are states of nature, and that fuzziness of boundaries is by no means a new thing. Fuzzy boundaries have been *en vogue* before now. Let me take the example of the firm. The firm has existed as a clearly discernible economic entity (in the modern sense that value-adding activities are formally organized on a continuing and sustainable basis with clearly and legally attributable control and ownership) for several millennia now. We have seen the size of what is regarded as efficient units vary, starting from about the first industrial revolution where production became centralized in the first factories, and gradually over the ensuing 200 years or so there has been a growth in the size of the optimal unit as centralization and economies of scale have increased. That is, there has been an expansion of activities that are undertaken intra-firm rather than through the market. This occurred both through horizontal integration and vertical integration. This centralization, this concentration of economic activity, occurred for various legal, political, social, financial and technological reasons. Since the middle of the twentieth century, there has been something of a reversal, with a growing popularity for decentralization, so much so that there has been talk of the Virtual Firm. Modularity of production and new process technologies have reduced the minimum efficient scale such that vertical integration is less of an imperative. Terms such as Global Production Networks (GPN) have been bandied about as heralding the advent of a new and revolutionary age (e.g., Ernst 1997, Borrus et al. 2000). Never mind that this decentralization predates centralization: prior to factories, production was undertaken by 'putting out', which was essentially coordinated outsourcing of specialized inputs from individual craftsmen before re-invention of the factory. These were flexible production networks with unclear boundaries of ownership and control. Flexible specialization through the use of networks of small firms remained commonplace (and coexisted alongside larger centralized production units) until the late nineteenth century (see Sabel and Zeitlin 1997). The use of half-way solutions for knowledge creation shares some important similarities with this era, because markets for innovation are also largely difficult to define. The organization of R&D through hierarchies, too, is imprecise, partly because it is new, and firms are not as yet sure of the most appropriate way to organize these activities (as evidenced by the continuing struggle of achieving optimal balance between external and internal proximity).

Chapters 4, 5 and 6 have illustrated that that firms are now using less traditional organizational forms of economic activity, sometimes forsaking pure internalization for quasi-internalization. Firms seek to outsource activities that they might once have done in-house, and form cooperative agreements to perform others. There are even such things as non-equity joint ventures. Companies can (in theory) have a much smaller physical existence because so much can be done through collaborative activities and outsourcing.

However, there are limits to how much firms can use non-internal means, as I have discussed in chapter 5. Firms still need to have the capacity to integrate outsourced technologies and knowledge sources into their products and processes and they must maintain a certain level of in-house capacity if they are to act efficiently as systems integrators (see also Paoli and Prencipe 1999, Brusoni et al. 2001).

All these developments do indeed make it difficult to understand where the boundaries of the firm lie. The last two decades have primarily seen a move away from vertical integration across borders, but not with more arm's-length transactions. Although equity-based ownership has declined, control has been maintained with quasi-internalized modes of operation. At the same time, an increase in horizontal integration and concentration has occurred. The growing reliance upon inter-firm cooperation – both through outsourcing and through strategic alliances – underlies firms' 'fuzzy' boundaries. The fuzziness arises from lack of clarity in what constitutes an economic entity. At what point can relations between economic entities which are physically independent and geographically disparate be seen to be inter-firm, and when are they regarded as intra-firm? But at what point do transactions become inter-firm?

This is not just an issue that is important for large MNEs. A considerable proportion of manufacturing activity is conducted by SMEs, most of which exist as suppliers to larger MNEs. And as the firms vertically disintegrate (and horizontally integrate), the firms that take up the slack are the SMEs.

Thus SMEs are at least as important as large firms in the scheme of things, if not more so. Although they may be small in relation to MNEs, they have not been immune to globalization. They have had to specialize, and depend on their network relationships with the MNEs. In addition, while they may be uni-national in their production, they are increasingly faced with international competition. The environment, then, has changed at least as much for SMEs as it has for MNEs, despite their uni-national status. However, SMEs do not have the advantages due to size and multinationality to adapt to changing conditions. Keep in mind too, that they are much more dependent on the large firm than vice-versa, so the bargaining power is not in the hands of the SME.[1]

The second outcome of globalization and technological change has been the increasingly blurred identity of the nation-state. On the one hand, countries remain sovereign and independent, while on the other hand, they are increasingly swayed by extra-national developments. Currencies are floating, their values are determined by the vagaries of currency traders the world over, and by political and economic developments not just in neighbouring countries. At the same time, there are clearly defined characteristics and patterns that are history-dependent and idiosyncratic, such as areas of specialization, technological competences, structure of markets, consumption patterns and culture. Government policies have to tread a thin line between responding to extra-national developments and to domestic priorities. This has led to what I have referred to as *de facto* economic integration. That is to say, unintended national-level economic integration has occurred, and this has gradually been acknowledged by *de jure* integration.

The shifting boundaries of the firm have affected the country-level fuzzy border problem. The increasing interdependence of firms has gone hand in hand with (or perhaps because of) improvements in the enforceability of contracts and the increased efficiency with which cross-border activity can be conducted. The main point is this: the growing intensity of international production has followed a natural co-evolutionary path with that of *de facto* economic integration, which in turn has been reinforced by *de jure* integration (Narula 2002b). Supra-national agreements such as the EU, NAFTA and WTO have reinforced, accelerated and created standardized regulation for economic activity, acting as a virtuous circle as regards economic integration that had been occurring as a matter of course. This process is by no means new, and is simply a natural progression of developments that go back at least 500 years. Underlying these developments has been an increasing similarity of product and process technologies across countries, and growing cross-border competition, not coincidentally associated with the post-World War II belief in the unhindered movement of goods and capital.

I think it is self-evident that these issues are even more crucial when we think of innovation and technology. For instance, as boundaries of the firm become fuzzy, the ownership and assignation of property rights of inventors and inventions become questionable. The policy implications are numerous. Where do R&D subsidies get spent? On a uni-national level it may mean that research incentives meant for a firm or a targeted sector may be utilized by another. Throw in the cross-border aspects. For it is clear that national borders are also increasingly fuzzy, with multi-country operations of MNEs, and multinational ownership of firms. Do financial incentives by the German government for Daimler Chrysler's R&D (say) get used directly by the firm in Stuttgart, or by its American subsidiary's Detroit facility? What of R&D that a MNE has outsourced from a completely independent company, located, say, in Russia? Is an SME really an SME if it has privileged status through strategic alliances to a large firm, or minority equity ownership by an MNE? If national technological policy is aimed at improving and enhancing the national innovation system, such issues are clearly important. But what may be sub-optimal for government policy is not necessarily so for the firm. Should the firm engage in R&D for which it can receive an R&D subsidy from the national government at 'home', but which it can only do sub-optimally at that location, or forgo the subsidy and use a more efficient source which may be located elsewhere in the world?

The 'fuzzy border problem' – for both firms and countries – suggests a looming crisis of defining national sovereignty, nationality and efficacy of all national regulation, especially for technology and industrial policy, but also for competition policy. The European Union has been learning to deal with these for a small group of countries, but the scope of such activity in the face of growing interdependent nature of firms and countries means that national governments need to think larger, and into the future.

7.2 The role of governments in innovation

Although most national governments agree on the need to intervene to improve and sustain created assets, not all agree on the optimal method to do so. It should be noted that the extent of government intervention through industrial policy varies considerably between countries, from a sporadic intervention in the case of the US, to a more systematic view taken by, say, France. Nonetheless, the differences between the views taken by individual industrialized countries would seem to be a matter of degree.

It is obvious that national governments have a strong interest in the ability of firms in a given location to conduct competitiveness-enhancing activities, and particularly those associated with the creation and deployment of knowledge capital. These reasons can be qualified under two main headings, namely, the promotion of wealth-creating assets of its firms (ownership advantages) and maintaining and improving indigenous resources and capabilities (location advantages). By doing so, it can help maintain and improve its own locational attractiveness to mobile and footloose investors (of whatever nationality) to conduct high value-adding activity. These two issues are strongly related, since the presence of highly competitive firms at a given location acts as a location advantage, often prompting a virtuous circle. Conversely, strong location advantages, such as the presence of support institutions and firms, infrastructure and skilled manpower, will enhance the ownership advantages of firms located there.

The role of governments in improving the quality of human capital cannot be overemphasized. One of the primary determinants behind technological accumulation and absorptive capacity is human capital. Qualified human resources are essential in monitoring the evolution of external knowledge and in evaluating its relevance, and for the integration of these technologies into productive activities. Human capital represents an important subset of absorptive capabilities, and this is well acknowledged by policy makers everywhere. However, the presence of a highly skilled labour force is not a *sine qua non* for improved innovativeness, although it is certainly a necessary condition. Simply providing tertiary-level education and skilled manpower does not lead to increased R&D, nor is there a direct connection between education and technological competence. The availability of a large stock of suitably qualified workers does not in itself result in efficient absorption of knowledge, as is well illustrated by the former centrally planned economies of Eastern Europe. But quality of the training and the ability of industry to exploit available skills in R&D or other technical effort matter a great deal.

In other words, the reduction of market imperfections in the creation and utilization of knowledge capital has considerable welfare benefits, which stem both from a direct result of these activities, and from externalities generated by them. It is also to be noted that governments may intervene for at least three other reasons which are only indirectly related to advancing competitiveness. Among these we might mention first to protect or advance economic or political sovereignty. The second is for strategic reasons, such as in defence-related issues. The third is where investment in R&D is primarily undertaken to promote social goals, such as in the health and environment sectors. In all of these cases, even though R&D may be undertaken by private firms for commercial application elsewhere, the interest of government is to limit diffusion (for example in the defence sector) of the technology to non-national firms, or to maximize diffusion (such as in the health and environment sectors) of innovations, by, for example, acquiring the property rights and providing it at marginal cost to all firms. However, in our current exposition we are interested in the role of governments in affecting commercial R&D activity, and so we shall not explore other issues in greater detail. We identify three main reasons that governments have an interest in fostering R&D activities.

Level of investment in R&D   Countries with low expenditures in R&D tend not to be as competitive (e.g., Archibugi and Pianta 1992). Therefore governments have an incentive to encourage R&D activities. Without government intervention, firms may tend to under-invest given their bounded rationality and the path-dependent nature of their activities. Firms prefer to engage in new activities closely linked to their current activities, and this may result in too little R&D investment, *relative* to other kinds of investment (Hall 1986). Further, greater uncertainty may arise from competition: another firm may be doing similar research. Neither the time when the research will be completed nor the identity of the winner of the race to innovate, is known. The risk from these and other problems is often reflected in the cost of capital to the firm intent on undertaking R&D, and the higher the risk, the more difficult it may be to acquire capital to undertake it. In the limit, financial capital may be unavailable for risky research projects. On the other hand, it is possible that too many, rather than too few, resources may be applied to R&D (Barzel 1968). This might occur, for example, where several firms are in a 'race' to solve a given technological problem, and this may lead to over-investment in R&D. In other words, there is (1) the danger of firms under-investing in new technologies with which they are unfamiliar, or are too risky; (2) the risk of over investment in a given project due to duplication of investment by several firms.

Problems from appropriability   Society is faced with the difficulty of sustaining economic growth through encouraging innovative activity by providing monopoly power to inventors so that they may continue to innovate at a socially optimal level on the one hand, but on the other, to maximize diffusion and availability of products at the lowest possible costs, generally by encouraging competition. However, firms will under-invest in R&D when they are uncertain of appropriating sufficient returns. This occurs for three reasons. First, because the value of an innovation is not always apparent to the market *ex ante*. Second, even where the value of the innovation is known to the inventor, a firm cannot convince others without revealing the details of the innovation, thereby losing some its value because of its public good will. Third, even where the firm overcomes these two hurdles, it cannot charge the market the actual value of the innovation, but the opportunity cost, or the value of the next-best option available on the market (Barzel 1968). Therefore, it will remain uncertain as to whether it can recuperate the costs of its investment, unless the government is able to act as a broker in this process. The traditional route by governments is to administer and issue patents, but these are highly imperfect tools to assign property rights, and are also inefficient. It is to be stressed that while government intervention is a possible solution it is not the *only* solution, and indeed there are several instances and situations where the market is able partially to rectify itself. Firms that are unable to patent utilize secrecy and lead times as methods to protect their property rights (Levin et al. 1987, Arundel and Kabla 1998), but are also unlikely to spread the risks and costs of R&D among the potential users of the innovation.

Industry structure and concentration   The third concern is the prevention of oligopolistic and/or monopolistic behaviour in asset creation and utilization. It is axiomatic that demand is necessary as a catalyst to innovation, and the competition to survive among firms in a given industry drives the generation and diffusion of technology. However, it remains unclear what the optimal level of competition is. Dasgupta and Stiglitz (1980) among others have shown that there is a positive relationship between competition in R&D and the level of innovation, but it is as yet unclear what the appropriate level of innovatory activity is. On the one hand, there is evidence to indicate that when there is a larger number of firms engaged in R&D in a given industry, the average level of R&D investment per firm falls, but the total investment in the industry rises. On the other hand, there is also evidence that would conform to the Schumpeterian idea that innovative activity may be encouraged by industry structures in which firms are few and concentration is substantial. This is a complex issue that remains unresolved, and is very much a question of country-specific policy. Certainly, it would appear that given the cost and risk of R&D in the age of globalization, a few large firms are more likely to be successful than a large number of small ones. How the implementation of R&D alliances affects the optimum industry structure is unclear, but in general governments have preferred to limit strategic alliances of firms in a given industry to pre-competitive research (for example, SEMATECH, ESPRIT).

7.3 Government intervention and innovative activity

A distinction needs to be made regarding the difference between three elements of R&D: basic research, applied research and development. While there is relatively little controversy regarding the role of government in basic R&D, this is not the case about government involvement in applied R&D activities, including R&D alliances. The roots of this controversy derive from the nature of knowledge capital and the problems of fully appropriating its benefits, due to its two contradictory aspects. On the one hand, knowledge is partly of a public-good nature, but on the other hand, in high-technology sectors, it is also highly tacit and context-specific in nature. Thus, owing to its inherent uncertainty, there tends to be sub-optimal R&D investment (including training programmes) by firms (e.g. Arrow 1962b). Therefore, one of the primary roles of governments is universally acknowledged as reducing the risks and costs and increasing the social benefits of the generation and diffusion of intellectual capital.

More controversially, however, there has been an increasing tendency among a number of industrialized-country governments towards direct intervention favouring particular domestic firms, in what has been described as 'techno-nationalism' (Ostry and Nelson 1995). That is, the decision of governments to 'target' certain firms in industries as primary recipients of government incentives to generate innovation. This chapter will examine techno-nationalism and the welfare implications on competitiveness, when applied to R&D alliances.

National governments attach great importance to the creation and diffusion of knowledge capital, which is regarded as the bedrock upon which the economic prosperity (that is, the competitiveness) of the advanced industrial countries is built. However, the influence of governments on the competitiveness of their economies has been somewhat diluted with the advent of globalization, and in its wake, alliance capitalism. To take a couple of examples:

- Governments find it much more difficult to enforce the appropriability of technology when intellectual property rights are violated in countries where such protection is limited, thereby perhaps raising the cost of products to domestic consumers, and further affecting the willingness of these firms to invest in R&D.

• There is increasing difficulty in identifying and determining where R&D investment is made, and who reaps the benefits therefrom, especially when the innovation is done in, say, the Philips R&D facility in the US, or, even more complex, when the innovation is from the UK laboratory of, say, the Anglo-Dutch conglomerate Unilever.

Ostry and Nelson (1995) suggest that because of the difficulties of enforcing and monitoring international compliance to property rights as well as the declining efficacy of patents, government support of R&D is the best way to induce industrial innovation, rather than relying on the market to provide an adequate return. This line of reasoning has a considerable following, not least among economists who advocate 'strategic trade theory', as well as most neo-Schumpeterian economists. Essentially the argument made is that since technology defines competitiveness, and the cost of R&D activity is rising, an oligopolistic market structure would be optimal. A small number of firms would reap higher profits, which would support higher wages. However, since every country would like its firms (or one of them) in each high-tech, capital-intensive sector to be among the surviving firms, this has led to a sort of 'techno-nationalism' where every country supports its national champions through various means in the bid to maintain its technological competitiveness.

However, this techno-nationalism has resulted in a sort of prisoner's dilemma, as globalization makes it much more difficult to identify what constitutes a national champion, as has proven to be the case with ICI or Rover. Indeed, Ostry and Nelson (1995) argue that policies that have sought to create national champions have actually furthered the process of transnationalization, since barriers to imports have encouraged foreign MNEs to establish local value-adding activities, and undertake alliances in order to receive national treatment.

Our discussion heretofore underlines the unresolved question of the prudence of government intervention in R&D activity. Indeed, there remains considerable variation between countries in the extent to which they intervene. For instance, although public sources in the US account for over 40 per cent of R&D expenditures, US intervention is by and large sporadic at the applied R&D level. On the other hand, France and Japan are much more systematically involved in subsidizing and coordinating applied research. Since R&D activity is highly uncertain in nature, especially when such R&D activity is close to or at the technology frontier, and where the R&D is basic and conceptual in nature, the efficacy of government intervention is unclear. This is for two reasons. First, governments need to target industries and sectors which offer promise in the medium and long term, and are not sunset industries. Besides there may be several different, competing technologies, but only limited funds. In such cases, choices have to be made, and firms do not have an incentive to reveal their true opinions, especially where the most 'deserving' firm is a rival one. As Farrell (1987) has emphasized, a central authority is bound to have less complete information than the firms in any given sector. When firms are engaged in R&D some distance away from the technological frontier, the direction in which investment is to be made is obvious since firms at the frontier (that is, the technology leaders) have already done so. (It is, however, necessary to emphasize the difference between firms that are a distance from the technology frontier, and those that are simply experiencing X-inefficiency. The latter group is simply using an inferior technology, while the former is operating at an earlier stage of the product life cycle.) However, non-intervention is not the answer either, since firms that are risk-averse will avoid investments in highly risky, economically less viable, 'blue sky' projects.

Second, where a 'worthy' project is defined, there are clear difficulties in identifying whether the government subsidies are being utilized for the purpose for which they were provided, or simply a mechanism for cross-subsidization of other R&D projects. This arises from the tacit nature of basic R&D in high-technology industries, since the output may not be patentable or have an identifiable, tangible form.

It is not my aim here to evaluate the wisdom of government involvement in promoting R&D activity, or to criticize techno-nationalism.[2] My position is based on the assumption that these are the implicit goals of national governments of the advanced industrial countries (for a review, see Ostry and Nelson 1995). However, the evidence reviewed so far indicates that firms must necessarily engage in asset exploitation on a global (or at least regional) basis if they are to remain competitive, and albeit to a lesser degree (but to a growing extent), develop and acquire new assets globally. The evidence reviewed would also indicate that, in general, firms are more willing to engage in collaborative R&D activities in overseas locations than engaging in wholly owned R&D activities, and this has much to do with techno-globalism (Archibugi and Michie, 1994).

This said, however, there is no consensus on the optimal way to boost the competitive advantage of firms through strategic alliances. On the one hand, countries such as the US have hitherto attempted to deal with the root causes of market failure by trying to make markets more efficient, but only directly intervening on a reactive, case-by case basis (for instance, in sectors where defence applications may exist). Countries such as France and Japan, on the other hand, have taken a more active, or direct role (see Nelson 1993).

7.4 R&D cooperation and governments: direct vs. indirect intervention

This disagreement about the extent to which intervention should be undertaken extends to the case of R&D alliance activity, although it is by now accepted that cooperative R&D can have net positive effects on the economy (see e.g. D'Aspremont and Jacquemin 1988, Katz 1986, Vonortas 1994, 1997). It should be noted that it is by no means necessary that national governments regard R&D cooperation as a first-best option, or even a second-best one: it is debatable, for example, whether R&D investment through alliances is quite at the same level as that achieved through internalized R&D activity by national firms. Certainly, it would seem obvious that government financial support to a collaboration between a national champion with a firm of another nationality may represent a subsidy to the foreign firm. Likewise, a firm may see R&D subsidies provided to it by the government as a substitute for its own R&D efforts rather than an additional source of investment, leading to a net reduction in R&D expenditures on a national level. However, the question is not whether R&D investment through STP is a better solution than R&D investment by domestic firms, but whether it represents a better solution than that offered by the free market, and there is good reason to suspect that the market will be unable to achieve a welfare optimum. The argument against intervention suggests that governments may not be able to do better than markets, and that since innovation occurs in response to market demand, it cannot be seriously sub-optimal (This line of reasoning is succinctly summarized in Hall 1986: 9–14.) Moreover, it is important to realize that it is not simply a question of maintaining the *level* of R&D investment, but also the *efficiency* of this investment.

Insofar as governments are concerned, their primary interests lie in strengthening the competitiveness of their national firms. The evidence would suggest that the role of governments, at least in the case of the industrialized countries, is most effective as a facilitator of competitive advantage, in terms of providing the complementary assets needed by firms, rather than as a direct intervention role. These assets are best described as the systems of innovation (see chapter 2). Innovation systems represent the location-bound resources and capabilities that sustain, complement and enhance the ownership advantages of firms. In other words, indirect intervention takes the form of improving the ownership advantages of firms by affecting the location advantages of the country. By direct intervention we refer, *inter alia*, to attempts by governments to enhance the ownership advantages of firms by fiat, through restrictions on domestic operations of foreign MNEs (for example, the US airline industry), through the provision of exclusive contracts to develop products for the use of governments (such as, the French TGV, Eurofighter project, space shuttle, etc.), through exclusive (or subsidized) access to public-sector research facilities. It must be noted that few countries desist completely from direct intervention. We will briefly discuss the options available to governments in connection with encouraging R&D alliances under these two headings.

7.4.1 Direct intervention

We identify five primary means by which governments can engage in direct intervention:

As a participant   Governments can engage as participants in R&D alliances through public organizations. This is especially common in basic-research projects, as public research institutes and universities have the human and capital resources to undertake fundamental R&D, or what is referred to as pre-competitive research by the EU. This is one of the means used by the EU to improve the competitiveness of European firms – indeed, almost 60 per cent of funding within the second and third framework programmes which covered the period 1987 to 1994, 12 billion ECUs was directed towards universities and public institutes (Geuna 1996). An additional advantage of such participation is that it is better able to monitor the utilization of the resources and act as an honest broker, and prevent the misallocation of funds by commercial (and profit-oriented) partners. NTT, the Japanese telecommunications giant, has played a similar role in enforcing the partnership agreements undertaken by firms in telecommunications and computers, by sponsoring complementary research to that of MITI, and allowing the consolidation of national champions in each of these industries (Levy and Samuels 1991).

By guaranteeing a market for the output of the alliance   This can be undertaken in at least three ways. First, by providing project-specific contracts to consortia of firms, as is the case with most EU aerospace projects, and US defence-related projects. This substantially reduces the risk associated with R&D, and at the same time improves the appropriability of the innovation. Second, by directly affecting the returns to the innovator by creating a market for the product. For example, in the 1970s the Japanese government established the Japan Robot Company which bought all the output from the robot manufacturers, and then leased the robots to the customers. Third, by establishing a particular technology standard, which may be proprietary to a particular firm, and requiring firms to adhere to them. This has the added advantage that it prevents duplication of investment in other, inferior, alternatives. This is achieved through establishing cross-licensing agreements. The most successful of these, the aircraft patent agreement among US firms which remained in force between 1917 and 1968, was established at the behest of the US government during World War I in order to standardize the use of the 'best-practice' technology in airframes across the various manufacturers (Bittlingmayer 1988). The difficulty in so doing is that, first, governments may not necessarily select *ex ante* what the most superior technology is, and, second, it requires a suspension of anti-trust regulations in most cases. In fact, the aircraft patent agreement was eventually terminated by the US Supreme Court, when it was deemed contrary to anti-trust regulations.

By bending anti-competition regulations   Collaboration between major players in any given industry treads dangerously close to representing collusive activity that contravenes anti-trust regulations. Under certain circumstances, a relaxation of such rules is permitted – particularly as regards pre-competitive (basic and applied research) – to encourage the sharing of risks and costs of otherwise prohibitively expensive projects. The Framework Programmes of the European Commission have encouraged R&D collaboration by public and private EU-based institutions, significantly relaxing anti-competitive regulations and providing subsidies to collaborative R&D, so as to allow European industry to compete more effectively, both on world markets and within the EU (Peterson and Sharp 1998).

By providing market access in exchange for technology to a domestic firm   Governments have sometimes insisted that a foreign-owned MNE have certain minimum local content, thereby creating linkages to the domestic innovation system, or by insisting that the MNE take a domestic partner in exchange for access to the domestic market. The case of both European and US voluntary export restrictions with Japanese firms led to an increase in local innovative activity (and alliance formation) during the 1980s. A similar approach was taken by Korea during the 1960s (Amsden 1989), where technology transfer was made a condition for market access.

By making participation in alliances a precondition for future government contracts   Both the direction of research and the availability of subsidies can be used as leverage to encourage firms to undertake collaborative research. This is the case with the Japanese computer industry, in which major Japanese firms were asked to collaborate on joint R&D, with the understanding that it affected future subsides from MITI. Levy and Samuels (1991) note that, when Matsushita left the computer industry in 1964, it was unable to enter MITI-sponsored computer alliances for two decades.

7.4.2 Indirect intervention

The literature is replete with policy prescriptions to improve the location advantages and the quality of location-bound resources, and there is no reason to revise this literature here. The enhancement and improvement of location advantages has received considerable attention in various guises and is thus relatively uncontroversial: there is therefore no need to develop an exhaustive typology of options here. We shall, however, highlight two important issues regarding countries' indirect intervention.

First, although governments are unable to prevent alliances from being unstable or, indeed, from reducing the inherent risk of R&D activity – whether collaborative or otherwise – there is a role for governments in providing information to help identify synergies, complementarities and opportunities, since there are market imperfections in the *market for partners*. Governments can help diffuse the results of basic-research output produced by either government research institutes or private establishments to interested parties by creating a sort of 'market-place' where potential partners can meet and exchange information. This is undertaken on a regular basis through trade fairs, but also directly through government institutions (Niosi 1995). Even where governments do not own the technologies, they can play an important role in match-making firms.

Second, there is an important and growing role for governments in encouraging and monitoring cross-border R&D alliances, and reducing uncertainty attached to this. First, this can be done by the development of binding multilateral intellectual property rights protection through agencies such as the World Trade Organization, thereby improving appropriability of innovation, both domestically and internationally. There is a very real danger of cross-border duplication of activity, especially in terms of multiple (and not necessarily compatible) standards which can be potentially sub-optimal in terms of expenditure on a global basis. Recent initiatives by the G7 members jointly to subsidize space research is such an example. The failure to develop a common standard on HDTV has largely affected its successful commercial launch. However, inter-governmental initiatives are, in general, the exception rather than the rule.

7.4.3 Areas in which government intervention is futile

Despite the best efforts of governments, there nonetheless remain considerable risks associated with success or failure of an alliance (see Inkpen and Beamish 1997). Even where complementarities exist, and potential partners are identified, there are several hazards that exist. Das and Teng (1996) suggest that these can be viewed as being of two types. *Relational risk* occurs as a result of one or more of the partners in an alliance being unwilling to work towards the mutual interest of the partnership, thereby breaching the agreement. Such behaviour may be rational or irrational, and includes asymmetrical learning, or a lack of trust. There is limited scope for government intervention in such an instance, since we would have to assume perfect information *ex ante* of the failure of a partner to provide inputs in the prescribed manner. Given the nature of R&D alliances, such an assumption is clearly unrealistic, and in the case of basic R&D the asymmetrical learning may not be evident in the short term. Nor, it must be said, does relationship risk arise only from the failure of partners to maintain the agreement, but also where they interpret the agreement literally. Lastly, relational risk may be unintentional, since partners may have different objectives. The second sort of risk, *performance risk*, occurs when all partners have cooperated fully, but the partnership has none-theless not achieved its objective, and represents the opposite prob-lem. The role of government here is also limited, except where such alliances had received government subsidies, since the question is whether in fact the failure of the partnering was due to inefficient and/or inappropriate use of the funds, or that the research trajec-tory was 'too far' from commercialization for any tangible output to be generated. Such questions have been raised about the ESPRIT programme of the European Commission (Mytelka 1991).

It is important to realize that the extent of government intervention is idiosyncratic and country-specific. Therefore the motive for sup-porting R&D alliances, and the nature of the intervention, may vary according to different government policies. I have noted five means which are most favoured by countries in intervening directly, and two by which governments do so indirectly, all of which are utilized to differing extents by policy makers. My most fundamental advice, based on the preceding analyses, is to avoid picking 'winners', in terms of both specific firms and particular technological trajectories, as this is bound to lead, *ceteris paribus*, to sub-optimal outcomes in the long run. In specific terms, my advice to policy makers, based on the analyses, can be succinctly summarized as follows:

1   View strategic technology partnering as a complementary to domestic R&D, rather than as a substitute. There is a danger that firms may see R&D subsidies provided to it by the government as a substitute for their own R&D efforts rather than an additional source of investment, leading to a net reduction in R&D expenditures on a national level. It is also important to note that even though the level of investment may have gone up, what is more crucial is whether the efficiency in using this investment has increased. That is to say, R&D alliances may lead to greater R&D expenditures, and it is by no means certain that such inputs will lead to a proportional increase in output, as the benefits may accrue to other projects and firms, since learning in an alliance is not always symmetrical.

2   Furthermore, a distinction needs to be made regarding the various aspects of R&D: basic research, applied research and devel-opment. There is relatively little controversy about basic research and the need for governments to subsidize it, although the ability of governments to pick whom to subsidize is another matter. However, strategic technology partnering is also relatively uncontroversial in basic research. The debate primarily revolves around applied re-search and development. It is not the role of governments to try to enhance the ownership advantages of its firms, to the exclusion of

foreign-owned establishments, nor can they expect to do so in this age of alliance capitalism. Instead, the stress should be on improving the location advantages of countries and the ownership advantage-augmenting resources such as education and training, infrastructure, institutions, intellectual property rights protection, and other non-specific R&D support. Nonetheless, in many other ways, competitiveness of countries does matter, since markets are imperfect, and resources are mobile, thereby making government intervention necessary. Its urgency is further enhanced by the fact that the current extent of involvement by governments represents a sort of prisoner's dilemma, since no country is likely to back down from the current competitiveness-enhancing 'war'. We would be safe in concluding that, in this age of strategic trade policies and targeted industrial development, nations that rely only on market forces to determine outcomes are not just not playing on a level playing field, but are playing on a different playing field altogether.

3   The evidence on globalization and alliance capitalism would seem to point towards a role for governments in improving the efficiency of R&D activities on an international basis. It is understandable that countries duplicate R&D investments for strategic and political reasons, especially in basic research, but the failure to create international standards, in many instances, leads to considerable misallocation of resources, particularly in applied R&D. Furthermore, several countries are often, unknowingly, engaged in subsidizing the same projects by trans-national firms. There is clearly a growing need to address these and other issues on an international basis, as is currently been undertaken within the framework of the WTO for intellectual property rights.

4   There is a role for governments in providing information to help identify synergies, complementarities and opportunities, since there are market imperfections in the *market for partners*. Governments can help diffuse the results of basic-research output produced either by government research institutes or private establishments to interested parties by creating a sort of 'marketplace' where potential partners can meet and exchange information. This is undertaken on a regular basis through trade fairs, but also directly through government institutions (Niosi 1995).

7.5 On innovation systems and learning: some policy issues

Policies to promote innovation and technological competitiveness cannot be made by focusing solely on promoting firm-level R&D

and promoting inter-firm cooperation. Providing tax credits and other fiscal incentives for firm-level R&D activities has not been proven to be a sufficient means to achieve this end.[3] Indeed, such a view assumes that knowledge domains and competences are easily developed, acquired or transferred, and that learning is largely instantaneous. Further, simply promoting firm-level innovation as a solution for weaknesses in technological competitiveness without a view to developing the appropriate non-firm sector is a recipe for failure. It is for this reason that I have taken a systems view of learning and the location of R&D in chapters 2 and 3. For instance, firms must have access to skilled human capital if they are to create or absorb efficiently: it is no accident that firms often locate R&D facilities in physical proximity to locations with the best knowledge infrastructure. If (say) universities do not produce sufficient quantities of researchers at an internationally competent level, firms will locate their R&D facilities elsewhere. But the systemic nature of policy means that, if universities are to achieve this target, they need to have the financial and technical wherewithal to attract and retain the best scholars. Sustaining or strengthening firm-level innovatory capacity requires developing the capacity of the non-firm sector. Any industrial policy to build up competitiveness in a targeted sector without concerning itself with education policy is doomed to failure. Firms need to have the capacity to absorb and innovate, and this is embodied in people. Perhaps the single biggest determinant of India's successful software industry derives from its considerable investment in higher education. In addition to providing skilled manpower, universities and other non-firm R&D performers are an important source of knowledge for firms (Arundel and Geuna 2001).

The importance of education policy as a fundamental condition for technological competitiveness and industrial development should by now be seen to be axiomatic. This has been emphasized by almost every major international organization and academic institution. I will not dwell on this point at any length here, but rather emphasize a related point, that while the provision of high-quality education and the improvement of human capital represents a core aspect of absorptive capacity, its presence *per se* is not a *sine qua non* for knowledge accumulation. While both physical and human capital are necessary inputs for industrial development, the lack of appropriate incentives for production and investment can compromise the success of the technological upgrading (Lall 1992). There is a need, in other words, for a *systemic view*. Educational policies cannot be divorced from industrial policy, because *they are all part of an indivisible system*.

Systems – be they of innovation or of production – are not meant to imply a *systematic* organization of their constituent elements, but a *systemic* relationship between the various facets. To single out any one of these elements as being of singular or exceptional importance is a commonplace error. Rather, it is the cumulative causation of all elements within a system in the sense proposed by Myrdal (1957) (see James 2001 for a discussion). Myrdal's concept of cumulative causation is complementary to that of inertia. Neither concept suggests a net positive outcome. Not all systems have a virtuous outcome in that they result in a vibrant and internationally competitive firm sector. This may be because some aspects of the innovation are absent, atrophied, or simply do not work well together. In this sense they can be incomplete. Their incompleteness may stem from a sub-standard aspect of the system due to (for instance) poor infrastructural facilities. There are two points worth noting here. First, that innovation systems are similar in character to the concept of industrial clusters or districts, a subject much studied by economic geography. Successful innovation systems are often co-located with successful clusters. Creating and sustaining agglomerations of economic activity is the holy grail of economics, although there is as yet no consensus on how an unsuccessful cluster of innovation systems can be made into a successful one. Despite the best efforts of many, no one has successfully replicated Emilia-Romana, Silicon Valley or Baden-Württemberg. Indeed, some industrial clusters have developed in spite of a lack of any planning on the part of governments.[4] The causes of successful clustering have been much studied, and I do not intend to go through the literature here. However, most researchers seem to agree that the location-specific advantages and the ownership specific assets of the firms in that location need to be complementary to each other and need to be spatially clustered if they are to be deployed with optimum efficiency (Storper and Scott 1995).

The second point worth noting is that while 'incompleteness' may be at a national level, in several industries – particularly those that are more knowledge-intensive and amenable to globally rationalized production – the national level may be the wrong unit of analysis. India's software sector has overcome deficiencies in its other components of the innovation system by being part of a more global innovation system/global production network, *inter alia* depending as it does on capital and infrastructural investment by US firms and entrepreneurs: it is part of an international cluster. Note that being able to integrate into a global or pan-national innovation system is an option specific to certain industries with particular characteristics: it cannot be generalized for all sectors (see Borrus et al. 2000 for a discussion). Other innovation systems may be more regional in nature, such as (say) the Nordic pulp and paper industry. Likewise, Singapore has positioned itself (as have the Netherlands, Belgium, Finland and a score of other small open economies) to exploit complementary resources and markets elsewhere,[5] thereby overcoming the exogenous limits on national capabilities and resources. This is not necessarily a strange concept: MNEs have sought to exploit the best of various separate national systems. It seems reasonable to argue that innovation systems can seek to complement each other in much the same way as MNEs coordinate and rationalize their global activities.

Getting locations to coordinate their activities on a multilateral basis is, of course, an extreme scenario, requiring *de facto* economic and political integration much like the blueprint of the European Union. It is also not immediately evident whether a similar approach to that of coordinated pan-EU planning can successfully be undertaken elsewhere. Such complex and deep integration requires considerable time, investment and political courage. The political will required to accept short- and medium-term losses at a national level to achieve the long-term goal of rationalizing a sector on a pan-regional basis is best illustrated by the integration of the European aerospace industry. But this is an example of a successful cooperation to rationalize to achieve critical mass. In the European biotechnology industry, for instance, policies and infrastructure continue to be fragmented and lack critical mass (Senker et al. 1996). This is despite the fact that the biotechnology industry possesses characteristics that form the basis for a 'complex interdependence within a global system' (Bartholomew 1997). Indeed, the European industrial landscape is littered with examples of failures. Critics of supra-national organizations belabour the impotence of these institutions to implement policy and intervene to overcome market imperfections and failure, as the current political climate seeks to transfer responsibilities from the nation-state to the private sector (Boyer and Drache 1996).

A much more realistic option to governments (in the absence of sufficiently powerful supra-national organizations) is to coordinate industrial policy strategically on a unilateral basis to most effectively utilize external resources and capabilities to enhance domestic resources and capabilities. This requires the acceptance of the realities of domestic limitations and global opportunities. Countries can enhance their own created assets and knowledge base by attracting human capital and firms with access to alternative knowledge bases. The strength of the US as a technological hegemony derives partly from its being able to attract the best minds from around the planet (Kogut 2000): well over 50 per cent of all PhDs in science and engineering are foreign-born, and a good percentage eventually stay on in the US. However, it takes more than arranging visas and scholarships. The US is a society where people are naturally footloose. It is not unusual for people to relocate from New York to California or vice versa with little thought.[6] In contrast, 90 per cent of European researchers live within 100 km of their birthplace. Too many institutions (in the sense of routines and procedures) in Europe are unwritten or difficult to transmit, embedded as they are as part of various cultures and traditions. The US, by contrast, has a relatively transparent set of institutions, at least as far as day-to-day activities are concerned. For instance, the process of acquiring tenure in Italian or German universities is an incredibly opaque one, evident from the very small numbers of non-indigenous university professors in any given university. Nonetheless, locales such as Taiwan, Singapore and Hong Kong have thrived by encouraging the inflow of specialists and skill manpower. Other countries have encouraged knowledge diversity through educating and training indigenes abroad, and systematically encouraging their return (see e.g., Pack 2001). This is much more important for small countries than large countries where there is a danger of knowledge 'in-breeding'. No country can possibly expect to provide world-class competences in all technological fields. Even the largest, most technologically advanced countries cannot provide strong innovation systems to all their industries, and world-class competences in all technological fields. The cross-border flow of ideas is something that has always been seen as fundamental to firms, and this imperative has increased with growing cross-border competition, and international production. Domestic economic actors need access to foreign sources of knowledge in a globalizing world. This is the message emphasized in chapters 2 and 3.

The flow of knowledge embodied in people is further enhanced through the presence of MNE subsidiaries, as has been the case in countries such as the Netherlands, Belgium, Singapore, Taiwan and China. (e.g., Pack, 2001, Amsden 1989, van Hoesel 1999, van Hoesel and Narula 1999, Sachwald 2001). In the case of the countries that are home to competitive MNEs with well-developed international networks of foreign affiliates, there is also the possibility of improving the domestic knowledge base through reverse technology transfer.

However, countries that have been historically inward-looking have also always regarded the need to import technologies as a sign of national weakness, and have a tradition of techno-nationalism. That is, they have sought to maintain in-country competences at whatever the cost. This problem is aggravated by the trend towards multi-technologies even in mature industries. The strategy of technological self-sufficiency is particularly untenable in economies that have limited resources. They must either spread their resources thinly across many technological competences or concentrate on a few. The case of Norway, discussed in chapter 3, illustrates this well.

It is one thing to propose changing policies that have previously championed self-sufficiency, and quite another to change the attitudes of policy makers and organizations that implement policy. Institutions (in the sense of routines and procedures) create the milieu within which economic activity is undertaken and establishes the ground rules for interaction between the various economic actors, and represents a sort of a 'culture'. Institutions are both formal and informal, and will probably have taken years – if not decades – to create and sustain. To modify and develop institutions is a complex and slow process, particularly since they cannot be created simply by government fiat. Witness the difficulties that former centrally planned economies of Eastern Europe face in adjusting to the market economy, developing countries such as India and Brazil (with a strong import-substituting milieu), or for that matter, France. Such change is even more complex where the new institutions require synchronization between countries (Narula 2002b). The Triad countries have taken fifty years to adjust and reform institutions, but even here there is an inertia. The EU, for instance, has failed to reform its agricultural sector. Norway remains largely mired in an import-substituting world, with a strong tendency towards central planning and state-owned economic actors. Nonetheless, systems do change, because the costs of supporting inefficient institutions may far outweigh the benefits of change. Systems and institutions are also evolutionary processes which require imitation, experimentation, learning and forgetting, and this most often means that change is gradual, slow and cumbersome (for an illustration of how ideas and practices diffuse between different innovation systems see Kogut 2000).

Promoting national champions by limiting foreign participation to arm's-length acquisition of knowledge is not an unviable option. However, just as there are limits to the firm's use of non-internal sources of knowledge, there are limits to how much countries can rely on technologies acquired through arm's-length means. That is, innovation based largely on improving and modifying external sources of technology acquired through arm's-length means is an option available only *as long as there is something to imitate*. As countries approach the technological frontier, there are two problems. First, it may not be possible to buy cutting-edge technologies, since firms that own these technologies are reluctant to license or sell them. The reluctance has to do with the nature of technology (in that a price cannot be put on an unproven knowledge base for which no market exists) and the fact that firms will seek to maximize the rent from their inventions as long as they are in a monopoly position. To sell their new technologies would be to create a competitor. Second, imitation is not possible *at* the frontier, since it is difficult to predict *ex ante* which technology (of several competing nascent technologies) will become paradigmatic. This explains the popularity of strategic technology partnering at and around the frontier, because firms seek to collaborate when it helps to reduce uncertainty and reduce the innovation time span. They therefore seek partners who can improve the probability of 'winning', and these firms are those that have complementary resources to offer (see chapter 4). The poor participation levels of developing countries in R&D alliances noted in chapter 6 has much to do with the fact that they bring little to barter with in an alliance situation.

As they approach the frontier, countries must have the capacity not just to absorb and imitate technological development created by others, but also the ability to generate inventions of their own. This requires technological capabilities that are non-imitative. In other words, learning-by-doing and learning-by-using have decreasing returns as one approaches the frontier, and in-house learning and learning–by-alliances become more efficient options.

The case of Korea (Amsden 1989, Kim 1995, Sachwald 2001) illustrates the evolution of the ability to assimilate R&D spillovers during the catching-up process. Korea relied on technology licensing and imports of capital goods from developed countries in acquiring external knowledge till the 1980s, but this enabled it only to access second-best practice technologies. Korea is now almost at the technological frontier in many sectors. Its asset-creating facilities (*inter alia* deriving from its education system) are, however, geared towards absorption through imitation rather than in-house learning (see Kim 1995, Suh 2000). In addition the difficulty of further assimilation connected to the more tacit nature of advanced knowledge and the reluctance of industrialized countries to transfer technology to Korean firms for fear of losing their technological advantage has aggravated this process. There is now an increasing emphasis on technological capability building and on reverse technology transfer, that is, through outward FDI by Korean MNEs (Sachwald 2001, Lee 2001).

The level to which governments can intervene – or the extent to which is desirable that they do so – varies considerably. The conventional wisdom today points towards a balance between an interventionist role for governments where governments attempt to 'pick winners', and one which seeks to overcome market failures and imperfections with an intention to establish the appropriate milieu or 'ecology' for innovation (e.g., Giesecke 2000). There are numerous examples that justify either a strong interventionist approach or a laissez-faire view focusing solely on improving the innovation milieu.

Selecting sectors is a task fraught with pitfalls, not least because selecting the 'right' industry to target becomes more difficult the closer the country is to the technological frontier. When governments attempt to select preferred industries in which to focus some distance away from the technological frontier, the direction in which investment is to be made is fairly obvious since firms at the frontier (the technology leaders) have already determined the direction in the past. That is to say, the further a country is from the technological frontier, the easier it is to 'pick' industries that will be successful. The relative success of MITI in picking winners in the 1950s and 1960s, and their subsequent less successful interventions in the 1980s and 1990s, well illustrates this point. Although there is a danger in investing limited resources in niche sectors which become obsolete, or get replaced by a new technological paradigm, this need not happen if broader sectors are targeted that are complementary to, and help upgrade, existing competences and skills. The development of Singapore's biotechnology sector illustrates this well (Lall 1997). As Stopford (1997: 473) explains,

> To nurture clusters, work needs to be done to identify specific technologies that can reinforce the position of existing leaders, or that suit the skills of the workforce or even that satisfy the demand that is particularly sophisticated in the nation. Investment in 'market-friendly' aspects of the underlying technologies can, as in Singapore, create a vital base for the building of firm-specific advantages by either local or foreign firms.

On the other hand, in the era of globalized production, it is easier to create production clusters from scratch. Because of the abilities of

MNEs to locate different parts of their value-added chain in several locations to achieve global efficiency, there is an increased opportunity for specialization.

It seems to me that interdependence between economic units is set to increase, rather than contract, over the foreseeable future. Policy makers need to take a pragmatic view of this situation, seeking not to prevent or deny the powerful forces of change, but to embrace them, and to seek to respond proactively to these developments. But because systems of innovation are bound by institutions that are complex organisms which evolve slowly, the 'fuzzy border problem' – for both firms and countries – suggests a looming crisis of defining national sovereignty and the efficacy of national regulation for technology and industrial policy, and also competition policy. This does not mean that we need to surrender industrial policies to the market, for markets are imperfect, but to accept the need for more effective supra-national policy making, and to regulate the rate of change to a level that allows institutions and systems to evolve successfully. The European Union has been learning to deal with these for a small group of countries, but the scope of such activity in the face of the growing interdependent nature of firms and countries means that we need to think larger, and into the future.

Notes

Introduction

1 I am grateful to Chris Freeman for highlighting this point in comments on an earlier draft.
2 See also Nelson (1987), Dosi (1982), Smith (2000).
3 Notably all kinds of knowledge, organizational and institutional capital.
4 See e.g. Dowrick and Gemmell (1991), Dowrick (1992), Verspagen (1993), Quah (1996).
5 However, the divergence trend of productivity growth is true only for the industrial sector, while in agriculture there has been catch-up by poorer economies (Dowrick 1992).

Chapter 1 Technology and the Causes of Globalization

1 The definition of the MNE (and indeed the firm) rests on the issue of control, rather than ownership. This is a very crucial point that is often ignored, because statistical offices tend to equate ownership with control. It is well known, however, that many MNEs use shell companies (located in third countries) as intermediaries in making investment. For instance, many Taiwanese firms have used Hong Kong as a base to invest in China, and indeed, Chinese firms have used affiliates in Hong Kong to re-invest funds into mainland China, in what is known as 'round-trip investment'. The Netherlands Antilles and the Virgin Islands are also often used as intermediary locations to reduce tax liabilities. What matters, then, is who is the *ultimate beneficiary owner*, and more importantly, to what extent do they actively exert control over the management of the affiliate? Without such direct influence, the investment may actually be a portfolio investment, even though it may technically be recorded as a FDI.

2 See e.g., the annual *World Investment Report* produced by United Nations Conference for Trade and Development (UNCTAD), Ietto-Gillies (2002), Hirst and Thompson (1996), Dunning (1993).
3 Strictly speaking, the two numbers are not comparable, because GDP is a flow figure. Nonetheless, it is generally accepted that FDI stock is a monotonic function of value added, so the change in this ratio gives us a general idea of how the significance of FDI activities has changed.
4 Authors such as Walter Rodney (1981) have made much of the role of European capital in systematically underdeveloping Africa. Much comment has likewise been made on US investments in South America, and the intervention of the US on behalf of American economic interests through direct and indirect military and political means (see Wade 2002). The dangers of an MNE-dominated world-view is also provided by Hymer (1970).
5 See Bruton (1998) for an excellent overview, which forms the basis of the discussion on import-substitution here.

Chapter 2 Cross-border Interdependence

1 For an excellent discussion on the differences between product and process innovations (which includes organizational innovation) from a systems of innovation perspective, see Edquist et al. (2001).
2 See Freeman and Lundvall (1988), van Hoesel and Narula (1999), Van den Bulcke and Verbeke (2001).
3 Some scholars assert that exports of British machine tools and steam engines were still nominally prohibited until much later on and special 'friends' had to be found to get round the regulations.
4 The concept of social capability was first introduced by Ohkawa and Rosovsky (1973).
5 The technological frontier is defined as the set of all production methods which at any given time are either the most economical or most productive in the world.

Chapter 3 Innovation and 'Inertia' in R&D Location

1 However, as Patel and Pavitt (2000) show, high levels of international production do not automatically translate to high levels of international R&D.
2 It should also be noted that firms in more mature sectors are more likely to be large, because concentration tends to be higher in such sectors than in more rapidly evolving sectors.
3 Of course, some innovation systems are more 'national' than others, and the term is indicative rather than definitive. For instance, smaller

countries' SI may have a larger dependence on non-national actors. Others have argued that innovation systems need to be viewed from an industry level (Nelson and Rosenberg 1993). It is true that certain sectors (such as biotechnology) are less national and more global, while others are regional.

4 Grabher does not use the term 'systemic lock-in' but refers to three simultaneous lock-ins: functional lock-in, cognitive lock-in and political lock-in.

5 Ehrnberg (1996) and McKelvey (1997) both argue that technological discontinuities do not always have a disruptive effect, depending on how the new technologies relate to an existing set of technologies.

6 See Dunning and Narula (1994), Belderbos (2001, 2003).

7 It is a paradox that both exit and voice are options that are more suited to larger firms. Smaller firms have tended to exploit their greater innovativeness to compensate for their resource limitations, particularly in new and innovative sectors. But their survival has always been dependent on their ability to cooperate with larger firms.

8 At the time of the sample selection, NOK 7.5 = US$1

9 Given the relatively small sample size, the very specific nature of their products and competences, and the small number of firms in each industry, it is difficult to give a detailed overview of the firms included in the sample, without breaching confidentiality.

10 See Hauknes (1999), Reve et al. (1992). Although both studies broadly agree, there is some disagreement as to which clusters are 'complete' and which are not. This is partly due to differences in definition and classification of the various clusters.

11 There have been several waves of nationalization of foreign-owned assets during the first half of the twentieth century. In addition, most German assets were acquired by Norway immediately after World War II. Most prominent was the acquisition of the majority ownership of Norsk Hydro by the Norwegian state (Stonehill 1965).

12 It is worth noting that the OECD estimates that barriers to trade and investment are still on average at least double those in most EU countries, and compared to countries such as Germany, UK and Italy more than three times as high (OECD 2000).

13 From the 1950s, the focus was on heavy industry, particularly electro-chemical industries, electro-metallurgical industries, shipbuilding and the like. The primary asset – and backbone – of the industrialization programme was the cheap and plentiful supply of electrical power. In the mid-1960s, considerable government investment was made in 'modernization', with a focus on infrastructural projects, particularly telecommunications, as well as defence. The core focus was in new technologies, focusing on electronics-related industries. In the words of one interviewee, 'up to 1980, Norway had the most heavily subsidized electronics industry in the world'. After the OPEC oil crisis, the emphasis was on developing the petroleum industry (Nygaard and Dahlstrom 1992).

14 In particular, four or five foreign-owned affiliates (which include ABB, Siemens, Ericsson and Alcatel) account for an estimated NOK 1 billion in R&D expenditure.

15 Data from Statistics Norway suggest that there are approximately 600 firms that undertake R&D in the business sector. This suggests that 400–500 firms account for approximately NOK 2 billion, which provides us with an average estimate of less than NOK 0.5 million per firm. These figures, although rough, allow us to estimate that approximately 80 per cent of firms in Norway which undertake innovation have fewer than one full-time equivalent R&D employee each.

16 Many of the firms interviewed were unwilling to provide data on level of sales or production for their foreign affiliates.

17 When asked to estimate their position vis-à-vis their competitors, many of the respondents said, 'we are number – in Europe', but these respondents were generally unable to indicate their global ranking.

18 Kvinge and Narula (2001) examine the growth of foreign companies in Norway, and note that there is a higher concentration of foreign firms in sectors that were formerly protected.

19 Although inward FDI into Norway has grown quite considerably over the last two decades, a considerable amount of FDI is still import-substituting in character, and tends to have low R&D intensity, except where access to Norwegian markets was provided with the condition that R&D be undertaken. A study by Benito (2000) noted that 42.7 per cent of the firms in his survey of 255 foreign subsidiaries regarded development as an activity undertaken in Norway, and 25.1 per cent regarded research as part of their profile. Given the high concentration of R&D expenditure by foreign firms, it would suggest that the R&D activities of a majority of foreign MNEs is on a rather small scale.

20 Although this is not always the case, some firms have also enjoyed hitherto protected domestic markets.

21 In 1997 the universities had an expenditure of NOK 4,845 million, the institute sector of NOK 4,826 million, and the enterprise sector of NOK 8,517 million.

22 The extent to which the state continues to intervene is highlighted by a recent development, where Norsk Hydro decided to sell its aquaculture business to a Dutch MNE, apparently despite the objections of the Norwegian government. Labour, the Centre Party and the Christian Democrats all expressed views to the effect that this sale could affect Hydro's chances of receiving new shares in the State Direct Financial Interest (SDFI) in the petroleum sector (*Dagsavisen*, 6 April 2000).

23 Some of this funding goes through the Norwegian Industrial and Regional Development Fund (SND). The SND is not primarily oriented towards supporting R&D, but is concerned with firm development, particularly in promoting their location in the (non-urban) regions of Norway.

24　Even though a large amount of funding from NFR is ostensibly earmarked for SMEs, the general consensus from interviews was that much of the funding for SMEs was directed towards projects which involved activities by SMEs in their role as suppliers to large firms. In addition, the definition of SMEs used in Norway – fewer than 200 employees - excluded a large number of internationally competitive companies from accessing funds. However, because of the way in which data is collected, evidence for this is primarily anecdotal (see Christiansen et al. 1996).

25　Weighted averages adjust for the effect of smaller firms. The un-weighted average per centages are 6.3 per cent and 3.7 per cent for Group A and Group B respectively.

26　SINTEF has organized eight research areas. As of 1999, these were as follows (approximate turnover given in brackets): Applied chemistry (NOK 148 million), applied mathematics (NOK 36 million), civil and environmental engineering (NOK 168 million), electronics and cyber-netics (NOK 89 million), industrial management (NOK 146 million), materials technology (163 million), telecom and informatics (NOK 105 million), medical (NOK 101 million). In addition, SINTEF also controls four stock research companies: SINTEF petroleum research (100 per cent owned), SINVENT (100 per cent owned), MARINTEK (jointly owned with Veritas, and the ship industry association), and SINTEF energy research (jointly owned with the energy research organization and the electrical industry association).

27　In theory, this frees the universities to focus on basic research. How-ever, the consistent underfunding of universities means that compe-tent researchers at universities also compete for research funding from NFR and others, and engage in more applied research than basic research. In addition, funding for open-ended (and more basic, non-project related) R&D by SINTEF has also been considerably cut over the years, and they also undertake less basic research.

28　Of course, smaller firms may cooperate within an industry association to achieve greater clout, as indeed has been the case with several sectors in Norway.

29　From a dynamic perspective, researchers tend to evolve with the chang-ing knowledge base in any given field, as new discoveries are made. It is also true that the very best researchers tend to 'wander' between new fields which may or may not be related to their core interests.

Chapter 4 Cross-border Strategic Technology Partnering

1　For a discussion of organizational knowledge, see Inkpen (1996, 1998).
2　The next chapter will differentiate even further within types of net-work, developing the concept of outsourcing.

Chapter 5 In-house R&D, Outsourcing or Alliances?

1 These estimates are based on the results from two different surveys, Culpan and Costelac (1993), and Gugler and Pasquier (1997).
2 This line of reasoning is well developed – see e.g., Nelson and Winter (1982), Cyert and March (1963), Mitchell and Singh (1992) among others.
3 However, there are often other factors why firms may decide to undertake alliances. For instance, there may be several other alliances between firms in other technologies, for which alliances maybe necessary.
4 Although there exists an imperfect substitute (Macintosh). For a firm that wishes to enter the Wintel market, however, there is no choice.
5 Take for instance the case where proximity in necessary, such as in a customer–supplier agreement that requires just-in-time delivery. Where cooperative agreements are undertaken in such a case, such decisions are mainly cost-based.
6 Cowan et al. (2000) argue that while codification is never complete, the extent to which knowledge is codified depends on the costs and benefits of doing so. Although new technologies have lowered the costs of codification, certain kinds of knowledge are too expensive to codify, simply because the information is useful to only a small number of users.
7 Numerous examples of technically sub-optimal innovations defining the technological trajectory exist (e.g., Betamax vs. VHS, Macintosh vs. PC). Perhaps the best-documented example is of the QWERTY keyboard (David 1985).
8 Jeremy Webb, 'Crashing the Barriers', *New Scientist*, 7 November 1998, 42–7.
9 Microsoft is promoting its Windows CE as the standard, for both HPCs and PDAs (personal digital assistants), but unlike Psion does not manufacture its own hardware. It has established alliances with AT&T, Philips, Sharp, Hewlett Packard, among others. A rival operating system is offered by 3Com, which works only with PDAs, and which they have preferred to keep proprietary.
10 Where the innovator attempts to get the product to market before competitors, with enough lead time, such that by the time they imitate, the first innovator has progressed to a newer and better product.
11 *New York Times*, 19 January 1999 'Philips and Sony Set a Venture with Sun Microsystems'.

Chapter 6 STP and Catch-up in Developing Countries

1 Patent protection is a highly imperfect tool to protect an inventor from competition, especially in industries where technological change is

rapid and competition high. So, an innovating firm's only way of maintaining its competitive advantage may be by being 'first', and remaining in the lead in subsequent rounds of innovation (Levin et al. 1987).

2 Country-specific characteristics are a function of exogenous supply and demand conditions, such as country size and natural resource availability. For instance, Chinese firms, by virtue of their home country market size, are a much more desirable partner for industries where economies of scale are more important, than, say, in Taiwan. Furthermore, sectors which rely on natural resource-based inputs, such as, say, petroleum in the case of either Indonesia or Venezuela, are more likely to be industries in countries where domestic firms have a competitive advantage, or would like to acquire one.

Chapter 7 Technology, Globalization and Policy Issues

1 See Narula (2002a) for a discussion of the limitations of the SME in R&D collaboration.
2 See Krugman (1994) for such a critique.
3 See David et al. (2000) and Klette et al. (2000).
4 See e.g., Nadvi and Schmitz (1994), Nadvi (1996).
5 See also Mytelka (2000).
6 Kogut (2000) argues that the US represents an example of a open, global system (rather than a national one) which overcomes the weaknesses in its national system by utilizing foreign skilled workers, at the same time acting as supplier of innovation to the rest of the world.

References

Abernathy, W. and Utterback, J. (1978) 'Patterns of Industrial Innovation', *Technology Review*, 80, 97–107.

Abramovitz, M. (1986) 'Catching up, Forging Ahead, and Falling Behind', *Journal of Economic History*, June, 46 (2), 385–406.

Abramovitz, M. (1995) 'The Elements of Social Capability', in Perkins, D. and Koo, B. (eds), *Social Capability and Long-term Growth*, Basingstoke: Macmillan.

Acharya, R. (1996) *The Biotechnology Revolution*, Aldershot: Edward Elgar.

Agosin, M. and Mayer, R. (2000) *Foreign Investment in Developing Countries: Does it Crowd in Domestic Investment?* UNCTAD Discussion Papers, 146.

Alam, M. and Naseer, A. (1992) 'Convergence and Polarisation: Testing for an Inverted-U Relation between Growth Rates and GDP per Capita', *Applied Economics*, 24, 363–6.

Amsden, A. (1989) *Asia's Next Giant*, New York: Oxford University Press.

Antonelli, C. and Calderini, M. (1999) 'The Dynamics of Localised Technological Change', in Gambardella, A. and Malerba, F. (eds), *The Organisation of Economic Innovation in Europe*, Cambridge: Cambridge University Press.

Archibugi, D. and Iammarino, S. (1999) 'The Policy Implications of the Globalisation of Innovation', *Research Policy*, 28, 317–36.

Archibugi, D. and Iammarino, S. (2000) 'Innovation and Globalisation: Evidence and Implications', in Chesnais, F. Ietto-Gilles, G. and Simonetti, R. (eds), *European Integration and Global Technology Strategies*, London: Routledge, 95–120.

Archibugi, D. and Lundvall, B.-Å. (eds) (2001) *The Globalizing Learning Economy*, Oxford: Oxford University Press.

Archibugi, D. and Michie, J. (1994) 'The Globalisation of Technology: A New Taxonomy', *Cambridge Journal of Economics*, 19, 121–40.

Archibugi, D. and Michie, J. (1995) 'The globalization of technology: a new taxonomy', *Cambridge Journal of Economics*, 19, 121–40.

Archibugi, D. and Michie, J. (eds) (1998) *Technology, Globalisation and Economic Performance*, Cambridge: Cambridge University Press.

Archibugi, D. and Pianta, M. (1992) *The Technological Specialization of Advanced Countries*, Dordrecht: Kluwer Academic Publishers.

Archibugi, D. and Pietrobelli, C. (2002) *The Globalisation of Technology and its Implications for Developing Countries: Windows of Opportunity or Further Burden?*, mimeo, Rome: CNR.

Archibugi, D., Howells, J. and Michie, J. (eds) (1999) *Innovation Policy in a Global Economy*, Cambridge: Cambridge University Press.

Arora, A. and Gambardella, A. (1990) 'Complementarity and External Linkages: The Strategies of the Large Firms in Biotechnology', *Journal of Industrial Economics*, 37, 361–79.

Arora A. and Gambardella, A. (1994) 'The Changing Technology of Technological Change: General and Abstract Knowledge and the Division of Labor', *Research Policy*, 523–32.

Arrow, K. (1962a) 'The Economic Implications of Learning by Doing', *Review of Economic Studies*, 29 (80), 155–73.

Arrow, K. (1962b) 'Economic Welfare and the Allocation of Resources for Invention', in *The Rate and Direction of Inventive Activity*, National Bureau for Economic Research, Princeton: Princeton University Press, 609–25.

Arundel, A. and Geuna, A. (2001) *Does Proximity Matter for Knowledge Transfer from Public Institutes and Universities to Firms?* SPRU Electronic Working Paper Series, 73.

Arundel, A. and Kabla, I. (1998) 'What Percentage of Innovations are Patented? Empirical Estimates for European Firms', *Research Policy*, 27, 127–41.

Asheim, B. and Isaksen, A. (1997) 'Location, Agglomeration and Innovation: Towards Regional Innovation Systems in Norway', *European Planning Studies*, 5, 299–330.

Asheim, B. and Isaksen, A. (2002) 'Regional Innovation Systems: The Integration of Local "Sticky" and Global "Ubiquitous" Knowledge', *Journal of Technology Transfer*, 27, 77–86.

Bairoch, P. and Kozul-Wright, R. (1998) 'Globalization Myths: Some Historical Reflections on Integration, Industrialization and Growth in the World Economy', in Kozul-Wright, R. and Rowthorn, R. (eds), *Transnational Corporations and the Global Economy*, Basingstoke: Macmillan, 37–68.

Baldwin, R. (1997) 'The Causes of Regionalism', *World Economy*, 20 (7), 865–88.

Barclay, L. (2000) *Foreign Direct Investment in Emerging Economies: Corporate Strategy and Investment Behaviour in the Caribbean*, New York and London: Routledge.

Bartholomew, S. (1997) 'National Systems of Biotechnology Innovation: Complex Interdependence in the Global System', *Journal of International Business Studies*, 28, 241–66.

Barzel, Y. (1968) 'Optimal Timing of Innovations', *Review of Economics and Statistics*, 50, 348–55.

Belderbos, R. (2001) 'Overseas Innovations by Japanese Firms: An Analysis of Patent and Subsidiary Data', *Research Policy*, 30, 313–32.

Belderbos, R. (2003) 'Entry Mode, Organisational Learning, and R&D in Foreign Affiliates: Evidence from Japanese Firms', *Strategic Management Journal*, 24.

Bellak, C. and Cantwell, J. (1997) 'Small Latecomer Countries in a Globalising Environment: Constraints and Opportunities for Catching-up', *Development and International Cooperation*, 13, 139–79.

Benito, G. (1997) 'Divestment of Foreign Production Operations', *Applied Economics*, 29 (10), 1365–77.

Benito, G. (2000) 'Industrial Clusters and Foreign Companies' Centres of Excellence in Norway', in Holm, U. and Pedersen, T. (eds), *The Emergence and Impact of MNC Centres of Excellence: A Subsidiary Perspective*, Basingstoke: Macmillan, 97–112.

Benito, G., Grogaard, B. and Narula, R. (forthcoming) 'The Effect of Regional Integration on Subsidiary Roles: The Heterogeneity of Subsidiaries in the Nordic Countries', *Journal of International Business Studies*.

Bitlingmayer, G. (1988) 'Property Rights, Progress, and the Aircraft Patent Agreement', *Journal of Law and Economics*, 31, 227–48.

Blanc, H. and Sierra C. (1999) 'The Internationalisation of R&D by Multinationals: A Trade-Off between External and Internal Proximity', *Cambridge Journal of Economics*, 23, 187–206.

Borensztein, E., De Gregorio, J. and Lee, J. (1998) 'How does FDI Affect Economic Growth?', *Journal of International Economics*, 45, 115–35.

Borrus, M., Ernst, D. and Haggard, S. (eds) (2000) *Rivalry or Riches: International Production Networks in Asia*, London: Routledge.

Boyer, R. and Drache, D. (1996) 'Introduction', in Boyer, R. and Brache, D. (eds), *States against Markets: The Limits of Globalisation*, London: Routledge, 1–30.

Braczyk, H.-J, Cooke, P. and Heidenrich, M. (1998) *Regional Innovation Systems*, London: UCL Press.

Braudel, F. (1992) *The Wheels of Commerce: Civilisation and Capitalism 15th–18th century*, Berkeley: University of California Press.

Brewer, T. and Young, S. (1998) *The Multilateral Investment System and Multinational Enterprises*, Oxford: Oxford University Press.

Bruland, K. (1989) *British Technology and European Industrialization: The Norwegian Textile Industry in the Mid-nineteenth Century*, Cambridge: Cambridge University Press.

Bruland, K. (ed.) (1991) *Technology Transfer in Scandinavian Industrialisation*, New York and Oxford: Berg Publishers.

Brusoni, S., Prencipe, A. and Pavitt, K. (2001) 'Knowledge Specialization and the Boundaries of the Firm: Why do Firms Know More than they do? ', *Administrative Science Quarterly*, 46, 597–621.

Bruton, H. (1998) 'A Reconsideration of Import Substitution', *Journal of Economic Literature*, 36, 903–36.

Buckley, P. and Casson, M. (1976) *The Future of the Multinational Enterprise*, New York: Holmes & Meier.

Buckley, P. and Casson, M. (1998) 'Models of the Multinational Enterprise', *Journal of International Business Studies*, 29 (1), 21–44.

Buckley, P. and Chapman, M. (1998) 'The Management of Cooperative Strategies in R&D and Innovation Programmes', *International Journal of the Economics of Business*, 5, 369–81.

Cantwell, J. (1987) 'The Reorganization of European Industries after Integration: Selected Evidence on the Role of Multinational Enterprise Activities', *Journal of Common Market Studies*, 26 (2), 127–51.

Cantwell, J. (1989) *Technological Innovation and Multinational Corporations*, Oxford: Basil Blackwell.

Cantwell, J. (1991) 'The Theory of Technological Competence and its Application to International Production', in McFetridge, D. (ed.), *Foreign Investment, Technology and Economic Growth*, Calgary: University of Calgary Press.

Cantwell, J. (1995) 'The Globalization of Technology: What Remains of the Product Cycle Model?' *Cambridge Journal of Economics*, 19, 155–74.

Cantwell J. and Iammarino, S. (2003) *Multinational Corporations and European Regional Systems of Innovation*, London: Routledge.

Cantwell, J. and Janne, O. (1999) 'Technological Globalisation and Innovative Centres: The Role of Corporate Technological Leadership and Locational Hierarchy', *Research Policy*, 29, 119–44.

Cantwell, J. and Janne, O. (2000) 'The Role of Multinational Corporations and National States in the Globalization of Innovatory Capacity: The European Perspective', *Technology Analysis and Strategic Management*, 12 (2), 243–62.

Cantwell, J. and Sanna-Randaccio, F. (1990) 'The Growth of Multinationals and the Catching Up Effect', *Economic Notes*, 19 (July), 1–23.

Cantwell, J. and Santangelo, G. (1999) 'The Frontier of International Technology Networks: Sourcing Abroad the Most Highly Tacit Capabilities', *Information Economics and Policy*, 11 (1), 101–23.

Carlsson, B. and Jacobsson, S. (1997) 'Diversity Creation and Technological Systems: A Technology Policy Perspective', in Edquist, C. (ed.), *Systems of Innovation: Technologies, Institutions and Organisations*, London and Washington: Pinter.

Carton, A. (1987) 'EUREKA: A Western European Response to the Technological Challenge Posed by the SDI Research Programme', in Brauch, H. (ed.), *Star Wars and European Defense*, New York: St Martin's Press, 311–28.

Castellani, D. (2001) 'Export Behaviour, Foreign Direct Investments and Firms' Productivity', Ph.D. thesis, University of Ancona.

Chandler, A. (1990) *Scale and Scope: The Dynamics of Industrial Change*, Cambridge, Mass.: Belknap.

Chenery, H. (1979) *Structural Change and Development Policy*, New York: Oxford University Press.

Chenery, H. and Taylor, L. (1968) 'Development Patterns: Among Countries and Over Time', *Review of Economics and Statistics*, 50 (4).

Chenery, H., Robinson, S. and Syrquin, M. (1986) *Industrialization and Growth*, Washington: World Bank.

Christiansen, M., Møller, J. and Smith, K. (1996) *Innovation Policies for SMEs in Norway*, Oslo, STEP report R-11.

Coase, R. (1937) 'The Nature of the Firm', *Economica*, 4 (4).

Cohen, W. and Levinthal, D. (1989) 'Innovation and Learning: The Two Faces of R&D', *Economic Journal*, 99, 569–96.

Cohen, W. and Levinthal, D. (1990) 'Absorptive Capacity: A New Perspective on Learning and Innovation', *Administrative Science Quarterly*, 35, 128–52.

Contractor, F. and Lorange, P. (1988) *Co-operative Strategies in International Business*, Lexington, Mass.: D. C. Heath.

Cooke, P. (1998) 'Introduction: Origins of the Concept', in Braczyk, H., Cooke, P. and Heidenrich, M. (eds), *Regional Innovation Systems*, London: UCL Press, 2–25.

Cowan, R. and Gunby, P. (1996) 'Sprayed to Death: Path Dependence, Lock-in and Pest Control Strategies', *Economic Journal*, 106, 521–42.

Cowan, R., David, P. and Foray, D. (2000) 'The Explicit Economics of Knowledge Codification and Tacitness', *Industrial and Corporate Change*, 9, 211–53.

Criscuolo, P. and Narula, R. (2001) 'Asset Seeking R&D Investment as a Channel for Reverse Technology Transfer', Paper presented at the second AITEG workshop, Instituto Complutense de Estudios Internacionales, Madrid, Spain, 26–7 June.

Criscuolo, P. and Narula, R. (2002) *A Novel Approach to National Technological Accumulation and Absorptive Capacity: Aggregating Cohen and Levinthal*, MERIT Research Memorandum 2002–16.

Criscuolo, P., Narula, R. and Verspagen, B. (2002), *The Relative Importance of Home and Host Innovation Systems in the Internationalisation of MNE R&D: a patent citation analysis*, MERIT Research Memorandum 2002–26.

Croisier, B. (1998) 'The Governance of External Research: Empirical Test of Some Transaction-Cost Related Factors', *R&D Management*, 28, 289–98.

Culpan, R. and Costelac, E. (1993) 'Cross National Corporate Partnerships: Trends in Alliance Formation', in Culpan, R. (ed.), *Multinational Strategic Alliances*, New York: International Business Press, 103–22.

Cyert, R. and March, J. (1963) *A Behavioral Theory of the Firm*, Englewood Cliffs: Prentice-Hall.

Dahlman, C. and Nelson, R. (1995) 'Social Absorption Capability, National Innovation Systems and Economic Development', in Perkins, D. and Koo, B. (eds), *Social Capability and Long-term Growth*, Basingstoke: Macmillan.

Das, T. and Teng, B.-S. (1996) 'Risk Types and Inter-Firm Alliance Structures', *Journal of Management Studies*, 33, 827–43.

Dasgupta, P. and Stiglitz, J. (1980) 'Uncertainty, Industrial Structure and the Speed of R&D', *Bell Journal of Economics*, 11, 1–28.

D'Aspremont, C. and Jacquemin A. (1988) 'Cooperative and Non-cooperative R&D in Duopoly with Spillovers', *American Economic Review*, 11, 33–7.

David, P. (1985) 'Clio and the Economics of QWERTY' *American Economic Review*, 75 (2), 332–7.

David, P. (1991) *The Dynamo and the Computer: An Historical Perspective on the Modern Productivity Paradox*, Paris: OECD.

David, P., Hall, B. and Toole, A. (2000) 'Is Public R&D a Complement or Substitute for Private R&D?', *Research Policy*, 29, 497–529.

Dicken, P. (1998) *Global Shift: Transforming the World Economy*, London: Paul Chapman.

Dodgson, M. (1993) 'Organizational Learning: A Review of Some Literatures', *Organization Studies*, 14, 375–94.

Dosi, G. (1982) 'Technological Paradigms and Technological Trajectories: A Suggested Interpretation of the Determinants and Directions of Technical Change', *Research Policy*, 11, 147–62.

Dosi, G., Pavitt, K. and Soete, L. (1990) *The Economics of Technical Change and International* Trade, New York: New York University Press.

Dowrick, S. (1992) 'Technological Catch Up and Diverging Incomes: Patterns of Economic Growth 1960–88', *The Economic Journal*, 102, 600–10.

Dowrick, S. and Gemmell, N. (1991) 'Industrialisation, Catching Up and Economic Growth: A Comparative Study across the World's Capitalist Economies', *Economic Journal*, 101, 263–75.

Drucker, P. (1997) 'The Global Economy and the Nation State', *Foreign Affairs*, 76, 159–71.

Dunning, J. (1992) 'The Competitive Advantages of Countries and the Activities of Transnational Corporations', *Transnational Corporations*, 1 (1).

Dunning, J. (1993) *Multinational Enterprises and the Global Economy*, Wokingham: Addison-Wesley.

Dunning, J. (1995) 'Reappraising the Eclectic Paradigm in the Age of Alliance Capitalism', *Journal of International Business Studies*, 26, 461–91.

Dunning, J. (1997) *Alliance Capitalism and Global Business*, London: Routledge.

Dunning, J. and Narula, R. (1994) 'Transpacific Direct Investment and the Investment Development Path: The Record Assessed', *Essays in International Business*, 10 (May), 1–64.

Dunning, J. and Narula, R. (1995) 'The R&D Activities of Foreign Firms in the United States', *International Studies of Management & Organization*, 25 (1–2), 39–73.

Edquist, C. (1997) *Systems of Innovation: Technologies, Institutions and Organisations*, London and Washington: Pinter.

Edquist, C. and Johnson, B. (1997) 'Institutions and Organisations in Systems of Innovation', in Edquist (1997).

Edquist, C., Hommen, L. and McKelvey, M. (2001) *Innovations and Employment: Process versus Product Innovation*, Cheltenham: Edward Elgar.

Ehrnberg, E. (1996) *Technological Discontinuities and Industrial Dynamics*, Göteborg: Chalmers University of Technology.

Ehrnberg, E. and Jacobsson, S. (1997) 'Technological Discontinuities and Incumbents' Performance: An Analytical Framework', in Edquist, (1997).

Ernst, D. (1997) 'Partners in a China Circle? The Asian Production Networks of Japanese Firms', in Naughton, B. (ed.), *The China Circle*, Washington: Brookings Institution Press.

Etzkowitz, H. and Leydesdorff, L. (2000) 'The Dynamics of Innovation: From National Systems and "Mode 2" to a Triple Helix of University–Industry–Government Relations', *Research Policy*, 29 (2), 109–23.

Fagerberg, J. (1994) 'Technology and International Differences in Growth Rates', *Journal of Economic Literature*, 32, 1147–75.

Fai, F. (2002) *Corporate Technological Competence and the Evolution of Technological Diversification*, Cheltenham: Edward Elgar.

Fai, F. and Cantwell, J. (1999) The Changing Nature of Corporate Technological Diversification and the Importance of Organisational Capability, in Dow, S. and Earl, P. (eds), *Economic Knowledge and Economic Coordination: Essays in Honour of Brian Loasby*, Cheltenham: Edward Elgar.

Fai, F. and von Tunzelmann, N. (2001) 'Industry-specific Competencies and Converging Technological Systems: Evidence from Patents', *Structural Change and Economic Dynamics*, vol 12, 141–70.

Farrell, J. (1987) 'Information and the Coase Theorem', *Economic Perspectives*, 1, 113–29.

Florida, R. (1997) 'The Globalisation of R&D: Results of a Survey of Foreign-Affiliated R&D Laboratories in the US', *Research Policy*, 26, 85–103.

Freeman, C. (1987) *Technology Policy and Economic Performance*, London: Pinter.

Freeman, C. (1992) 'Formal Scientific and Technical Institutions in the National System of Innovation', in Lundvall, B. (ed.), *National Systems of Innovation: Towards a Theory of Innovation and Interactive Learning*, London: Pinter.

Freeman, C. and Hagedoorn, J. (1994) 'Catching Up or Falling Behind: Patterns in International Inter-Firm Technology Partnering', *World Development*, 22, 771–80.

Freeman, C. and Lundvall, B. (1988) *Small Countries Facing the Technological Revolution*, London: Pinter.

Freeman, C. and Soete, L. (1997) *The Economics of Industrial Innovation*, 3rd edn, London: Pinter.

Frost, T. (1998) 'The Geographic Sources of Innovation in the Multinational Enterprise: U.S Subsidiaries and Host Country Spillovers, 1980–1990', Ph.D. thesis, Massachusetts Institute of Technology.

Gambardella, A. and Torrisi, S. (1998) 'Does Technological Convergence imply Convergence in Markets? Evidence from the Electronics Industry', *Research Policy*, 27, 445–63.

Gerlach, M. (1992) *Alliance Capitalism*, Oxford: Oxford University Press.

Gertler, M., Wolfe, D. and Garkut, D. (2000) 'No Place like Home? The Embeddedness of Innovation in a Regional Economy', *Review of International Political Economy*, 7, 688–718.

Geuna, A. (1996) 'The Participation of Higher Education Institutions in European Union Framework Programmes', *Science and Public Policy*, 23, 287–96.

Giesecke, S. (2000) 'The Contrasting Roles of Government in the Development of Biotechnology Industry in the US and Germany', *Research Policy*, 29, 205–23.

Glaister, K. and Buckley, P. (1996) 'Strategic Motives for International Alliance Formation', *Journal of Management Studies*, 33, 301–32.

Goey, de F. (1999) 'Dutch Overseas Investments in the Very Long Run (c.1600–1900)' in Hoesel, R. and Narula, R. (eds), *Multinationals from the Netherlands*, London: Routledge, 32–60.

Gomulka, S. (1990) *The Theory of Technological Change and Economic Growth*, London: Routledge.

Grabher, G. (1993) 'The Weakness of Strong Ties: The Lock-in of Regional Development in the Ruhr Area', in Grabher, G. (ed.), *The Embedded Firm*, London: Routledge.

Granstrand, O. (1998) 'Towards a Theory of the Technology Based Firm', *Research Policy*, 27, 465–90.

Granstrand, O. and Oskarsson, C. (1994) 'Technology Diversification in "Multi-Tech" Corporations', *IEEE Transactions on Engineering Management*, 41, 355–64.

Granstrand, O. and Sjolander, S. (1990) 'Managing Innovation in Multi-technology Corporations', *Research Policy*, 19, 35–60.

Granstrand, O., Håkanson, L. and Sjolander, S. (eds) (1992) *Technology Management and International Business, Internationalisation of R&D and Technology*, Chichester: John Wiley and Sons.

Granstrand, O., Patel, P. and Pavitt, K. (1997) 'Multi-Technology Corporations: Why They Have "Distributed" Rather than "Distinctive Core" Competencies', *California Management Review*, 39, 8–25.

Gray, H. (1996) *Globalization and Economic Development*, mimeo, Rutgers University, Newark.

Gray, J. (1998) *False Dawn: The Delusions of Global Capitalism*, London: Granta Books.

Gugler, P. and Pasquier, M. (1997) 'Strategic Alliances of Swiss firms: Cooperative corporate strategies in the global race', *Die Unternehmung*, 2 (97), 133–44.

Hagedoorn, J. (1993) 'Understanding the Rationale of Strategic Technology Partnering: Inter-Organizational Modes of Cooperation and Sectoral Differences', *Strategic Management Journal*, 14, 371–85.

Hagedoorn, J. (1996) 'Trends and Patterns in Strategic Technology Partnering since the Early Seventies', *Review of Industrial Organization*, 11, 601–16.

Hagedoorn, J. (2002) 'Inter-Firm R&D Partnerships: An Overview of Patterns and Trends since 1960', *Research Policy*, 31, 477–92.

Hagedoorn, J. and Duysters, G. (2002) 'Learning in dynamic into firm networks: The Efficacy of multiple Contracts', *Organisation Studies*, 23, 525–666.

Hagedoorn, J. and Narula R. (1996) 'Choosing Modes of Governance for Strategic Technology Partnering: International and Sectoral Differences', *Journal of International Business Studies*, 27, 265–84.

Hagedoorn, J. and Narula, R. (2001) 'Evolutionary Understanding of Corporate Foreign Investment Behaviour: US Foreign Direct Investment in Europe', in Narula, R. (ed.), *Trades and Investment in a Globalizing World*, New York: Pergamon.

Hagedoorn, J. and Sadowski, B. (1996) 'General Trends in International Technology Partnering: The Prospects for Transition Economies', in Sedaitis, J. (ed.), *Commercializing High Technologies*, International Series on Technical Innovation and Entrepreneurship, New York: Rowman & Littlefield.

Hagedoorn, J. and Sadowski, B. (1999) 'Exploring the Potential Transition from Strategic Technology Partnering to Mergers and Acquisitions', *Journal of Management Studies*, 36, 87–107.

Hagedoorn, J. and Schakenraad, J. (1993) 'A Comparison of Private and Subsidised R&D Partnerships in the European Information Technology Industry', *Journal of Common Market Studies*, 31, 374–90.

Hagedoorn, J. and Schakenraad, J. (1994) 'The Effect of Strategic Technology Alliances on Company Performance', *Strategic Management Journal*, 5, 291–311.

Håkanson, L. and Nobel, R. (2000) 'Technology Characteristics and Reverse Technology Transfer', *Management International Review*, 40, 29–48.

Håkanson, L. and Nobel, R. (2001) 'Organisational Characteristics and Reverse Technology Transfer', *Management International Review*, 41, 395–420.

Hall, P. (1986) 'The Theory and Practice of Innovatory Policy: An Overview', in Hall, P. (ed.), *Technology, Innovation and Economic Policy*, New York: St Martin's Press.

Hannan, M. and Freeman, J. (1984) 'Structural Inertia and Organisational Change', *American Sociological Review*, 49, 149–64.

Harding, R. (2001) 'Competition and Collaboration in German Technology Transfer', *Industrial and Corporate Change*, 10, 389–417.

Harrigan, K. (1988) 'Strategic Alliances and Partner Asymmetries', in Contractor, F. and Lorange, P. (eds) *Cooperative Strategies in International Business*, Lexington: Lexington Books.

Harris, J. (1998) *Industrial Espionage and Technology Transfer. Britain and France in the Eighteenth Century*, Aldershot: Ashgate.

Hauknes, J. (1996) *R&D in Norway 1970–1993: An Overview of the Grand Sectors*, Step Report W2–96.

Hauknes, J. (1999) '*Norwegian Input–Output Clusters and Innovation Patterns*' in OECD, *Boosting Innovation: The Cluster Approach*, Paris: OECD, 61–90.

Havas, A. (1996) *Evolution and Structure of Strategic Technology Alliances in Hungary*, mimeo, University of Maastricht.

Held, D., McGrew, A., Goldblatt, D. and Perraton, J. (1999) *Global Transformations: Politics, Economics and Culture*, Cambridge: Polity.

Helper, S. (1993) 'An Exit-Voice Analysis of Supplier Relations: The Case of the US Automobile Industry', in Grabher, G. (ed.), *The Embedded Firm*, London: Routledge.

Henderson, R. and Clark, K. (1990) 'Architectural Innovation: The Reconfiguration of Existing Product Technologies and the Failure of Established Firms', *Administrative Sciences Quarterly*, 35, 9–30.

Hennart, J. (1993) 'Explaining the Swollen Middle; Why Most Transactions are a Mix of Market and Hierarchy', *Organization Science*, 4, 529–47.

Hikino, T. and Amsden, A. (1994) 'Staying Behind, Stumbling Back, Sneaking Up, Soaring Ahead: Late Industrialization in Historical Perspective', in Baumol, W., Nelson, R. and Wolff, E. (eds), *Convergence of Productivity: Cross Country Studies and Historical Evidence*, New York: Oxford University Press.

Hill, C., Hwang, P. and Kim, W. (1990) 'An Eclectic Theory of the Choice of International Entry Mode', *Strategic Management Journal*, 11, 117–28.

Hirschman, A. (1970) *Exit, Voice and Loyalty*, Cambridge, Mass.: Harvard University Press.

Hirst, P. and Thompson, G. (1996) *Globalization in Question*, Cambridge: Polity.

Hobday, M. (1995) *Innovation in East Asia: The Challenge to Japan*, Aldershot: Edward Elgar.

Hodne, F. (1993) 'The Multinational Corporations of Norway', in Jones, G. and Schröter, G. (eds), *The Rise of Multinationals in Continental Europe*, Aldershot: Edward Elgar, 128–51.

Hoesel, R. van (1996) 'Taiwan: Foreign Direct Investment and the Transformation of the Economy', in Dunning, J. and Narula, R. (eds), *Foreign Direct Investment and Governments: Catalysts for Economic Restructuring*, London: Routledge, 280–315.

Hoesel, R. van (1999) *New Multinational Enterprises from Korea and Taiwan*, London: Routledge.

Hoesel, R. van and Narula, R. (1999) 'Outward Investment from the Netherlands: Introduction and Overview', in Hoesel and Narula, R (1999) 1–31.

Hoesel, R. van and Narula, R. (eds) (1999) *Multinationals from the Netherlands*, London: Routledge.

Hogenbirk, A. (2002) *Determinants of Inward Foreign Direct Investment: The Case of the Netherlands*, Maastricht: Datawyse.

Hood, N. and Young, S. (1979) *The Economics of the Multinational Enterprise*, London: Longman.

Howells, J. (1999) 'Regional Systems of Innovation?' in Archibugi et al. (1999), 67–93.

Hughes, K. (1992) 'Trade Performance of the Main EC Economies Relative to the US and Japan in 1992–Sensitive Sectors', *Journal of Common Market Studies*, 30, 437–54.

Hymer, S. (1970) 'The Efficiency (Contradictions) of Multinational Enterprises', *American Economic Review*, 60, 441–8.

IDB (2000) *Periodic Note on Integration and Trade in the Americas*, mimeo, Washington: Inter-American Development Bank.

Ietto-Gillies, G. (2002) *Transnational Corporations: Fragmentation amidst Integration*, London: Routledge.

Inkpen, A. (1996) 'Creating Knowledge through Collaboration', *California Management Review*, 39, 123–40.

Inkpen, A. (1998) 'Learning and Knowledge Acquisition through International Strategic Alliances', *Academy of Management Executive*, 12 (4) 69–80.

Inkpen, A. and Beamish, P. (1997) 'Knowledge, Bargaining Power, and the Instability of International Joint Ventures', *Academy of Management Review*, 22, 177–202.

Ito, T. and Krueger, A. (2000) 'Introduction', in Ito, T. and Krueger A. (eds), *The Role of Foreign Direct Investment in East Asian Economic Development*, Chicago and London: University of Chicago Press.

Jaffe, A. and Trajtenberg, M. (1996) *Flows of Knowledge from Universities and Federal Labs: Modeling the Flow of Patent Citations over Time and across Institutional and Geographical Boundaries*, NBER Working Paper 5712, Cambridge Massa.

Jaffe, A., Trajtenberg, M. and Henderson, R. (1993) 'Geographic Localization of Knowledge Spillovers as Evidenced by Patent Citations', *Quarterly Journal of Economics*, 108, 577–98.

James, J. (2001) 'Information Technology, Cumulative Causation and Patterns of Globalisation in the Third World', *Review of International Political Economy*, 8, 147–62.

Johanson, J. and Vahlne, J. (1977) 'The Internationalization Process of the Firm: A Model of Knowledge Development and Increasing Foreign Market Commitments', *Journal of International Business Studies*, 8 (1), 23–32.

Johnson, B. (1992) 'Institutional Learning', in Lundvall, B. (ed.), *National Systems of Innovation: Towards a Theory of Innovation and Interactive Learning*, London: Pinter.

Jones, G. (1996) *The Evolution of International Business*, London: Routledge.

Katrak, H. (2002) 'Does Economic Liberalisation Endanger Indigenous Technological Developments? An Analysis of the Indian Experience', *Research Policy*, 31, 19–30.

Katz, M. (1986) 'An Analysis of Cooperative Research and Development', *Rand Journal of Economics*, 17 (4), 527–43.

Kay, N. (1991) 'Industrial Collaborative Activity and the Completion of the Internal Market', *Journal of Common Market Studies*, 29, 347–62.

Kay, N. (1997) *Pattern in Corporate Evolution*, Oxford: Oxford University Press.

Kim, L. (1995) 'Absorptive Capacity and Industrial Growth: A Conceptual Framework and Korea's Experience', in Perkins, D. H. and Koo, B. H. (eds), *Social Capability and Long-term Growth*, Basingstoke: Macmillan.

Klette, T., Møen, J. and Griliches, Z. (2000) 'Do Subsidies to Commercial R&D Reduce Market Failures? Micro-Economic Evaluation Studies', *Research Policy*, 29, 471–95.

Knickerbocker, F. (1973) *Oligopolistic Reaction and the Multinational Enterprise*, Cambridge, Mass.: Harvard University Press.

Kogut, B. (1988) 'Joint Ventures: Theoretical and Empirical Perspectives', *Strategic Management Journal*, 9, 319–32.

Kogut, B. (2000) *The Transatlantic Exchange of Ideas and Practices: National Institutions and Diffusion*, Notes de l'IFRI, 26.

Kogut, B. and Zander, U. (1993) 'Knowledge of the Firm and the Evolutionary Theory of the Multinational Enterprise', *Journal of International Business Studies*, 24, 625–46.

Kondratieff, N. (1925) 'The Long Wave in Economic Life', *Review of Economic Statistics*, 17, 105–15.

Krugman, P. (1994) 'Competitiveness: A Dangerous Obsession', *Foreign Affairs*, 73, 28–44.

Kuemmerle, W. (1996) '*Home Base and Foreign Direct Investment in R&D*', Ph.D. dissertation, Harvard Business School.

Kumar, N. (2001) 'Determinants of Location of Overseas R&D Activity of Multinational Enterprises: The Case of US and Japanese Corporations', *Research Policy*, 30, 159–74.

Kuznets, S. (1962) 'Inventive Activity; Problems of Definition and Management', in Nelson, R. (ed.), T*he Rate and Direction of Inventive Activity*, Princeton: Princeton University Press.

Kvinge, T. and Narula, R. (2001) *FDI in Norway's Manufacturing Sector*, TIK Working Paper 9.

Laestadius, S. (2000) *Hidden or Not So Important? Reflections on Innovative Activity in the 90 per cent of Industrial Sectors which are Labelled Low-Tech*, mimeo., Stockholm: KTN.

Lall, S. (1979) 'The International Allocation of Research Activity by U.S. Multinationals', *Oxford Bulletin of Economics and Statistics*, 41, 313–31.

Lall, S. (1992) 'Technological Capabilities and Industrialization', *World Development*, 2 (2), 165–86.

Lall, S. (1997) 'East Asia', in Dunning, J. (ed.), *Governments, Globalization and International Business*, Oxford: Oxford University Press, 407–30.

Lall, S. (2000) 'Foreign Direct Investment and Development: Policy and Research Issues in the Emerging Context', *QEH Working Paper Series*, 43.

Lam, A. (2000) 'Tacit Knowledge, Organizational Learning and Societal Institutions: An Integrated Framework', *Organisational Learning*, 21 (3), 487–513.

Le Bas, C. and C. Sierra (2002) 'Location versus Country Advantages' in R&D Activities: Some further results on multinationals' locational strategies', *Research Policy*, 31, 589–609.

Lee, K.-R. (2001) 'Technological Catching-Up through Overseas Direct Investment: Samsung's Camera Business', in Sachwald, F. (ed.) *Going Multinational. The Korean Experience of Foreign Direct Investment*, London: Routledge, 275–314.

Levin, R., Klevorick, A., Nelson, R. and Winter, S. (1987) 'Appropriating the Returns from Industrial Research and Development', *Brookings Papers on Economics Activity*, 3, 783–820.

Levy, J. and Samuels, R. (1991) 'Institutions and Innovation; Research and Collaboration as Technology Strategy in Japan', in Mytelka, L. (ed.) *Strategic Partnerships and the World Economy*, London: Pinter, 120–48.

List, F. (1885) *The National System of Political Economy* translated by Sampson S. Lloyd, downloaded from http://socserv2.socsci.mcmaster.ca/~econ/ugcm/3ll3/list/list1.

Lowe, J. and Taylor, P. (1998) 'R&D and Technology Purchase through License Agreements: Complementary Strategies and Complementary Assets', *R&D Management*, 28, 263–78.

Lundan, S. and Jones, G. (2001) 'The "Commonwealth Effect" and the Process of Internationalization', *World Economy*, 24 (1), 99–118.

Lundvall, B. (1988) 'Innovation as an Interactive Process: From User–Producer Interaction to the National System of Innovation', in Dosi et al. (eds), *Technical Change and Economic Theory*, London and New York: Pinter.

Lundvall, B. (ed.) (1992) *National Systems of Innovation: Towards a Theory of Innovation and Interactive Learning*, London: Pinter.

Lundvall, B. and Johnson B. (1994) 'The Learning Economy', *Journal of Industry Studies*, 1 (2), 23–42.

McKelvey, M. (1997) 'Using Evolutionary Theory to Define Systems of Innovation', in Edquist (1997).

McKelvey, M. (1998) 'Evolutionary Innovations: Learning, Entrepreneurship and the Dynamics of the Firm', *Journal of Evolutionary Economics*, 8, 157–75.

McKelvey, M. (2000) *Evolutionary Innovations: The Business of Biotechnology*, Oxford: Oxford University Press.

McKelvey, M. and Texier, F. (2000) 'Surviving Technological Discontinuities through Evolutionary Systems of Innovation: Ericsson and Mobile Communication', in Saviotti, P. and Nooteboom, B. (eds), *Technology and Knowledge: From the Firm to Innovation Systems*, Cheltenham: Edward Elgar.

Madhok, A. (1997) 'Cost, Value and Foreign Market Entry Mode: The Transaction and the Firm', *Strategic Management Journal*, 18, 39–61.

Madhok, A. and Phene, A. (2001) 'The Co-evolutional Advantage: Strategic Management Theory and the Eclectic Paradigm', *International Journal of the Economics of Business*, 8, 243–56.

Mansfield, E. (1984) 'R&D and Innovation: Some Empirical Findings' in Griliches, Z. (ed.), *R&D, Patents, and Productivity*, Chicago and London: University of Chicago Press and NBER.

March, J. (1991) 'Exploration and Exploitation in Organizational Learning', *Organizational Science*, 2, 71–87.

Maurseth, P. and Verspagen, B. (2001) *Knowledge Spillovers in Europe: A Patent Citations Analysis*, mimeo, Eindhoven University of Technology and Norwegian Institute of Foreign Affairs.

Mitchell, W. and Singh, K. (1992) ' "Incumbents' " Use of Pre-entry Alliances before Expansion into New Technical Subfields of an Industry', *Journal of Economic Behaviour and Organisation*, 18, 347–72.

Myrdal, G. (1957) *Economic Theory and Under-developed Regions*, London: Duckworth.

Mytelka, L. (1991) 'States, Strategic Alliances and International Oligopolies', in Mytelka, L. (ed.) *Strategic Partnerships and the World Economy*, London: Pinter, 182–210.

Mytelka, L. (1995) 'Dancing with Wolves: Global Oligopolies and Strategic Partnerships', in Hagedoorn, J. (ed.), *Technical Change and the World Economy*, Aldershot: Edward Elgar, 182–204.

Mytelka, L. (2000) 'Local Systems of Innovation in a Globalised World Economy', *Industry and Innovation*, 7, 15–32.

Mytelka, L. and Delapierre, M. (1987) 'The Alliance Strategies of European Firms in the Information Technology Industry and the Role of ESPRIT', *Journal of Common Market Studies*, 26, 231–53.

Nadvi, K. (1996) '*Small firm industrial districts in Pakistan*', D.Phil. thesis, University of Sussex.

Nadvi, K. and Schmitz, H. (1994) *Industrial clusters in less developed countries: Review of experiences and research agenda*, Institute of Development studies Discussion Paper 339, University of Sussex.

Nagarajan, A. and Mitchell, W. (1998) 'Evolutionary Diffusion: Internal and External Methods Used to Acquire Encompassing, Complementary, and Incremental Technological Changes in the Lithotripsy Industry', *Strategic Management Journal*, 19, 1063–77.

Nakamura, T. (1981) *The Post-war Japanese Economy*, Tokyo: University of Tokyo Press.

Narula, R. (1993) 'Technology, International Business and Porter's "Diamond": Synthesising a Dynamic Competitive Development Model', *Management International Review*, 33, 85–107.

Narula, R. (1996a) *Multinational Investment and Economic Structure*, London: Routledge.

Narula, R. (1996b) 'Forms of International Cooperation between Corporations', in Jepma, C. and Rhoen, A. (eds), *International Trade: A Business Perspective*, Harlow: Longman, 98–122.

Narula, R. (1999) 'Explaining Strategic R&D Alliances by European Firms', *Journal of Common Market Studies*, 37(4), 711–23.

Narula, R. (2001a) 'Strategic Partnering by EU firms: A Rejoinder', *Journal of Common Market Studies*, 39, 159–64.

Narula, R. (2001b) 'Choosing between Internal and Non-internal R&D Activities: Some Technological and Economic Factors', *Technology Analysis & Strategic Management*, 13, 365–88.

Narula, R. (2002a) 'R&D Collaboration by SMEs: Some Analytical Issues and Evidence', in Contractor, F. and Lorange, P. (eds), *Cooperative Strategies and Alliances*, Oxford: Pergamon Press.

Narula, R. (2002b) 'Regional Integration and the Strategies of Multinational Firms', in *Trade and regional Integration in the Development Agenda*, Washington: Inter-American Development Bank.

Narula, R. (2002c) 'Switching from Import Substitution to the "New Economic Model" in Latin America: A Case of *not* Learning from Asia', paper presented at Strategic Management Society meeting, Paris, September.

Narula, R. and Dunning, J. (1998) 'Explaining International R&D Alliances and the Role of Governments', *International Business Review*, 7, 377–97.

Narula, R. and Dunning, J. (1999) 'Developing Countries versus Multinationals in a Globalising World: The Dangers of Falling Behind', *Forum for Development Studies*, 2, 261–87.

Narula, R. and Dunning, J. (2000) 'Industrial Development, Globalization and Multinational Enterprises: New Realities for Developing Countries', *Oxford Development Studies*, 28, 141–67.

Narula, R. and Hagedoorn, J. (1999) 'Innovating through Strategic Alliances: Moving towards International Partnerships and Contractual Agreements', *Technovation*, 19, 283–94.

Narula, R. and Portelli, B. (2002) *Is FDI a sine qua non for Development? The Realities of LDCs of Leveraging FDI for Industrial Upgrading*, mimeo, University of Oslo.

Nelson, R. (1987) *Understanding Technological Change as an Evolutionary Process*, Amsterdam: North Holland, 75–6.

Nelson, R. (ed.) (1993) *National Innovation Systems*, New York: Oxford University Press.

Nelson, R. and Rosenberg, N. (1993) 'Technical Innovation and National Systems', in Nelson, (1993), 3–28.

Nelson, R. and Winter, S. (1982) *An Evolutionary Theory of Economic Change*, Cambridge, Mass: Belknap Press.

NIFU (1999) *Science and Technology Indicators*, Oslo: NIFU.

Niosi, J. (1995) *Flexible Innovation: Technological Alliances in Canadian Industry*, Montreal: McGill-Queens University Press.

Niosi, J. (1999) 'The Internationalisation of R&D: From Technology Transfer to the Learning Organisation', *Research Policy*, 28, 107–17.

Nonaka, I. and Takeuchi, H. (1995) *The Knowledge-Creating Company*, New York: Oxford University Press.

Nonaka, I., Toyama, R. and Konno, N. (2000) 'SECI, Ba and Leadership: A Unified Model of Dynamic Knowledge Creation', *Long Range Planning*, 33, 5–34.

Nygaard, A. and Dahlstrom, R. (1992) 'Multinational Company Strategy and Host Country Policy', *Scandinavian Journal of Management*, 8, 3–13.

OECD (1999) *Measuring Globalisation: The Role of Multinationals in OECD Countries*, Paris: OECD.

OECD (2000) *Economic Survey of Norway*, Paris: OECD.

Ohkawa, K. and Rosovsky, H. (1973) *Japanese Economic Growth*, Stanford: Stanford University Press.

Ørstavik, F. and Nås, S. (1998) *Institutional Mapping of the Norwegian System of Innovation*, STEP Report A-01.

Osborn, R. and Baughn, C. (1990) 'Forms of Inter-Organisational Governance for Multinational Alliances', *Academy of Management Journal*, 33, 503–19.

Osborn, R. and Hagedoorn, J. (1997) 'The Institutionalisation and Evolutionary Dynamics of Inter-Organizational Alliances and Networks', *Academy of Management Journal*, 40, 261–78.

Ostry, S. and Nelson, R. (1995) *Techno-Nationalism and Techno-Globalism: Conflict and Cooperation*, Washington: Brookings Institution.

Ozawa, T. (1995) 'Structural Upgrading and Concatenated Integration', in Simon, D. (ed.), *Corporate Strategies in the Pacific Rim: Global versus Regional Trends*, London: Routledge, 215–46.

Ozawa, T. (1996) 'Japan: The Macro-IDP, Meso-IDPs and the Technology Development Path (TDP)', in Dunning, J. and Narula, R. (eds), *Foreign Direct Investment and Governments: Catalysts for Economic Restructuring*, London: Routledge, 423–41.

Pack, H. (2001) 'The Role of Acquisition of Foreign Technology in Taiwanese Growth', *Industrial and Corporate Change*, 10, 713–33.

Paliwoda, S. (1995) *Investing in Eastern Europe. Capitalizing on Emerging Markets*, New York: Addison-Wesley.

Paoli, M. and Prencipe, A. (1999) 'The Role of Knowledge Bases in Complex Product Systems: Some Empirical Evidence from the Aero Engine Industry', *Journal of Management and Governance*, 3, 137–60.

Patel, P. (1996) 'Are Large Firms Internationalising the Generation of Technology? Some New Evidence', *IEEE Transactions on Engineering Management*, 43, 41–7.

Patel, P. and Pavitt, K. (1991) 'Large Firms in the Production of World Technology: An Important Case of Non-Globalisation', *Journal of International Business Studies*, 22, (1), 1–21.

Patel, P. and Pavitt, K. (2000) 'National Systems of Innovation Under Strain: The Internationalisation of Corporate R&D', in Barrell, R., Mason, G. and O'Mahoney, M. (eds), *Productivity, Innovation and Economic Performance*, Cambridge: Cambridge University Press.

Patel, P. and Vega, M. (1999) 'Patterns of Internationalisation and Corporate Technology: Location versus Home Country Advantages', *Research Policy*, 28, pp. 145–55.

Pavitt, K. (1998) 'Technologies, Products & Organisation in the Innovating Firm: What Adam Smith tells us and Joseph Schumpeter doesn't', *Industrial and Corporate Change*, 7, 433–52.

Pearce, R. (1989) *The Internationalisation of Research and Development by Multinational Enterprises*, London: Macmillan.

Pearce, R. (1999) 'Decentralised R&D and Strategic Competitiveness: Globalised Approaches to Generation and Use of Technology in Multinational Enterprises (MNEs)', *Research Policy*, 28, 157–78.

Pearce, R. and Singh, S. (1992) *Globalising Research and Development*, London: Macmillan.

Peterson, J. (1991) 'Technology Policy in Europe: Explaining the Framework Programme and Eureka in Theory and Practice', *Journal of Common Market Studies*, 29, 269–90.

Peterson, J. and Sharp, M. (1998) *Technology Policy and the European Union*, Basingstoke: Macmillan.

Pisano, G. (1990) 'The R&D Boundaries of the Firm: An Empirical Analysis', *Administrative Science Quarterly*, 35, 153–76.

Polanyi, M. (1967) *The Tacit Dimension*, London: Routledge & Kegan Paul.

Polanyi, M. (1969) *Knowing and Being: Essays*, London: Routledge.

Porter, M. (1990) *The Competitive Advantage of Nations*, New York: Free Press.

Porter, M. and Fuller, M. (1986) 'Coalitions and Global Strategy', in Porter, M. (ed.), *Competition in Global Industries*, Boston: Harvard Business School Press.

Pottelsberghe de la Potterie, B. van and Lichtenberg, F. (2001) 'Does Foreign Direct Investment Transfer Technology across Borders?', *Review of Economics and Statistics*, 83 (3).

Quah, D. (1996) 'Empirics for Economic Growth and Convergence', *European Economic Review*, 40, 1353–75.

Ramsay, H. (1995) 'Le Défi Europeén: Multinational Restructuring, Labor and EU Policy', in Amin, A. and Tomaney (eds), *Behind the Myth of European Union*, London: Routledge, 174–97.

Reich, R. (1990) 'Who Is Us?', *Harvard Business Review*, January–February, 53–64.

Reinhardt, N. and Peres, W. (2000) 'Latin America's New Economic Model: Micro Responses and Economic Restructuring', *World Development*, 28(9), 1543–66.

Reve, T., Lensberg, T. and Gronhaug, K. (1992) *Et Konkurransedyktig Norge*, Oslo: Tano.

Rodney, W. (1981) *How Europe Underdeveloped Africa*, Washington, DC: Howard University Press.

Rosenberg, N. (1982) *Inside the Black Box: Technology and Economics*, Cambridge: Cambridge University Press.

Rugman, A. (1980) 'Internalisation as a General Theory of Foreign Direct Investment: A Reappraisal of the Literature', *Weltwirtschaftliches Archiv*, 116, 365–79.

Rugman, A. (1991) 'Diamond in the Rough', *Business Quarterly*, winter.

Rugman, A. and D'Cruz J. (1993) 'The Double Diamond Model of International Competitiveness: The Canadian Experience', *Management International Review*, 33, 17–39.

Rugman, A. and Verbeke, A. (1993) 'Foreign Subsidiaries and Multinational Strategic Management: An Extension and Correction of Porter's Single Diamond Framework', *Management International Review*, 33, 71–84.

Sabel, C. and Zeitlin, J. W. (eds), (1997) *World of Possibilities: Flexibility and Mass Production in Western Industrialization*, Cambridge: Cambridge University Press.

Sachwald, F. (1998) 'Cooperative Agreements and the Theory of the Firm; Focusing on Barriers to Change', *Journal of Economic Behaviour and Organisation*, 35, 203–25.

Sachwald, F. (2001) 'Globalisation and Korea's Development Trajectory', in Sachwald, F. (ed.), *Going Multinational: The Korean Experience of Foreign Direct Investment*, London: Routledge, 361–82.

Sally, R. (1996) 'Public Policy and the Janus Face of the Multinational Enterprise: National Embeddedness and International Production', in Gummett, P. (ed.), *Globalisation and Public Policy*, Cheltenham: Edward Elgar.

Santangelo, G. (2000) 'Corporate Strategic Technological Partnerships in the European Information and Communications Technology Industry', *Research Policy*, 29, 1015–31.

Santangelo, G. (2002) *Innovation in Multinational Corporations and the Information Age*, Cheltenham: Edward Elgar.

Schumpeter, J. (1939) *Business Cycles: A Theoretical, Historical and Statistical Analysis of the Capitalist Process*, 2 vols, New York: McGraw-Hill.

Senker, J., Joly, P. and Reinhard, M. (1996) *Overseas Biotechnology Research by Europe's Chemical/pharmaceuticals Multinationals: Rationale and Implications*, STEP Discussion Paper 33.

Sjöholm, F. (1996) 'International Transfer of Knowledge: The Role of International Trade and Geographic Proximity', *Weltwirtschaftliches Archiv*, 132, 97–115.

Skoie, H. (1997) *Norway: A Province of Science in a Changing World*, STS Report 32.

Smith, K. (1997) 'Economic Infrastructures and Innovation Systems', in Edquist, (1997).

Smith, K. (2000) 'Innovation as a Systemic Phenomenon: Rethinking the Role of Policy', *Enterprise and Innovation Management Studies*, 1, 73–102.

Soete, L. (1987) 'The Impact of Technological Innovation on International Trade Patterns: The Evidence Reconsidered', *Research Policy*, 16, 101–30.

SPRU (2001) *European Biotechnology Innovation System*, University of Sussex, October.

Stiglitz, J. (2002) *Globalisation and its Discontents*, London: Penguin.

Stonehill, A. (1965) *Foreign Ownership in Norwegian Industries*, Oslo: Central Bureau of Statistics.

Stopford, J. (1997) 'Implications for National Governments', in Dunning, J. (ed.), *Governments, Globalization, and International Business*, Oxford: Oxford University Press, 457–80.

Stopford, J. and Strange, S. (1991) *Rival States, Rival Firms: Competition for World Market Shares*, Cambridge: Cambridge University Press.

Storper, M. and Scott, A. (1995) 'The Wealth of Regions', *Futures*, 27 (5), 505–26.

Strange, S. (1998) 'Who are EU? Ambiguities in the Concept of Competitiveness', *Journal of Common Market Studies*, 36, 101–14.

Suh, J. (2000) *Korean Innovation System: Challenges and New Policy Agenda*, mimeo, Maastricht: UNU-INTECH.

Teece, D. (1977) 'Technology Transfer and by Multinational Firms: The Resource Cost of Transferring Technological Know-how', *Economic Journal*, 22, 242–61.

Teece, D. (1986) 'Profiting from Technological Innovation: Implications for Integration, Collaboration, Licensing and Public Policy', *Research Policy*, 15, 285–305.

Teece, D. (1996) 'Firm Organisation, Industrial Structure and Technological Innovation', *Journal of Economic Behaviour and Organisation*, 31, 193–224.

Tidd, J. and Trewhella, M. (1997) 'Organizational and Technological Antecedents for Knowledge Creation and Learning', *R&D Management*, 27, 359–75.

Trajtenberg, M., Henderson, R. and Jaffe, A. (1997) 'University versus Corporate Patents : A Window on the Basicness of Invention', *Economics of Innovation and New Technologies*, 5, 19–50.

UNCTAD (2001) *World Investment Report 2001*, Geneva and New York: United Nations.

UNCTAD (2002) *World Investment Report 2002*, Geneva and New York: United Nations

United Nations (1993) *Small and Medium-Sized Transnational Corporations*, New York: United Nations.

Van den Bulcke, D. and Verbeke, A. (2001) *Paradoxes of Globalization: The Case of the Small Open Economy*, Cheltenham: Edward Elgar.

Vernon, R. (1996) 'Passing Through Regionalism: The Transition to Global Markets', *Journal of World Trade*, 19 (6), 621–33.

Verspagen, B. (1993) *Uneven Growth between Interdependent Economies: An Evolutionary View on Technology Gaps, Trade and Growth*, Aldershot: Avebury.

Veugelers, R. (1997) 'Internal R&D Expenditures and External Technology Sourcing', *Research Policy*, 26, 303–15.

Veugelers, R. and Cassiman, B. (1999) 'Make and Buy in Innovation Strategies: Evidence from Belgian Manufacturing Firms', *Research Policy*, 28, 63–80.

Vonortas, N. (1994) 'Inter-firm Cooperation with Imperfectly Appropriable Research', *International Journal of Industrial Organization*, 12 (3) 413–35.

Vonortas, N. (1997) *Cooperation in Research and Development*, Dordrecht: Kluwer Academic Publishers.

Vonartas, N. and Safioleas, S. (1997) 'Strategic Alliances in Information Technology and Developing Countries Firms: Recent Evidence', *World Development*, 25(5).

Wade, R. (2002) 'America's Empire Rules an Unbalanced World', *International Herald Tribune*, 5 January.

Walsh, V. (1988) 'Technology and Competitiveness of Small Countries: A Review', in Freeman, C. and Lundvall, B. (eds), *Small Countries Facing the Technological Revolution*, London: Pinter, 37–66.

Wibe, M. and Narula, R. (2002) 'Interactive Learning in an Innovation System: The Case of Norwegian Software Companies', *International Journal of Entrepreneurship and Innovation Management*, 2002, 2, 224–44.

Wilkins, M. (1986) 'The History of European Multinationals: A New Look', *Journal of Business Economic History*, 15, 483–510.

Wilkins, M. (1988) 'European and North American Multinationals, 1870–1914: Comparisons and Contrasts', *Business History*, 30, 8–45.

Williamson, O. (1975) *Markets and Hierarchies: Analysis and Anti-Trust Implications*, New York: Free Press.

Xu, B. (2000) 'Multinational Enterprises, Technology Diffusion, and Host Country Productivity Growth', *Journal of Development Economics*, 62, 477–93.

Zander, I. (1995) *The Tortoise Evolution of the Multinational Corporation: Foreign Technological Activity in Swedish Multinational Firms 1890–1990*, Stockholm: IIB.

Zander, I. (1999) 'How do you Mean "Global"? An Empirical Investigation of Innovation Networks in the Multinational Corporation', *Research Policy*, 28, 195–213.

Zander, I. and Zander, U. (1996) 'Sweden', in Dunning, J. and Narula, R. (eds), *Foreign Direct Investment and Governments: Catalysts for Economic Restructuring*, London: Routledge.

Zanfei, A. (2000) 'Transnational Firms and the Changing Organisation of Innovative Activities', *Cambridge Journal of Economics*, 24, 515–42.

Index